HARVEY "SMOKEY" DANIELS  :LMAN

SUBJECTS MATTER

Exceeding Standards Through Powerful Content-Area Reading

SECOND EDITION

Heinemann

Portsmouth, NH

Heinemann
361 Hanover Street
Portsmouth, NH 03801–3912
www.heinemann.com

Offices and agents throughout the world

The authors and publisher wish to thank those who have generously given permission to reprint borrowed material:

Excerpts from the Common Core State Standards © Copyright 2010. National Governors Association Center for Best Practices and Council of Chief State School Officers. All rights reserved.

Excerpt from *E = mc²: A Biography of the World's Most Famous Equation* by David Bodanis. Copyright © 2000 by David Bodanis. Reprinted by permission of Walker and Company.

Credits continue on page viii

Library of Congress Cataloging-in-Publication Data
Daniels, Harvey.
    Subjects matter : exceeding standards through powerful content-area reading / Harvey "Smokey" Daniels and Steven Zemelman.—Second edition.
      pages cm.
    Includes bibliographical references and index.
    ISBN 978-0-325-05083-6
    1. Content-area reading—United States.   2. Reading (Middle school)—United States.   3. Reading (Secondary)—United States.   I. Title.
LB1050.455—D36 2014
428.4071'2-dc23
                                                   2013048071

Acquisitions Editor: Tobey Antao
Production Editor: Patty Adams
Cover and Interior Designs: Suzanne Heiser
Cover Photographer: David Stirling
Typesetter: Gina Poirier, Gina Poirier Design
Manufacturing: Steve Bernier

Printed in the United States of America on acid-free paper
18   17   16   15   14   PAH   1   2   3   4

CONTENTS

LESSONS

Preface

In the ancient times of 2004, we published the first edition of *Subjects Matter*. The book was based on the most current research at the moment, and was brought to life by the savvy classroom strategies of twenty master teachers from across the curriculum and all around the country. We two also chipped in some insights from our own teaching experience, which by then included working with kids and teachers in thirty-two states.

Since the book's debut, tens of thousands of educators have used its key ideas to help young people dive into nonfiction reading—in articles, books, websites, blogs, primary sources, magazines, and, yes, even a few textbooks. We've been cheered to see kids willingly embark on closer, second helpings of text, discussing and debating ideas with peers, digging deeper and building knowledge that lasts. We celebrate when students go beyond just-finish-the-assignment obedience to feel genuine curiosity. They invest themselves in subject matter texts about real-world issues, coming to care, and sometimes taking action. And we've been especially gratified to hear from special educators and teachers of English language learners that the strategies in our first edition worked for their kids, too.

But in these ten short years, the times have changed—and how! Exciting new reading research has emerged, national standards have been adopted (and vigorously debated and challenged), and amazing teachers have stepped forward to share even more powerful instruction in content-area reading—in English, mathematics, science, history, and social studies, not to mention the arts, business, foreign languages, music, and technology.

The Common Core State Standards call for every teacher in America to be (or promptly become) a teacher of reading. What a great challenge and opportunity for us all. There's no task more urgent for every individual student—nor one more satisfying for any teacher—than opening up the domains of knowledge for young people to explore, savor, sift, challenge, treasure, and put to use.

And where do we begin? At McDonald's, where else?

—Smokey and Steve

CHAPTER OPENERS

SUBJECTS MATTER

The Core Purposes of Reading

A McDonald's restaurant in downtown Chicago, Wednesday, lunchtime. On the street out front, a sidewalk preacher testifies to passersby with the aid of a portable PA system. Inside, the store is filled with shoppers, tourists, well-inked students from the Art Institute, and traders from the nearby commodities exchange, wearing their distinctive yellow numbered vests. Customers contentedly chew their Big Macs and chicken nuggets. The air is thick with conversation and the smell of french fries.

The door swings open and two teenage boys walk in. They're big kids, about seventeen or eighteen years old, one Hispanic and one African American. They weave through the tables, up to the crowded window where people are ordering. Michael is carrying a stack of blue flyers, which he quietly places on the counter, where customers can easily pick one up while waiting for their food.

The flyer is headlined "What's in the meat we love?" and depicts the headless carcass of a steer hanging upside down, just as it would be in a slaughterhouse. Below is a grinning likeness of Ronald McDonald, swinging a butcher knife high over his head, with a caption underneath asking "Who profits from the killing floor?" The text warns readers of the prevalence of food-borne illnesses, especially those carried by the beef served in fast-food restaurants. As its source, the flyer cites the book *Fast Food Nation: The Dark Side of the All-American Meal* by Eric Schlosser (2002).

Customers waiting for their burgers gradually become aware of the handout, and a few idly pick one up. Reactions differ: some look disgusted, some annoyed, some amused. There is a growing audience now, as the boys begin walking from table to table. Antonio approaches a middle-aged white woman who's eating alone, reading a book. He asks if she is familiar with

E. coli poisoning. Has she heard about the notorious cases of fast-food restaurants sickening their customers? No, she patiently replies, looking down at her lunch, spread out on its yellow paper wrapping. Does she know that every day in America, two hundred people are sickened—and fourteen die—from bacteria commonly found in hamburger meat? From his back pocket, Antonio pulls out his dog-eared copy of *Fast Food Nation* and points out some key statistics on page 195. She leans down to read the page, heavily highlighted in yellow, with cryptic annotations in the margins.

> *... teenagers should not be "getting ready" to be lifelong learners, but should be acting like them **right now***

"See," he concludes, gesturing at her lunch, "it tastes good and it's quick to get, but it could be a manure sandwich, is what I'm saying."

The woman nods, but seems a little stunned by all this passionate attention to her health. Or perhaps she's put off by Antonio's barnyard analogies.

Meanwhile, the thirtyish manager has been alerted to the disturbance by his counter crew. He scoops up the leftover flyers and walks up behind Antonio, tapping him on the shoulder.

"You can't bother my customers like this," he says firmly. "And you can't hand these out either." He calmly dumps the sheaf of blue flyers into a nearby wastebasket, right on top of the ketchup-soaked napkins and empty soda cups. Antonio and Michael look at each other, silently deciding whether to raise the ante.

Discretion rules, and they shrug as the manager points to the way out. They go, but not quickly and not quietly. All the way to the door, as the manager herds him along, Antonio half-playfully hollers remarks over his shoulder:

"Listen up, listen up people!

"Coming soon, the new truth about McDonald's!"

"You gotta know what your food contains!"

"You might be having a shit sandwich for lunch up in here!"

And finally, at the door, he gives the manager one for the road: "You gonna put me out 'cause I'm black and I'm tellin' the truth?"

Michael and Antonio were students at Best Practice, a small public high school we helped to design and open in Chicago in 1996 (Daniels, Bizar, and Zemelman, 2001). A core value of Best Practice High School (BPHS) was deep and close reading—real reading—in all content areas, across the curriculum. The boys' truth-squad assault on the McDonald's at State and Jackson happened after they had spent a month reading about the fast-food industry and how it affects our health, agriculture, values, laws, economy, and society. The unit was designed by a cross-disciplinary team of senior teachers representing science, social studies, English, and special education, in partnership with faculty from math, technology, and art.

Like other lessons at BPHS, the fast-food project was built on the assumption that teenagers should not be "getting ready" to be lifelong learners, but should be fully engaged *right now*. The school's faculty knew that feeding students a steady stream of textbook chapters is not a healthy reading diet—or a grown-up one. So they supplemented kids' intake with generous servings of newspapers, magazines, websites, and nonfiction trade books—the same range of texts that thoughtful, curious members of the adult community around them might read.

In the fast-food unit, the kids read widely and dug deep. First, each student received the paperback edition of *Fast Food Nation*. Reminiscent of Upton Sinclair's *The Jungle*, but ranging even more widely, Schlosser's book is an old-fashioned muckraking exposé that lambastes every link in the chain of industrialized agriculture, up to its ultimate crudescence in fast-food restaurants. (In middle schools, we have also used Schlosser's equally disturbing 2007 abridged version, *Chew on This* [Schlosser and Wilson 2007].) We used some grant funds to buy every student a copy, for two reasons: first, because we simply wanted them to own the book, since our kids generally don't own a lot of books; and second, because we planned to use some reading strategies that required kids to actively mark up, highlight, and annotate the text.

But the book was just the start. For scientific background (and also because the content is mandated in the citywide curriculum), the kids read their biology textbook's chapters on nutrition, digestion, viruses, and bacteria. Each student also read several magazine articles, among them a *Fortune* magazine piece about lawsuits brought (and dismissed) against fast-food restaurants for causing obesity; one from *Science* magazine, debunking the "fat myth," and arguing that fat may actually be good for you; and another from *Harper's* about how fast-food companies intentionally target poor urban neighborhoods. Students chose from six articles about animal cruelty downloaded from the PETA (People for the Ethical Treatment of Animals) website, sparking lively discussion about whether, for example, harvesting eggs or milking cows constitutes animal abuse. The more the kids and teachers dug into the topic, the more often relevant sources seemed to pop up—books, articles, and websites everywhere. One juicy favorite was the American Restaurant Association's stinging rebuttal called "The Truth About *Fast Food Nation*," a web-launched press release quoting the book's few negative reviews, and pounding home the point that Schlosser wanted to deny people "the food they love." (Today's ongoing McDonald's ad campaign, taglined "I'm lovin' it," continues to promote the idea that people should be *loving* the high-fat, high-salt, fiber-free junk food peddled by Ronald and crew.)

The school faculty didn't just assign all these disparate readings and hope that kids would comprehend them. All year long, they had been teaching specific practical **thinking strategies** that help kids to dig meaning out of a document in any content field. As a result, these kids knew how to:

> visualize ideas and situations in the text
>
> make connections with their own background knowledge
>
> notice and ask questions
>
> draw inferences (e.g., make predictions)
>
> evaluate and determine what's important
>
> summarize and synthesize information
>
> notice and analyze the author's craft and style
>
> monitor and adjust thinking while reading

Further, the teachers embodied these thinking strategies in concrete **tools** that helped students understand and remember what they read. In this unit, for example, the teachers made use of text coding tools, book clubs, dialogue journals, bookmarks, Post-it notes, text annotation, admit slips, and exit slips, among others (all covered in Chapter 5). With these kinds of scaffolding, students were able to enter some very challenging texts, make sense of them, monitor their thinking, bring ideas back to discussions, and apply what they had read to their own lives.

And, of course, lots of classroom and community-based activities grew out of and extended the readings. Kids made anthropological observations at fast-food joints, interviewed restaurant workers, kept personal diet journals, searched the Web for nutrition information, and joined in two elaborate simulations, one about life as a teenage employee in a fast-food restaurant and another that dramatized the unionization of a slaughterhouse. The outcome of all this reading and experience was eighty kids with a lot of questions, concerns, and opinions. And that made things pretty easy when it came to the culminating experience—finding a public audience with whom to share some of their ideas about the fast-food industry.

Not all the kids chose in-your-face actions like Michael and Antonio. Jaisy, who was upset by the horrific conditions faced by immigrant workers in modern meat-packing plants, very diplomatically wrote her congressman:

Dear Representative Davis,

My class and I are reading Fast Food Nation. *This book addresses a lot of issues, however the one I find to be most disturbing is the conditions of slaughterhouses, especially for the cleanup crews. That portion of the book was really hard for me to read. The descriptions were way too vivid for my liking! I am writing you because I want to know what can the average person do to increase the chances of workers having good working conditions in slaughterhouses . . . I plan to make every effort to convince you to take action to better the conditions in the slaughterhouses. If you haven't read* Fast Food Nation, *I strongly urge you to; that will be the strongest influence over you.*

Sincerely,
Jaisy R. Geans

Jaisy also created a petition made up of direct quotes from the book, and then solicited signatures around the school and the neighborhood. Jaisy brought her own special style to the petition process: she'd approach you in the hall, hand you the petition, and ask you to read the quotes. After about three seconds, she'd start asking: "Isn't that awful? Isn't that just terrible?" And when you'd nod, she'd command, "Well, sign it, then!!"

> *. . . the teachers made use of text coding tools, book clubs, dialogue journals, bookmarks, Post-it notes, text annotation, admit slips, and exit slips, among others.*

Sean, Nely, Jenny, and Elvira wrote and illustrated a picture book called "What's in Your Happy Meal?" ("See the cow. See Jack kill the cow. See the potatoes. See the french fries soaked in grease.") After making arrangements with an interested teacher in the elementary school downstairs, the teen authors visited a first-grade class to read the book at story time and talk about fast food with the children. Of course the younger children were upset with the idea of killing animals for food—but the teenagers were too, which is why they wrote the book. Indeed, of all the issues encountered during the unit, this was the one with the greatest emotional wallop; adolescents could care less what their cholesterol is, but once they learn what goes on in a slaughterhouse, it can change their thinking forever.

Another group of kids documented their own miserable school lunches by taking digital photos of each item being served and by collecting wrappers from the other food sold in the cafeteria. Using these assorted materials, they created a huge collage and superimposed it on the U.S. Department of Agriculture's "food pyramid," the chart that specifies the officially recommended diet for Americans. Enhancing the 3-D effect were some napkins and plastic "sporks" hanging from the corner of the piece.

To drive home their point, the kids drew arrows from each cafeteria item (hot dogs, nachos with cheese sauce, Snickers bars) to the appropriate level of the food pyramid. The graphic was dramatic: almost all the arrows pointed to the top of the pyramid—to fats and oils, sugars, and red meat, categories of foods that people are advised to eat very sparingly. Fruits and vegetables, which are supposed to dominate a healthy diet, were virtually absent from the school food residue.

Some of these projects may seem a little naive, heavy-handed, or even—what's the word we're looking for—adolescent? Admittedly, hectoring innocent diners in a restaurant or reminding six-year-olds that their lunch began as Bossie does seem a little indelicate. But the thing was, these teenage readers were actually angry and concerned. They had learned things that really got them thinking, got them agitated, got them activated. The self-reflections at the end of the unit showed how deeply many students (though not all—hey, this is a real school) were affected by what they learned.

> I really don't like eating McDonald's anymore. Before I read this book I had already stopped eating beef and pork, and this book really makes you wanna quit.

> After this book, now at a fast food restaurant I don't eat the burgers—only apple pies and fries. (I'm not going to starve myself!)

> For about 1–2 weeks I couldn't eat meat. However, that really sucked because I didn't have too much to eat without meat. Finally I was pushed to the edge of hungriness and I ended up eating a chicken sandwich. I will definitely be more conscious of what I eat.

> Will this change my eating habits? No way, except that I'll think about the facts and laugh ironically before I eat a delicious meal at Burger King or McDonald's.

> Ever since I read fast Food Nation I only ate fast food one time. I thought differently about it and started to reduce my fast food servings.

> I can't really eat any meat without thinking about the animal it used to be.

Read This for Friday

Mr. Cosgrove's biology class, Thursday, second period.

"All right . . . Jamie, sit down, please. All right. Everyone, before the bell rings, let me give the assignment for tomorrow. I want you to read Chapter 17 in the textbook and answer the questions at the end of the chapter. You're gonna turn those in at the start of class tomorrow, so be sure to use our regular format—name, date, and period in the upper right— you know the drill. Now, a word to the wise. Are you listening, Kathy? I would suggest that you pay special attention to the section on photosynthesis, because we might have a quiz on that one of these days. OK? Did everyone hear that? I said, we might have a pop quiz on photosynthesis sometime very soon. Any questions? OK. See you tomorrow."

Cut to Friday. The kids straggle in, and after a gentle reminder, begin hunting in their backpacks for the homework. As usual, Jamie whines, "Oooh, Mr. C, can I go to my locker? I think I left my homework in there." As Mr. Cosgrove roams the aisles, collecting papers, a few routine excuses pop up ("I had soccer last night"; "I think it's on my kitchen table"). But most of the kids have done the work—and here comes Jamie back from his locker, triumphantly clutching a crumpled sheet of notebook paper.

Flipping through the stack, Mr. Cosgrove is not especially displeased. Though some students' responses are more complete than others, almost every kid has written down something for each of the twelve questions from the textbook.

"OK, gang," Mr. Cosgrove announces, "Remember my words to the wise yesterday— it's quiz time. Please clear your desks."

Pro forma resistance immediately breaks out. "Aw, Mr. C, that's not fair! You only said *maybe* a quiz!" "But we just had a quiz on Tuesday!" Inevitably, the ten-item multiple-choice quiz is distributed, and the kids gradually quiet down and bend to the task. There's some background sighing and pencil-tapping, and a few students gaze steadily up in the air, as if the correct answers might miraculously appear on a ceiling tile. When Mr. Cosgrove calls time and collects the test papers, he notices a lot of blank, unanswered questions.

Once the quizzes are stacked on his desk, it is time for some class discussion. "So, guys," Mr. C asks, "what's the big picture here? Why is photosynthesis so important to life?" Twenty-seven eighth graders simultaneously look down at their desktops, apparently finding something utterly fascinating in the grain of the wood. "Who wants to start us off? Why is photosynthesis so important?" Mr. C scans the room, but no eye contact seems to be available, no twitch of volunteerism emerges. Call on one of the reliable ones, he thinks. Christine, maybe. But as he gazes her way, she drops her pen on the floor and turns, in ultraslow motion, to retrieve it. The silence is profound.

"Geez, guys, give me a break here. We read this stuff last night, you just had it on the quiz." Blank stares. "OK, why don't you take your books out and open up to Chapter 17 again." The kids heft the six-pound science books back onto their desks, opening to the chapter.

"OK, everybody with me now? All right here's an easy one: what's the green stuff that is the key to photosynthesis?" There's the sound of pages flipping. And flipping. And flipping. "Come on, you gotta know this."

More silence, and then, finally, a first tentative hand is raised.

"Uh, would that be carbon dioxide?" wonders Diane.

The phrase "pulling teeth" flashes through Mr. Cosgrove's head. For a split second, he sees himself in a white dentist's smock, holding a shiny pair of pliers in one hand; the students arrayed before him resemble rows of deeply impacted, unpullable teeth—definitely *not* of the "wisdom" type.

"All right, guys, maybe this just isn't a good day for a discussion. Tell you what, let's just turn to Chapter 18 and start reading that for tomorrow. I'll give you the last fifteen minutes of class to get a head start on the homework. And be ready for a quiz on Monday."

Later, grading the tests, Mr. C tallies two As, four Bs, seven Cs, seven Ds, and eight Fs. All the kids needed was to get six out of ten answers halfway right. Sixty percent! Was that too much to ask? Apparently, even sitting at home last night, with the textbooks right in front of their noses, students couldn't memorize the most straightforward points—even the ones sitting right there in boldface type. They read it, but they just didn't get it.

Not only do they not get it—they don't seem to care. And this bothers Steve Cosgrove most of all. Steve went into teaching because he loved science—especially ecology. Back in college, he took an advanced ecosystems course, where he studied global warming with a group of classmates. His life changed the day he read about scientists who drilled into air pockets in Antarctica to find samples of the atmosphere trapped centuries ago. They proved that in the year 1700 the earth's air had a third less carbon dioxide than it has now. When he read that study, Steve was stunned, concerned, and hooked.

Here at Barnum Middle School, Steve's goal in teaching has never been just to push kids through the textbook, or help them pass a state assessment, though he cares about both of those necessary outcomes. Steve hopes for more. He wants his students to really understand how the earth works, how life interlocks, how thin and fragile the biosphere really is.

He hopes to awaken in young people a sense of wonder at the complexity of life. He hopes that they will feel concern, maybe get involved, see themselves as stewards of the environment, friends of the planet. But these kids, they can't even (or won't even) read the book.

Two Visions of Reading

So what's the difference between these two stories of reading? Well, to begin with, one of these stories really happened and the other was made up. Steve Cosgrove is not a real teacher, and there is no Barnum Middle School, as far as we can Google. We created "Steve's" story to display some common problems that teachers of all subjects struggle with when we assign content-area reading "the regular way." We tried to portray Steve as a nice person and a hard worker, because that's what teachers are. He's approaching reading the way he was taught in his methods class, and probably the same way he experienced it in his own schooling, in middle school, high school, and college. Admittedly, we did engineer every conceivable problem into Steve's classroom; here's hoping none of us ever encounters a real class as discouraging as his photosynthesis-proof group!

Obviously, we think the fast-food story has a lot more to recommend it—and not only because it is about our own students, whom we love even when they go a little over the top. If your teaching experience is like ours, you might agree that we don't see teenage readers this engaged very often. When we assign students to read pages 234–245 in the textbook and answer the questions at the end of the chapter, they hardly ever get on a bus and go share their learning with fellow citizens across town. And maybe you also feel the way we do—that we'd prefer to see students overly worked up than not worked up at all. We'd rather help a kid simmer down and find productive outlets for her outrage, than try to wake her up in the back row of the classroom, where she is snoozing face-down on a textbook. In a deep sense, this is what *Subjects Matter* is all about: effectively inviting kids to engage in our subjects, to think, remember, build knowledge—and to care.

Why Content Teachers Care About Reading

Studies consistently show that most of us are like Steve C: we middle and high school teachers chose our profession mainly because we love a *subject*—physics, mathematics, art, history, political science, biology, chemistry, literature, a language. Elementary teachers, on the other hand, most commonly say they elected teaching because they "like being with children."

That's a big difference. It doesn't mean we secondary types don't like young people (most of us are quite fond of them, actually), but we have another powerful dynamic going in our heads: we care deeply about a particular field, a body of knowledge, a special set of tools and procedures, an intellectual tradition, a heritage.

Looking back over our careers, we can feel the truth of this. We didn't sign up for this occupation, go to school for four or five years, get ourselves certified, and agree to this pitiful pay scale just to push some state assessment score up a half percent. Our imagination wasn't fired by some list of standards to be met in the first semester of ninth grade. We got into this job because we were hooked on a field, usually our college major, and we wanted to transmit that excitement to young people. We wanted students to share our enthusiasm, our fascination, our wonder at the beauty and importance of ideas. We had something powerful and precious to share: knowledge.

We imagined students catching our fever of ideas. We pictured them exploring a Civil War battlefield on a summer vacation, looking through a telescope in their backyard, writing their own software on a home computer, sketching a great artwork in a museum gallery, or writing their own collection of poems. After having us as teachers, after we had lit the fire, we saw our students moving on to take more courses in math, in science, in literature, in art. We envisioned them going on to major in our subject in college—the greatest compliment a secondary teacher can get. They would make our subject a special part of their own lives, just like we did; some would even join the field, make a contribution, become fellow enthusiasts, colleagues, and peers.

But even in these professional fantasies, we were realistic. We knew we'd never get them all; not every student would commit their working life to our subject area. However, we expected every kid to grasp the big ideas, to respect the field, to remain curious about it through life. When our ex-students read the daily paper, they'd encounter stories about the subject and understand the basic issues. Perhaps some would subscribe to *Discover*, *National Geographic*, *American Heritage*, or *The New Yorker*. Others would work through books of math puzzles, just for fun. Maybe they'd read popular books in the field: *1491: New Revelations of the Americas Before Columbus*; *Zero: Biography of a Dangerous Idea*; *Salt: A World History*; *The Future of Life*; *Into the Wild*; or *The Glass Castle*. And who knows? Maybe at least a small number of our alumni might be the kind of people who join in monthly book discussion groups, meeting with friends to talk about the latest novels or nonfiction trade books. Or even become teachers themselves.

Of course, between our long-term dreams and the immediate realities, things can intrude. Here sit our students before us, first period, today. Before they can become lifelong learners and pillars of their intellectual communities, there might be a few obstacles to overcome. Maybe these kids aren't ready to explore genetics at the level that makes our grown-up DNA quiver. Maybe, right at this moment, they are grappling with personal or developmental issues that mute the majesty of the pyramids. Perhaps their previous experience in school hasn't delivered them to our classrooms ready to tackle tariffs. And quite possibly, our proliferating standards, mandated curricula, departmental exams, and tests, tests, tests are undermining our own ability to teach with passion and personality.

Yes, there are a lot of obstacles to young people falling in love with math, science, history, language, and the arts. But that doesn't mean that our idealism is sentimental and misplaced, or that we should give up the dream that binds us to this profession. It is right and reasonable to hope that kids can have a lifelong engagement with at least one, hopefully several fields of knowledge—and that they'll pursue it through reading, for years to come.

Reading and School Reform

We teachers are not the only people worried about kids' reading these days. A powerful reform movement, backed by both political parties, a host of business leaders, national foundations, and Washington think tanks, has swept American schools. Among other changes, these corporate-model reformers have created America's first-ever national reading standards, high-stakes tests to enforce them, and a scheme to reward or punish teachers based on their students' scores (Common Core State Standards, 2010). Why have these bold policy changes been needed? The reformers hold a dim view of reading achievement and instruction in America schools. And, at first glance, it seems they have plenty of evidence to back up their case.

Reading failure continues to be a prime cause of students leaving school early. Our high school dropout rate, nationally about 7.5 percent, has dire personal and social consequences for millions of young people. In Chicago, where we still work regularly, the official dropout rate is listed as around 30 percent, though many insiders peg the number closer to 50 percent. If you look over the enrollment records of Chicago high schools in poor, all-minority neighborhoods, you might find that they list 600 freshmen, 450 sophomores, 300 juniors—and just 150 seniors left to march at graduation. And these tragic outcomes are replayed in big-city school systems around the country, where most of America's 3.9 million dropouts between ages sixteen and twenty-four can be found, unemployed, demoralized, and already trapped in the school-to-prison pipeline.

Among the majority of teenage students who do stay in school, their scores on state and national standardized tests are often disappointing and evoke worrisome headlines. One *Washington Post* piece, titled "SAT Reading Scores Hit a Four-Decade Low," intoned:

> Reading scores on the SAT for the high school class of 2012 reached a four-decade low, putting a punctuation mark on a gradual decline in the ability of college-bound teens to read passages and answer questions about sentence structure, vocabulary and meaning on the college entrance exam. (Layton and Brown, 2012)

Sounds pretty bad. And the equally influential American College Testing Program (ACT) showed a similar decline in its reading scores over the same period. However, the *Post* reporters appropriately went on to note that the main reason for the dropoff in college entrance tests was the "changing pool of test takers," with more poor kids signing up for the exams in recent years.

As savvy teachers know, most state and national tests are subject to year-to-year variance, constant rejiggering by test makers and/or politicians, and ever-shifting "cut scores" that determine which kids are "proficient." In contrast, the National Assessment of Educational Progress, sometimes called the "Nation's Report Card," is the one test that has been engineered to provide consistently meaningful data about American students' learning over years and decades. So its findings deserve special weight. Interestingly, if you look at NAEP eighth-grade reading scores since the test was begun in 1992, you see not a decline or a steep upward trend, but a stable, slightly rising pattern over two decades.

*U.S. schools with less than 10 percent poverty scored **first in the world** in reading.*

Although the-sky-is-falling rhetoric dominated the media and animated reformers over this time period, the actual story was one of slow progress. In 1992, the average eighth grader scored 260 in reading; on the 2013 test, that had risen to 268. In high school, scores looked similar. The average twelfth grader scored 288 in 2009, up from 287 in 2002. But looking back to 1992, the average score at that time was 290. (The next round of twelfth-grade NAEP results will be announced after this book goes to press.) While some might be outraged at this flat score pattern over many years, it doesn't seem mathematically accurate to use words like *decline*, *plummet*, *steep*, *crisis*, or *tragedy* to describe this phenomenon.

International educational comparisons are constantly cited as evidence that American schools require big, immediate changes in the interest of "global economic competitiveness." Many of these exams show American kids performing at the middle, or even toward the bottom, of world achievement levels. Perhaps the most quoted example has been the PISA test, which stands for the Programme for International Student Assessment sponsored by the Organization for Economic Cooperation and Development. Their 2009 report on the reading skills of fifteen-year-olds in dozens of countries was a shocker. American teenagers ranked fourteenth on the list, below such nations as Canada, Korea, Estonia, Poland, and Iceland, not to mention several provinces of China. The 2012 scores are now out, and while U.S. performance held steady, a number of countries advanced, dropping us to 24th place in reading.

Some Americans think that the United States already is, or soon should be, number one in everything, and they'd probably be disappointed by anything less than first place on international assessments. To folks who don't know anything about this issue except the final rankings of countries on the test, we can see how this kind of logic might sound like an excuse. However, as we will see in a moment, this might actually have been a bit of overperforming by the United States.

Most significant is what we find when viewing international test scores by poverty level (McCabe, 2010, Riddle, 2010). To begin with, none of the top-scoring countries have anywhere near the levels of deep, enduring poverty of America. When you disaggregate PISA scores by family income, here's what you find: U.S. schools with less than 10 percent poverty scored *first in the world* in reading. In schools with between 10 and 25 percent poverty, American teens scored *third in the world.* Even in schools with 25 to 50 percent poverty, our students were *tenth in the world.* But in schools with over 75 percent poverty, the scores were *last in the developed world.* So, when you average the results from America's economically and racially bipolar school system, you get an "average" score of fourteenth in the world. What a sad and telling statistic that is. We do *not* have a "mediocre" school system in this country; we have many centers of true excellence, and we also have some shockingly underserved students and communities. In this light, it now seems entirely appropriate to use words like *crisis* and *tragedy.*

Still, at this point, it may not matter what "data sets" like NAEP or SAT or PISA actually show in terms of schools' efficacy. The significance of these numbers is effectively moot, since school reformers have already sold the narrative of a sudden, precipitous decline. Exculpating data analyses from inside the profession don't have much clout with a citizenry that's been convinced that the public schools are a mess. In 1992, 58 percent of U.S. citizens polled by Gallup had "a great deal" or "quite a lot" of confidence in the public schools; today, that proportion has dropped to 29 percent (Smith, Turner, and Lattanzio, 2012). It is probably not incidental that just between 2008 and 2012, at the height of the Race to the Top and Common Core reforms, teachers who rated themselves as "very satisfied" with their job dropped from 62 percent to 39 percent (Met Life, 2013).

Now, don't get us wrong because we are disputing the bad news about reading among America's kids. We are not cheerleaders for the status quo, and we sure aren't happy with the current state of reading instruction. We believe that all of our kids can do better, know more, be more engaged—and we certainly know firsthand that many American schools have a really long way to go. And making reading a more meaningful, more effective, and more profound learning experience is something that we teachers can start tackling today, in our own classrooms—even as we address new standards and prepare our kids for new tests.

Content-Area Reading and the Common Core State Standards

The great majority of U.S. states have committed to implementing the Common Core State Standards (CCSS) and to presenting their students for national tests based on those standards. Other states, like Texas, have developed their own quite similar targets and exams outside the Core. Still others are opting in and out of various aspects of the standards/testing movement to this day. But while this larger school reform movement remains controversial, what is not open to debate is whether such standards will have a big impact on students and teachers: they already have. The CCSS, and state standards like the TEKS in Texas, are already challenging and transforming the work of everyone in schools.

Here's what you need to know if you are a middle or high school teacher of any subject, in any state: *we are all teachers of reading now*. According to the new standards, our students are supposed to:

* read much more
* read more nonfiction (historical, scientific, technical, explanatory, and argumentative text)
* read more closely and thoughtfully
* read increasingly complex and challenging materials
* discuss what they read with peers
* write about their reading

And all of us, not just the English teachers, have to pitch in, according to the Common Core:

Instruction in reading, writing, speaking, listening, and language are to be a shared responsibility within the school. The grades 6–12 standards are divided into two sections, one for English language arts and the other for history/social studies, science, and technical subjects. This division reflects the unique, time-honored place of ELA teachers in developing students' literacy skills while at the same time recognizing that teachers in other disciplines must play a strong role in this development as well. Part of the motivation behind the interdisciplinary approach to literacy promulgated by the standards is extensive research establishing the need for college- and career-ready students to be proficient in reading complex informational text independently in a variety of content areas (CCSS, 2010).

And just in case you think you're exempt because your subject isn't specifically mentioned, check this: [L]iteracy standards in other areas, such as mathematics and health education, modeled on those in this document, are strongly encouraged to facilitate a comprehensive, schoolwide literacy program (CCSS, 2010).

The Common Core Standards themselves can be dizzying (over three hundred pages, if you tackle all the appendices). But we can winnow them down to what matters most. In the chart on pages 16–17, we have combined information from several sections of the standards with content-area teachers in mind. All of the standards related to reading—whether they're for language arts or content-area classes—are built on the same ten core ideas. For example, you'll see that Standard 1 always deals with recalling and making inferences, even though the particulars vary across subjects: in history, students might be making inferences about a primary source's origin; in science, students might be examining precise details as part of an analysis; in English, students might be using both recall and inference to construct meaning. The purpose and specific requirements change across subjects, but the essential skills stay the same. In every class, students are expected to be skillful readers.

The Common Core has grouped these ten standards into four categories, which send a pretty clear message about what the standards value:

* key ideas and details (comprehending the text)
* craft and structure (considering why and how the text was written)
* integration of knowledge of ideas (analyzing text and making connections)
* range of reading and level of text complexity (reading a lot, including some difficult text)

While the Common Core might seem to focus on wringing meaning out of text without any consideration for what students need or are interested in, that doesn't mean that you need to drain the joy out of your work (and theirs). On the contrary: getting students engaged and passionate about what they're studying is likely the only way that they'll end up exceeding what the standards ask them to do.

		History/Social Studies	Science and Technical Subjects	English Language Arts
Key Ideas and Details	**Recall and Infer** 1	Cite specific textual evidence to support analysis of primary and secondary sources, attending to such features as the date and origin of the information.	Cite specific textual evidence to support analysis of science and technical texts, attending to the precise details of explanations or descriptions.	Cite strong and thorough textual evidence to support analysis of what the text says explicitly as well as inferences drawn from the text.
	Summarize 2	Determine the central ideas or information of a primary or secondary source; provide an accurate summary of how key events or ideas develop over the course of the text.	Determine the central ideas or conclusions of a text; trace the text's explanation or depiction of a complex process, phenomenon, or concept; provide an accurate summary of the text.	Determine a central idea of a text and analyze its development over the course of the text, including how it emerges and is shaped and refined by specific details; provide an objective summary of the text.
	Analyze 3	Analyze in detail a series of events described in a text; determine whether earlier events caused later ones or simply preceded them.	Follow precisely a complex multistep procedure when carrying out experiments, taking measurements, or performing technical tasks, attending to special cases or exceptions defined in the text.	Analyze how the author unfolds an analysis or series of ideas or events, including the order in which the points are made, how they are introduced and developed, and the connections that are drawn between them.
Craft and Structure	**Acquire Academic Vocabulary** 4	Determine the meaning of words and phrases as they are used in a text, including vocabulary describing political, social, or economic aspects of history/social studies.	Determine the meaning of symbols, key terms, and other domain-specific words and phrases as they are used in a specific scientific or technical context relevant to grades 9–10 texts and topics.	Determine the meaning of words and phrases as they are used in a text, including figurative, connotative, and technical meanings; analyze the cumulative impact of specific word choices on meaning and tone (e.g., how the language of a court opinion differs from that of a newspaper).
	Analyze Text Structure 5	Analyze how a text uses structure to emphasize key points or advance an explanation or analysis.	Analyze the structure of the relationships among concepts in a text, including relationships among key terms (e.g., *force, friction, reaction force, energy*).	Analyze in detail how an author's ideas or claims are developed and refined by particular sentences, paragraphs, or larger portions of a text (e.g., a section or chapter).
	Purpose and Point of View 6	Compare the point of view of two or more authors for how they treat the same or similar topics, including which details they include and emphasize in their respective accounts.	Analyze the author's purpose in providing an explanation, describing a procedure, or discussing an experiment in a text, defining the question the author seeks to address.	Determine an author's point of view or purpose in a text and analyze how an author uses rhetoric to advance that point of view or purpose.

	History/Social Studies	Science and Technical Subjects	English Language Arts
Examine Text from Multiple Perspectives 7	Integrate quantitative or technical analysis (e.g., charts, research data) with qualitative analysis in print or digital text.	Translate quantitative or technical information expressed in words in a text into visual form (e.g., a table or chart) and translate information expressed visually or mathematically (e.g., in an equation) into words.	Analyze various accounts of a subject told in different mediums (e.g., a person's life story in both print and multimedia), determining which details are emphasized in each account.
Evaluate Reasoning and Evidence 8	Assess the extent to which the reasoning and evidence in a text support the author's claims.	Assess the extent to which the reasoning and evidence in a text support the author's claim or a recommendation for solving a scientific or technical problem	Delineate and evaluate the argument and specific claims in a text, assessing whether the reasoning is valid and the evidence is relevant and sufficient; identify false statements and fallacious reasoning.
Compare and Contrast Texts 9	Compare and contrast treatments of the same topic in several primary and secondary sources.	Compare and contrast findings presented in a text to those from other sources (including their own experiments), noting when the findings support or contradict previous explanations or accounts.	Analyze seminal U.S. documents of historical and literary significance (e.g., Washington's Farewell Address, the Gettysburg Address, Roosevelt's Four Freedoms speech, King's "Letter from Birmingham Jail"), including how they address related themes and concepts.
Read Widely and Deeply 10	By the end of grade 10, read and comprehend history/social studies texts in the grades 9–10 text complexity band independently and proficiently.	By the end of grade 10, read and comprehend science/technical texts in the grades 9–10 text complexity band independently and proficiently.	By the end of grade 9, read and comprehend literary nonfiction in the grades 9–10 text complexity band proficiently, with scaffolding as needed at the high end of the range. By the end of grade 10, read and comprehend literary nonfiction at the high end of the grades 9–10 text complexity band independently and proficiently.

Integration of Knowledge and Ideas

Range of Reading and Level of Text Complexity

For this particular chart, we chose the 9–10 "grade band." You can easily do the same for grade bands 6, 7, 8, or 11–12. The language at each level is very similar, with fine shadings of developmental difference with each higher band. First we grabbed the ten CCSS "anchor standards" for nonfiction reading, which are identical across all grade levels and subject areas. Then, under each anchor, we entered the subject-specific language for each of the three broad subject areas covered by the CCSS: history/social studies, science/technical subjects, and English language arts nonfiction.

All of the suggestions and strategies in this book work toward (and often beyond) the goals in the Common Core and other state standards.

Now, let's step back and appraise the general strengths of the content-area reading standards, and then grapple with the challenges they pose. Some of our pros and cons are evidenced in the above chart; others are derived from the review of other CCSS documents.

The Standards Help Because They:

* Focus on thinking and comprehension, not just decoding or factual recall.
* Call for a healthy balance of fiction and nonfiction during the school day and year, and across the curriculum.
* Guide students (and teachers) to look closely at texts to understand what they say, draw inferences from them, take note of their particular point of view, and assess the validity of their assertions.
* Stress the development of students' independence, which invites teachers to use the Gradual Release of Responsibility, a particularly effective instructional strategy (see page 89, 92).
* Integrate reading with content-area study, thereby aiding learning of subject matter.
* Elevate the importance of real-world texts and articles over textbooks, which do not lend themselves to the kinds of analysis the standards call for.
* Support the use of student discussion, debate, and research groups.
* Spread the development of reading across all subjects and throughout the school day.
* Invite students to write about what they read.

At the same time, the standards have some important limitations, and it's important not just to be aware of them but also to find ways to ameliorate them.

The Standards Need Fine-Tuning Because They:

* Sound *joyless*. When you read the text of the standards, it's mostly commands, duty, obedience, slogging, and work, work, work. There's no sense that studying school subjects can be exciting, engaging, or make a difference in the real world.

* Forget that young people are curious, creative, and eager for discovery. Sure, we can coerce students, with predictably uneven results. But when we bait the hook temptingly enough, then suddenly, kids want to know. There's no baiting in the CCSS.

* Assume that all adolescents will automatically and obediently leap into abstract thinking about extremely hard texts. Maybe we should be glad that the standards writers pledged to eschew pedagogy, but their manifest assumption that you can just assign anything and expect to get students' best efforts makes us wonder: "Have these guys ever taught for a day? A week?"

* Fail to describe reading as a form of thinking, and neglect to name the well-documented cognitive strategies of proficient readers. Skillful comprehenders visualize, connect, question, infer, determine importance, synthesize, and monitor their own comprehension while reading. Smart teachers model and explicitly teach these mental strategies in the context of important curricular materials.

* Repudiate modern comprehension research. The standards writers adhere to a fifty-year-old academic school called "New Criticism," which holds that a single fixed meaning resides within any text. Newer cognitive research shows that skilled readers actually "co-create" meaning with the author's words, bringing to bear all their prior knowledge, life experience, and even their misconceptions. Ignoring this mental reality cuts off most ways that young readers can enhance their comprehension, and incorrectly labels them as "bad readers" if they lack the background knowledge or thinking tools to crack a given text.

* Don't seem to care about whether kids learn from the content, concepts, or ideas they are exposed to in school. The English Standard 9 does mention a few "foundational" documents. But building subject-area knowledge is rarely emphasized as the *purpose* of reading. The standards focus on pushing kids up a ladder of complexity, rather than actually learning from and appreciating text, whatever its level.

* Ignore student choice of reading materials. Independent, self-chosen reading is highly correlated with school achievement (Allington and Gabriel, 2012). But the CCSS's preferred approach seems to be: the teacher chooses every text, which every student reads at the same time, accompanied by didactic, whole-class lessons, all year long. While some whole-class books and discussions can be valuable and energizing, this is not a balanced diet of reading. Students need a wide range of reading experiences, including both self- and teacher-chosen selections.

* Confuse the meaning of "independent reading." The CCSS define reading independently as reading complex teacher-assigned text without any help. In the everyday school world (as we implied just above), independent reading means reading for pleasure and interest books that you have chosen, at your own recreational reading level. Big difference. Both have validity, one as a goal and one as a means. The evidence shows that, to get to the CCSS kind of independence, you have to do a lot of regular independent reading—picking and reading and talking about lots of books that are *easy* for you (Allington, 2013).

* Offer a list of recommended readings that are narrow, monocultural, and sometimes archaic. Particularly for science, many of the "text exemplars" are sadly out of date: a book on the atom, for example, from 1965; one on astronomy from 1926. And for social studies, there are volumes of Founding Fathers idolatry, but a surprising lack of texts related to the Vietnam War, the 9/11 attack, developments in the Middle East, or other essential historical events. Fortunately, all the cited works are just suggestions, according to the CCSS (though some school districts are predictably treating the exemplar list as their curriculum, just to be on the safe side). In this climate, it is vital for teachers to gradually find and substitute more engaging, current, culturally representative, and balanced selections for their young readers.

* Assert that students can become better readers by reading text they cannot read. The level of the text exemplars is generally at the very high end of each grade band. But the research on this topic speaks loudly for the opposite (and commonsense) approach. Since our work as teachers is to

lead students on a year-long journey toward more challenging reading, rather than start them there, the appended list can be both misleading and unhelpful. We need books for the beginning of the year, not just the end (Afflerbach et al., 2008).

✱ Are contradicted by the "Publishers' Criteria" (Coleman and Pimentel, 2012). This separate and hotly debated document was created by two of the original Common Core standards writers, David Coleman and Susan Pimentel. While eventually approved by the CCSS after many debates and revisions, these guidelines began as a freelance opinion piece that unfortunately misled many school leaders. Maybe this is sounding a little like "inside baseball"—or just petty politics? True enough. But there is one lingering misconception from the Publishers Criteria we all need to watch for. If someone tells you that the Common Core does not allow you to preview text and build kids' background knowledge before they read a selection, an alarm should go off in your head. Not only does this assertion not make instructional sense, it is also *not* what the standards say. Don't hold back; give kids the scaffolding they need to cope with the text.

The Goals of This Book

There are two main problems with reading in secondary subject fields: students are reading the wrong stuff and they don't understand what they read. Other than that, everything is fine! Students consume a drastically unbalanced and unhealthful reading diet, with negative side effects like low test scores, ignorance of vital information, and negative attitudes toward reading. They read too many textbooks and not enough "real" books and articles. And while we assign plenty of reading, we don't teach kids *how* to understand and remember what we assign. There are specific and documented mental processes that effective readers use, but these thinking skills are not being consistently taught or used in middle and high school courses (Daniels et al. 2011).

This book addresses both of these issues. We want to make sure that your students possess the cognitive strategies they need to understand the core written information in your field—and that you, the teacher, have a repertoire of tools and structures to make this happen. And further, we want to be sure that your students are exposed to the best possible samples, those just-right texts and critical documents that can ignite genuine interest and curiosity about your subject matter.

Here's a preview of the changes we will argue for in the coming pages, and a summary of what we mean by the *what* and the *how* of content reading experiences. As you look at these lists, you can think back over our two opening stories, about the fast-food unit and the attempted photosynthesis lesson.

More-Successful Content-Area Reading Activities

WHAT is read

* Kids may still use a textbook as a basic source of information, but they also venture far beyond it.
* The subject matter includes authentic, interesting, and current issues that affect young people's daily lives.
* Instead of relying on a single authority, students consult a variety of sources and voices on the topic, constructing their own understanding of what is fact, what is true, what is right.
* The students not only read about settled facts and closed questions; they also read in the arena of the unsettled, the debatable, the still-emerging.
* Students sample a wide variety of genres—textbooks and other reference works, newspapers, magazines, websites, blogs, and popular trade books.
* Reading selections have a range of lengths, from short newspaper, magazine, and online pieces to whole books.
* There's a premium on current information; many of the pieces used in a given unit were recently published or posted.
* Many of the texts take an interdisciplinary approach, using the tools of multiple disciplines, combining science, statistics, history, biography, and more.

HOW it is read

* The purpose for reading is not just to pass a test or get through the textbook. The students' work is to gather information, construct meaning, and apply knowledge about important issues.

* The teacher selects some, but not all, of the readings; students are also responsible for locating and choosing some selections on their own.

* Not every student reads the same texts. There are some common readings and some "jigsawing" of related but different texts.

* Teachers teach (and kids use) a repertoire of specific thinking strategies that help them enter, understand, and apply the material they read.

* Teachers offer students practical tools that help them process different kinds of texts.

* Teachers organize classroom structures and activities that deepen student engagement with key written materials.

* Reading is seen as a social, rather than a solitary, activity; there is plenty of collaborative work in pairs, teams, book clubs, inquiry groups.

* Instead of an exclusive focus on "right answers," there's room for debate and discussion, for differences of opinion and interpretation.

* Instead of receiving a string of 180 daily reading assignments, students do their subject-area reading as part of longer, coordinated themes or inquiries.

* Reading is linked to action in the real world: young readers engage in research, documentation, correspondence, and advocacy.

* The assessment of kids' reading relies less on quizzes and worksheets, and more on complex performances, products, and exhibitions.

In the coming pages, we will show how content teachers can take steps—carefully and thoughtfully— toward more promising reading activities. In the next chapter, we'll look at how our own brains work when we read, so we can explain the tricks of the trade to students. Reading is not some unknowable "black box" of cognition; it's actually quite easy to surface our own reading strategies, name them, and then model them for students.

Next, students need a new and more healthful diet of reading materials—and we address this issue in Chapters 3 and 4. After exploring the specific limitations of textbooks, we'll give you lists of the specific books, magazines, journals, and websites that have energized the curiosity of many young readers, across the whole range of content areas. We will invite you to join us on the book's website to extend those lists with your kids' favorites. And we'll show how teachers have integrated these new materials into their curricula, alongside the textbook, in harmony with the Common Core Standards, and with success on high-stakes tests.

In the edge-tinted pages of Chapter 5, we offer a large repertoire of practical classroom structures and strategies that help kids understand and remember what they read—whether it comes from a textbook, a website, or a novel. Some of the most powerful of these strategies take only a few minutes of class time to implement, and can reap huge dividends in comprehension. We cover a wide range of activities, from quick getting-started exercises to structures that guide kids through longer, harder texts. We'll show you how to make sure that students enter texts thinking, demanding clarity along the way, and connecting their learning to real-life issues.

Improving reading in middle and high school can be a victory for everyone involved, a rare win-win-win deal.

In Chapter 6, we return to the world of textbooks—this time, not to critique but to celebrate ways of working with the newer, better models that are now coming onto the market and onto the Web. Next, before moving into longer-term, more complex reading projects, we show in Chapter 7 how you can create a responsible, collaborative climate in which kids can effectively read and discuss with peers. Then, in Chapters 8, 9, and 10, we explore three key structures for sustained content-area learning: reading workshop, book clubs, and inquiry units. In Chapter 11 we explicitly translate all these ideas for kids who struggle with learning, reading, or English.

Chapter 12 is our research report. In these times, it is vital to show that suggested classroom activities really enhance student learning, that they have been validated by both quantitative and qualitative research of careful design. Happily, more than sixty years of research show the value of a varied reading diet and careful reading-as-thinking instruction, as measured by standardized test scores as well as improved reading habits and attitudes. In the interest of getting right to the classroom stuff, we have placed our research summary at the back of the book. But for people who want to see the proof right away, or for administrators or parent leaders who must consider policy questions first, you may want to begin with Chapter 12, and return to the instructional ideas later.

Improving reading in middle and high school can be a victory for everyone involved, a rare win-win-win deal. To meet the state mandates and pass standardized tests in any subject area, as well as to find personal meaning in a field, young people must be able to read key materials fluently, skillfully, strategically, and critically. To fulfill our entirely reasonable dream that every kid will fall in love with at least one field of knowledge, students must encounter each field's most galvanizing, tantalizing, and pivotal documents. This means we teachers must do more than just assign reading, and we must help our students venture well beyond "the basics."

But what an energetic and hopeful adventure this can be, with payoffs for everyone: for schools, to show the public what their students can do; for the kids, to lock in lifelong reading skills and maybe find a passion; and, for us teachers, to realize that vision we always dream of—"the light going on" in lots of kids' heads, and maybe hooking a few of them on the ideas that changed our own lives. Sound good? Let's get to work.

How Smart
Readers Think

We often complain that students "can't read" (or *won't* read) the materials in our subject areas. And indeed, if flunked quizzes, unfinished homework, and low test scores prove anything, then we have plenty to worry about. And we do worry. Sometimes in the faculty lounge, agonizing about this problem, when we hit a really low moment—we'll cast aspersions on our colleagues in the lower grades: "Weren't these kids supposed to learn to read in elementary school?" we wonder.

To figure out what skills our students are missing, let's start with ourselves as skillful, experienced, mature readers. Now, don't give us that "aw, shucks, not me" stuff, apologizing because you haven't read a novel in ten years or guiltily copping to your TV habit. Let's give ourselves some credit. We are grown-ups who have done tons of reading in our lives, inside and outside of school. We've successfully digested enough written material to earn at least a bachelor's degree, maybe even a master's. Every day we deal with reams of text: the morning paper (if we have time), memos from the principal or the department chair, the textbook and all the supplementary materials we use in class, students' work, magazine or journal articles—it really adds up when you inventory everything. So it's true: teachers have print-heavy jobs, and we do know a lot about reading, understanding, and remembering a wide variety of written material, whether we're highly conscious of it or not.

So, please read the following text.

The Batsmen were merciless against the Bowlers. The Bowlers placed their men in slips and covers. But to no avail. The Batsmen hit one four after another along with an occasional six. Not once did their balls hit their stumps or get caught.

OK, that was a trick, sorry. But we think you might have just learned a few things about yourself as a reader. What did you notice about your own thinking process? How was your comprehension? Your attitudes or feelings? Many teachers with whom we have read this passage have found it to be difficult in some ways, and a somewhat irritating experience as well. We certainly don't want to irritate you, so here's some help: it's about cricket. You know, that goofy sport that the British are so obsessed with? Now, go back and read the passage again.

Makes a little more sense now, right? And since no reading exercise would be complete without a quiz, it's time for the questions-at-end-of-the-chapter. Please answer:

1. Who were merciless against the Bowlers?
2. Where did the Bowlers place their men?
3. Was this strategy successful?
4. Who hit an occasional six?
5. How many times did the Batsmen's balls hit a stump?

See, you got 100 percent! Congratulations! What? You say you didn't *really* understand it? Hmmm. Now we're starting to see content-area reading from a kid's-eye view: how students can read every word on a page without deep understanding; how they can sometimes pass tests on concepts they don't really grasp; how they can go through a whole book or unit, and end up with no long-term memory of what they've studied.

Reading Lessons

How can our own reading of the cricket passage help us as teachers of math, science, art, English, or history? We know that much of the knowledge in our subject fields is stored in print, and we urgently want that material to be open, available, and readable for our students. So exactly what do we need to know about the mental process called "reading" to help students access our content?

Reading is more than "decoding"

In the cricket passage, were there any letters that you couldn't sound out? Any words you had never seen before? Probably not. Whatever makes this passage hard to read goes way beyond phonics, phonemics, or decoding skills. This is important to remember, especially these days, when there is a national recognition in the Common Core State Standards that reading is about comprehension and thinking. Sometimes, middle and high school teachers wonder if kids who struggle with a textbook or novel might be suffering from a lack of phonics. But "phonics" just means the sound-symbol correspondence between spoken and printed language. Beginning readers learn which letters in English can make each of the forty sounds used in the spoken language. This task is supposed to be completed by the end of second grade, and for the great majority of American kids, it is. True, a small fraction of students (no more than 5 percent nationally) manage to arrive in middle school or even high school with lingering decoding problems, and those few kids should have long ago been identified for services from the special education department. In other words, if large numbers of our older students are having trouble reading content-area texts, it is not because they were shorted on phonics in elementary school and now can't "sound out the words"—any more than your problems with the cricket passage two minutes ago were phonetic in origin.

Reading is an active, constructive process

If this chapter's "test passage" had been a paragraph about teaching teenagers in America, instead of about cricket, you might have sailed through it without stopping, with genuinely high comprehension, and with no particular awareness of your reading process. Sometimes we call such smooth, unobstructed reading "clicking," meaning that you are just clicking along through the text. So instead, to make your reading process more conscious and visible, we assigned you a "hard" passage, one that for most Americans has more clunk than click.

> All these mental acrobatics remind us that readers actively build and construct meaning from a text.

As you were trying to read the cricket piece, you could probably *feel* yourself thinking—maybe even struggling or battling for meaning. Instead of clicking, you were clunking, getting this visceral sense of "I don't get it." If you're like us, the first clunk came pretty early, and many more followed. And your reading process probably became more conscious—or at least your feelings about it did. You can look back on it now, remembering the stops and starts, the moves you made, the tricks you tried to get the passage to make sense. You may have found yourself trying to picture what was going on, rereading to clarify meaning, making educated guesses (maybe it's about a game), comparing to your own experience (is it like baseball?), looking for word roots or alternative meanings (maybe the slips aren't underwear), posing questions (what's a cover?), and more.

All these mental acrobatics remind us that readers actively build and construct meaning from a text. Meaning does not simply reside on the page, ready to be understood whole, nor is it a message simply "sent" by an author and "received" by reader. The "message," if you think about it, is merely patterns of ink on a page. These squiggles have to be built into meaningful concepts by the mind of a hard-working reader.

Good readers have a repertoire of thinking strategies they use to comprehend texts

Those tricks you used, trying to make sense of the cricket text, weren't random and they weren't spontaneous. You were actually drawing from a set of specific thinking skills you have developed and used throughout your life as a reader. There are many ways to label these strategies (Harvey and Goudvis, 2007; Keene and Zimmerman, 2007), and no one set of terms is authoritative. Here's our own list:

Thinking Strategies of Effective Readers

* visualize (to make mental pictures or sensory images)
* connect (to connect to one's own experience, to events in the world, to other readings)
* question (to actively wonder, to surface uncertainties, to interrogate the text)
* infer (to predict, hypothesize, interpret, draw conclusions)
* evaluate (to determine importance, make judgments)
* analyze (to notice text structures, author's craft, vocabulary, purpose, theme, point of view)
* recall (to retell, summarize, remember information)
* self-monitor (to recognize and act on confusion, uncertainty, attention problems)

Do these feel real to you? Are you aware of having used one or more of these mental tools to try to crack the cricket passage? Maybe, because the passage forced you to work extra hard at comprehending, you were aware of this thinking.

But based on the bulk of your life reading experience, you might doubt that these cognitive choices actually exist in your head. "That's not how it feels to me," you might say. "Usually, I don't use all those different strategies. When some printed material comes into my life, I just read it." Fair enough. In fact, that's how reading does work, most of the time. As a mature reader, your mental strategies have become mainly automatic and unconscious. Have you ever noticed how you can drive your car across town to a friend's house, daydream all the way, and still arrive at your destination without much conscious attention to the steering wheel, brake pedal, turn signal, or rear-view mirror? To survive and arrive, you have to constantly monitor the movements of other cars behind, beside, and ahead of you; calculate stopping distances; time merges onto the busy expressway. While at the wheel, you are simultaneously dealing with issues of time, space, physics, and potentially, life and death—and all the while, you're wondering who's bringing the guacamole. The same happens with reading: you can "drive" through some text without explicit self-awareness, especially when the topic is as familiar as the directions to your friend's house. But this doesn't mean that, driving or reading, you aren't thinking. In both cases, you are using complex cognitive strategies, very actively and creatively, at the unconscious level.

> *. . . you can "drive" through some text without explicit self-awareness, especially when the topic is as familiar as the directions to your friend's house.*

However, if you're heading off to visit a *new* acquaintance, in a new neighborhood, then it's a different story. So maybe you study your GPS or directions first. You have to watch closely, questioning the street signs to make sure you're prepared to do what your GPS is telling you to execute. You're noticing the stores and subdivisions and comparing them in your head to the sort of area you visualized your new friend living in. You're watching the odometer or the GPS to see how much farther you need to go before the next landmark. If you do make a wrong turn (which we've done in spite of our GPS guidance), you start looking for someone to ask for help (unless you are a male). And if you have been driving someone else's car, an unfamiliar vehicle where you don't know how the pedals and switches and mirrors work, then you pay extra-conscious attention to every stop, turn, merge, and acceleration. *This* is more like what your students often need to consciously do as they navigate the unfamiliar territory of the textbook.

But we still have a reading problem. Even though we know the passage is about cricket, and we have deployed a pretty sophisticated array of comprehension tools to open it up (consciously or unconsciously), we still don't really understand what it says. And look out! Here comes some more:

> Inverarity viciously pulled Brown into the gully but was sent retiring to the pavilion by a shooter from Cox. Jones in slips and Chappel at silly mid on were superb, and Daniel bowled a maiden over in his first spell. Yallop took his toll with three towering sixes but Thompson had little to do in the covers. Grant was dismissed with a beautiful yorker and Jones went from a brute of a ball . . .

Whew. This must be how students feel with our textbooks, running their eyes over every word but just not getting it, dutifully "doing the reading," but not making satisfactory meaning. What else is missing?

Prior knowledge is the main determinant of comprehension

To look deeper into what makes content-area reading hard, let's use a couple more passages. Try this one first:

> With hocked gems financing him, our hero bravely defied all scornful laughter that tried to prevent his scheme. "Your eyes deceived," he had said. "An egg not a table correctly typifies this unexplored entity." Now three sturdy sisters sought proof. Forging along, sometimes through calm vastness, yet more often over turbulent peaks and valleys, days became weeks as many doubters spread fearful rumors about the edge. At last from somewhere, welcomed winged creatures appeared, signifying momentous success.

Probably another puzzler for many of us. It has some familiar problems too, like common words that don't make sense. But now reread the passage using this one clue: Columbus.

Now it clicks just fine, right? That's because you have ample prior knowledge about Columbus and his explorations. When you were reading the passage for the second time, you were using the fund of information in your head about Columbus. Your prior knowledge did not need to be complete or perfectly authoritative to help you read. Indeed, your prior knowledge might even include some ideas that are not correct (Columbus captained the Pinta), notions that others might dispute (Columbus was humane to the native peoples he met), or just plain misconceptions (Columbus sailed the ocean blue in 1482).

Cognitive researchers have found that we human beings store our knowledge in mental patterns called **schemata**.

But you have more in your head than just a bunch of prior knowledge. Notice that a one-word clue opened up the whole passage for you, giving the key to a dozen terms that, a minute earlier, were deeply mysterious. What that key actually opened was your *schema* for Christopher Columbus. Cognitive researchers have found that we human beings store our knowledge in mental patterns called *schemata* (don't worry, you don't have to explain this to the students). It helps to think of a schema as a web that stores and connects all the information in your mind related to a given topic. You have a schema in your head for your mother, one for hospitals, another for football, for weddings, for rivers, for Star Wars movies. Most of us adult Americans have a schema for Columbus, which both contains and interconnects all the bits and pieces of information we have about the explorer: words, pictures, stories, maps, images, readings, attitudes, and feelings.

So what just happened was that we helped you "switch on" your schema for Columbus, which allowed you to comprehend the passage. It turned out that all the information you needed to read that passage was right in your head, but until the right schema was activated, you "couldn't read" the paragraph. The same happens with students at times: approaching any given reading, they may actually have some good prior knowledge to build on, a usable schema to attach information to, but they don't activate it—with the result that they do not understand or remember the material. That's why this book describes many specific ways of activating kids' prior knowledge and switching on their related schemata, so they can take in new information, remember, and understand. We need to give kids the "Columbus key" so they can read in all our content areas.

But the definition of reading is really shifting now. The ability to get meaning from print is dependent on what we already know. Those same brain scientists believe that the only way we can learn new information is by attaching it, connecting it, integrating it with information we already have. You have to assimilate the information into an existing schema or revise an old one to make the new stuff fit. Either way, you have to work with what is already in the mind; you can't build on nothing.

Build on nothing? Hey, that's what I do every day in my classroom. My students *don't know* algebra (history, chemistry, British literature)—that's why they're here! Do these kids have any schemata for federalism or the conservation of matter? Doesn't look like it to me. They're enrolled in my courses, for crying out loud, because they don't know this stuff.

OK. Let's take that description of our students' predicament seriously. How can you read stuff if you don't know something about it already? How do you operate (as our students often must) when the content is largely unfamiliar, and it's not easy to connect with things you already know? Let's shed some light on this with one last (we promise!) reading experiment.

The following paragraph was written by a well-known biochemist to describe one of his research interests, and was posted on his university website:

MS2 Phage Coat Protein—RNA Interaction. This system is being studied for several reasons: (1) it is an example of a sequence-specific RNA-protein interaction, (2) it participates in a well-behaved in vitro capsid assembly reaction, and (3) it is a good model system to study how protein finds a target on a large RNA molecule. Available are an X-ray crystal structure of the RNA-protein complex and an NMR structure of the free RNA hairpin target. Current efforts focus on understanding how the thermodynamic details of sequence-specific "recognition" is achieved. We have made mutations in all the amino acids believed to make contact with the RNA and are evaluating the affinity of the mutant proteins to the normal RNA target as well as to targets that have single atom changes in either the bases or the phosphodiester backbone. It is already clear that nearly all the contacts predicted by the co-crystal structure contribute to the total free energy of binding. Thus, unlike several protein-protein interfaces that have been analyzed in a similar way, there are no "hot spots" that dominate the affinity. However, we have several examples where affinity and specificity are defined by structural elements of the RNA in its free form. (—Olke Uhlenbeck, Interdepartmental Biological Sciences, Northwestern University, 2003)

Hey, could you science teachers please explain this to the rest of us? We used all of our sophisticated adult reading strategies on this passage—we questioned, we inferred, we analyzed like crazy, we even visualized some dancing double helices—but we still don't understand what this research is about. Maybe *your* capsid assembly reactions are well-behaved, but ours are acting like morons! Perhaps we just don't have the phosphodiester backbone for reading as tough as this.

> We need someone to get us ready for reading like this by giving us an overview ...

All biochemical jokes aside, what makes this passage hard to read is the *content*. We're not lost in Professor Uhlenbeck's paragraph because some hapless elementary teacher forgot to teach us a diphthong twenty years ago. The problem is, it's too damn hard. "Hard" meaning we don't have enough background knowledge, a good enough schema of this discipline, on which to build much meaning. There's no "Columbus key" to this passage for most of us, is there? Would it have helped if we gave you the clue "RNA research" for this passage? Probably not much, since, except for biochemists, that clue would not switch on a large enough web of preexisting information in our heads, the way it did before.

We need more help. We need someone to get us ready for reading like this by giving us an overview, telling us beforehand what some of the words mean, drawing us a picture, showing us a model, giving us an explanation—or maybe, taking us much further back, to the "basics" of this field. So perhaps having kids read mostly text like this is an incomplete experience, or even a wrong approach to our subject fields. Once again, that is what the rest of this book will try to do: show you how, with textbooks and novels, with lab reports and census tracts, to build up to the more challenging material in your field, guiding your students to seek out the larger concepts that underlie the technical details; to find connections with examples they *do* understand; to actively search for related readings more at their level of knowledge that will begin to bridge the gap; and to feel confident and curious enough to pursue such inquiry.

One more point about prior knowledge: some people misread the Common Core Standards as discouraging teachers from activating students' prior knowledge, instead asserting that students should create meaning just by struggling with the text itself. Our nonfiction examples show pretty starkly that this simply doesn't work. We suspect that some educators have come to this view out of their legitimate desire to see students become independent learners. And perhaps they're worried about some teachers who *tell* students what a text means, in place of having them read it. However, we're saying that by engaging learners in preparatory work, teachers help them *move toward* independence in their reading. The Common Core Standards are not about where we start with our students, but about the goals we are guiding them to attain. Further, the standards themselves call for students to read widely, and to compare texts—expectations that are, in fact, ready-made tools for building background knowledge.

> *. . . by engaging learners in preparatory work, teachers help them* **move toward** *independence in their reading.*

Reading is a staged and recursive process

Take a quick look back at the MS2 passage again, and see if you can remember how you worked your way through it even if you didn't understand it fully. What steps did you take—first, second, third, and so on after that? Your thinking steps may be hard to reconstruct (especially in sequence) because so much of it was unconscious. But we'll venture that you can identify some things you did before, during, and after reading. Before you hit the text, we purposely gave you an introduction about Dr. Uhlenbeck and his research, hoping to get you thinking, digging for prior knowledge, and searching for the right schema to activate. On your own, you might have scanned the title and started digging deeper for background information on RNA B, or maybe you started preparing yourself mentally: "Uh-oh, this is gonna be really technical science stuff." Then, as you worked your way into the passage itself, clicking and clunking along, you might have noticed yourself stopping, maybe going back and rereading, and so on. While your schema for DNA research may be very rickety and full of holes and blank spots, you probably started building on whatever scraps you *do* have (unless you simply gave up!). You may have read at some time in the past about how DNA and RNA molecules are long sequences of amino acids that work like letters in a code, and now seeing the words *sequence-specific recognition* and *target*, you started making some dim guesses, whether right or wrong, about using certain chemicals to locate a significant spot on the RNA molecule. Later, if your biochemistry teacher clarified it all, you'd recall these guesses and either congratulate yourself for being smarter than you thought, or replacing your mistaken surmise with something better: "Oh, now I get it!"

We could walk you through all the stages—right up to the after-reading part, where you may recall cursing us and our cutesy little reading tests. The point is: there are activities that skillful readers typically engage in before they start reading, other things they do while reading, and still other things they do after they have read a passage, all focused on the process of using, expanding, or altering what they know to make sense of new information. They do everything every time, but as we have learned, much of it is done unconsciously. Plus, just to make things extra complicated, smart readers don't just go through these activities in 1-2-3 order, but hop back and forth between stages, especially when the reading is complex or unfamiliar. You might have noticed this recursiveness in your own reading just now.

If we want to put this staged model of reading in a simple linear order, the sequence of tasks might look like this.

Stages of Reading

Before Reading
Set purpose for reading.
Activate prior knowledge.
Develop questions.
Make predictions.

During Reading
Sample text.
Visualize.
Hypothesize.
Confirm/alter predictions.
Monitor comprehension.

After Reading

Recall/retell.

Evaluate.

Discuss.

Reread.

Apply.

Read more.

There are many reading-process models like this one, and until we have traced all the participating neurons, no one version will be deemed "correct." But all the models shed a pretty dramatic light on the customary "read this for Friday" approach to reading in middle and high school. If the real task of reading, of making meaning from content-area texts, involves a complex series of cognitive operations like those listed here, it's no wonder that kids are often adrift. Inadvertently, we may be leaving them alone with many more jobs to do than we realized—and with much less support that they need.

All through this chapter we have been using ourselves—grown-up schoolteachers—as handy examples of how mature readers develop. But we now have to warn that there are limits to the generalizability of our experience. After all, as people who chose careers in education, we are not exactly "normal." That's not a slam—just a reminder that we were probably pretty successful students in school. We might have been better-than-average readers and students from the start, perhaps beginning with some out-of-school advantages (parents who read, or books in

> *As adult readers, we command an amazing array of mental processes.*

our homes, or a burning interest in a subject ignited at an early age). If we had struggled terribly with reading, and failed in school as a result, we probably wouldn't have elected to spend our whole working lives there.

But we stayed—and as adult readers, we command an amazing array of mental processes. Look at all we can do: We can use our phonics skills. We can predict, activate our prior knowledge, sample, reread, and confirm. We can generate and revise hypotheses. We can monitor our own reading process, and try a variety of ways to construct meaning. We can tap into a large repertoire of cognitive strategies—visualizing, questioning, connecting, analyzing, evaluating. We can work in a staged and stepwise manner. For crying out loud, we even have thousands of interlocking schemata in our heads that we can activate at will. Who knew?

For many educators (most definitely including the two of us), these operations were never explicitly named or taught in our own schooling. Instead, we cobbled together our inventory of reading/thinking skills from a mix of inconsistent school instruction and a lot of real-life trial and error experience. And we certainly didn't finish acquiring all these self-taught reading powers back in elementary school—we were still working on them in middle and high school. In fact, we recognize that our reading skills were honed in college and into adult life—and are still growing today.

But now, as we gaze out into our classrooms, we are *not* facing rows and rows of future teachers sitting there; they are not ranks of little us-es eagerly looking forward to a life of book work. Instead, we face a normal distribution of kids for whom neither reading nor school necessarily comes easy. So, yes, whatever subject we teach, we do need to understand reading a little better, including what makes it so hard for kids when they step into our disciplines and try to read our subject matter without some of the advantages and predilections that we enjoyed.

Various Kinds of Reading

The Common Core reading standards call for students to understand various ways that texts are structured, and many educators assert that recognizing a structure helps a student better comprehend the material. In this regard, teachers often speak of various text features, such as bold print, headings, information in boxes, and visuals, as they help students read textbooks and other material, but the differences go well beyond that. A typical set of nonfiction structures that are talked about includes

* chronological order
* cause and effect
* steps in a process
* problem and solution
* compare and contrast
* physical description

We should recognize, however, that these categories are somewhat limited in their usefulness. For one thing, there are still more structures to be aware of. An *analysis* of the various parts of a structure or organization is at least one we'd like to include. Analysis might involve some comparison and contrast, description, or cause and effect, but it's not necessarily any of those.

Another kind of text could be *question and answer*. And then there are topics that involve lots of questions, but the answers are not yet known.

Many—perhaps most—texts in the real world are complex combinations of these. Moreover, a category may not really tell a reader what to expect. Students might at first imagine that in a cause-and-effect piece, the cause would come first. However, in plenty of writing the author describes a mysterious event or phenomenon and then sets out to find the cause. Just think about mystery novels and much science reporting. A good example of mixed structures is a recent well-written report in the *New York Times* on low-income students' struggles with success in college, alternating throughout between a narrative tracing three young women's difficulties, data on college graduation for minorities and high- and low-income students, and interviews with high school and college counselors, who offered explanations for the various causes for this pattern.

One thoughtful reading teacher we talked with pointed out, though, that the text structure terms provide students with some vocabulary to talk about what they're reading. Kids can readily create their own categories, which sounds like more fun and still helps them understand how information is being presented. And the text structures for various genres of writing are surely quite different from one another.

Reading does differ markedly from one field to another, of course, but more in the kind of thinking that is involved, and the kinds of questions that informed readers bring to it. As recent studies tell us (Gillen and Vaughan, 2003; Heller and Greenleaf, 2007; Nokes, 2011; Hynd, 2013; Simonson, 2011; Shanahan et al., 2011), a scientist reads reports differently than a historian or a reader of novels. Mathematics involves yet another kind of reading. In each field, experts think and query information in particular ways. When reading a science paper, for example, a scientist may ask the following questions (Gillen and Vaughan, 2003):

* What prior work formed the basis for this paper?
* What methods did the author use?
* Are the experimental data convincing?
* Were the data analyzed and interpreted fairly?
* What literature did the author cite?
* What are the major conclusions of the study?

And a scientific paper is generally organized as follows:

* title
* abstract

* introduction
* methods
* results
* discussion
* acknowledgments
* literature cited

In contrast, a historian asks some very different questions that go well beyond the text itself, particularly if he or she is studying an original document (Nokes, 2011):

* What type of document is this?
* Who was the author?
* How was the author involved in the activity?
* When was the document produced?
* Who was the intended audience?
* Can this information be corroborated?
* Whose voices are omitted from this account?
* What might the author's potential biases have been?

Historians compare texts to seek corroboration or differences on particular facts, causes, or interpretations of them. They seek to determine the importance of particular documents. They develop a larger story that integrates information to describe an event or period, and provide arguments for why they believe the story to be accurate.

These accounts of reading are similar in some ways to what is described in the Common Core Standards, but they also differ in important ways. The science and history approaches to reading call for close attention to the ideas and information within a text as well as comparisons between texts, as the Common Core expects. But they also pose questions that go beyond the texts altogether. When historians ask about an author's potential biases, or scientists gauge the quality of an experimenter's interpretations of data, the evidence may well be outside the text itself. Mathematicians often omit many steps in their reasoning that they expect experienced fellow math wonks to work out for themselves. Historians provide arguments and evidence to back them up, which the standards ask students to analyze. But history texts also create narratives. And by the way, we're talking here about actual documents in the various fields, not the textbooks that boil real subject-area thinking down to mere summaries of information or concepts.

If That's What Reading Involves, What Does It Mean for Our Teaching?

If we understand that reading is not just "receiving a message," but actively building meaning upon prior knowledge, using staged, strategic thinking, then we will teach differently. If students need to learn to evaluate the nature and authority of a historical document rather than taking it at face value, they'll need help learning how to do that. So instead of saying "Read this for Friday" and popping out a quiz on the appointed day, we will first provide prereading activities that help kids activate their thinking, get ready for new vocabulary, and start making predictions about the text. Knowing that prior knowledge is the strongest determinant of understanding, and that new knowledge can only be built upon existing knowledge, we understand better where to begin—with students' conceptions and misconceptions about our subject, whatever they are, and with connections to ideas that the kids *do* know about within their own experience. We will work harder to activate, develop, build upon, shape, and add to our students' prior knowledge. Experts in the various academic fields stress that learning to read effectively, using the kinds of thinking that goes on in their areas, is a long, developmental process.

> *We will work harder to activate, develop, build upon, shape, and add to our students' prior knowledge.*

While students are reading, we will provide them tools and activities that help them question, interpret, and harvest their responses as they go, using us and their classmates to clarify ideas. And after students have read, we will talk over ideas to clarify, confirm, and deepen understanding. Maybe we'll even transmediate, which means moving ideas from one domain of expression (writing) into another (drawing, drama, dance), to ensure deep comprehension. Again, these are strategies specifically called for in the Common Core Standards.

In short: understanding what readers do, we will *teach* reading, not just assign it, though that doesn't mean we are turning into reading teachers. We are specialists—science, math, history, art, music, foreign language people—to the bone. The difference is, we'll break the work into steps for kids, and provide help along the way. We'll be using methods, tools, activities that are particular to our fields of learning, and engaging reading materials that help our students understand and remember our content better—and maybe even, dare we hope, get interested in it. Which is where we started.

What does this mean as we work to bring the Common Core Standards to life in our classrooms? First and most essentially, it tells us that as we support students' content-area reading, we are simultaneously helping them learn and engage more deeply in our subjects and responding to the Common Core recognition that strong literacy is needed for success in subject areas as well as in English language arts. It means that we are increasing students' reading of nonfiction to balance the novels, stories, and poetry they study in English, a balance that the Common Core recognizes as important to students' learning. We are showing students how to read in ways that the Common Core calls for, but also going beyond the standards when reading in our subjects requires that. We are using instructional tools to help students read closely and critically, identify important evidence and ideas in the texts they read, and analyze them in a variety of ways.

One big concern with the Common Core is its expectation that students will read increasingly complex texts—though the definition of "complex" in this case is itself, well . . . complex: it means not just a mix of more complex sentences, vocabulary, and ideas, but also a reliance on the level of students' prior knowledge and interest in the topic. Of course, our job as teachers is not just to throw the more complex readings at the kids, but to give them the tools to handle such material. And that's what good teaching about thinking, as students read and learn in our subjects, will accomplish.

> *For now, there are only a couple of elements you need to name, teach, and use explicitly in class.*

Of course, helping students read our materials more effectively will take some in-class time. We know—you didn't want to hear that. You hardly have enough time to cover the topics mandated by your district and included on the standardized tests. But we like to think of it as getting two-fers. When you teach students strategies for getting more out of their reading—and we'll describe a whole collection of such strategies in Chapter 5—you can do it with materials from your content, focused right on the topic students are learning about at that moment, or you can add more engaging materials as well. And the kids are gaining a better understanding of the topic through the reading lesson itself. So you're teaching your subject *and* the reading strategies at the same time. That is, you're getting a two-fer.

So what do we tell the kids? Let's keep all the theory to ourselves, OK? Middle and high students do not need to know all this reading terminology, cognition, and research. They can pursue schema theory in a college psychology course someday, if they want. For now, there are only a couple of elements you need to name, teach, and use explicitly in class. One is the list of thinking strategies on page 30. Students do need to know, consciously, that smart readers use a variety of cognitive lenses to crack the meaning in tough texts. And later, in Chapter 5, we'll introduce a family of specific reading activities—things like "written conversation," "KWL," and "multicolumn notes"—that everyone in the classroom should know how to operate. If teachers and kids share this modest vocabulary, these few key concepts, you can start to build a strong, energetic, high-performing community of readers in any subject, and across a school.

Why Textbooks
Are Not Enough

Next week, Jane Woodbury will start as a freshman at Burt Lake High School. So this warm August morning, following the instructions in a letter sent home to families, Jane and her mother have appeared at the school bookstore with an empty backpack. After enduring a short wait in line—and after Mom writes a large check—Jane's bag is stuffed with thick, glossy textbooks. As a set, they are stunningly heavy, more than thirty pounds.

Jane has been issued one textbook for each subject, along with some accompanying workbooks, a lab manual for science, and a couple of paperback novels for English class. The big textbooks are jammed with facts, lists, charts, information, photographs, places, dates, formulas, problems, sidebars, study questions and more study questions, and if you drop one, it weighs enough to break your foot. This is not an exaggeration. According to a fifteen-year-old international comparison of mathematics and science education (TIMSS, 1999), American students had the heaviest, thickest textbooks in the world. And, in spite of some online growth, it looks like we are maintaining our top international ranking, in this category at least. Today's textbooks have become so weighty that the American Academy of Orthopaedic Surgeons (2013) has issued a warning about the rising incidence of injuries among young people carrying their books to school. Indeed, our textbook obesity epidemic has spawned a whole new industry: rolling backpacks.

Jane's experience is repeated every fall all across the country, in public schools and private, in poor and rich neighborhoods. In a profound sense, textbooks *are* school. In the secondary grades, "reading" usually means reading a textbook. In some states, the predominance of textbooks among instructional materials is even enshrined in law. Some states have special "adoption commissions" that approve or ban the purchase of specific textbooks. Until recently in Illinois, it was actually illegal to spend state book money on anything but commercially published school textbooks—no state funds could be spent on novels or trade nonfiction books. Charles Dickens, Stephen Hawking, and Steven Ambrose need not apply in the Land of Lincoln.

So why do textbooks hold this seemingly unassailable place in classroom practice—and in school budgets? What exactly are the benefits and shortcomings of these ubiquitous and potentially injurious objects? What are kids risking their backs for?

The Central Role of Textbooks

If you are reading this page, you may well use a textbook in your classes every day. When you teach math, or Spanish, or earth science, or almost anything else in a secondary school, textbooks are a fact of life. And for many teachers, the content-area textbook is a treasured asset. The book may be one that you helped select after an extensive search process—reviewing all the competition, making a thoughtful match-up with your local curriculum, and (if you served on the adoption committee) even lobbying for this book over others. The textbook may have become a trusted companion over the years, traveling with you through your career. By now, you know its chapters, charts, diagrams, photographs, and study questions backward and forward. You may even have seen the book evolve through several editions, and once in a while (if you are as shallow as we are) you may have enviously fantasized about the royalty checks piling up in the authors' mailboxes.

On the other hand, the textbook used in your classes may be less of a choice and more of an imposition. The book may have been selected by others, as a departmental or district adoption that you had no voice in or that was already chosen when you joined the faculty. Maybe this particular text doesn't suit your teaching style, or your way of approaching the field, or your idea of what's really important. Perhaps the book has flaws, gaps, and problems that drive you nuts. Maybe it skimps on information in a key area, or introduces vocabulary too fast, or is just plain out of date. It might be somebody else's favorite—but not yours. Maybe, if you think about it, none of us ever finds the absolutely perfect textbook, even when we select it ourselves.

Similarly, *how* you use your textbook may be under your own control, or it may be tightly constrained. Some teachers are free to "pick and choose" from the textbook, inviting kids to dig deeper into some chapters while skipping or scanning others. They can dip into the textbook occasionally, use it mainly as a reference book, or even make it a supplement to other materials and activities. Other teachers are more locked into the textbook, perhaps because they love it, or because they lack any other materials to choose from. Still others may be trapped by coverage mandates, enforced by departmental or district-wide end-of-semester examinations. Some teachers are even required to keep their students on the same textbook page each day—literally, not metaphorically—with other students in the same course, or even in schools across the district.

Somewhat ironically, English teachers are less likely to have a single textbook play such a central role in their classes. While they may use a literature anthology or a skills textbook part of the time, language arts teachers often assign students separate novels, plays, or poetry as well. This may reflect a fundamental difference between fields. Yes, language arts does have *some* content: a canon of literature, the techniques of literary craft, grammar and the conventions of language use. But much English instruction is focused on processes (reading, writing, speaking, and listening) rather than a hierarchical body of knowledge. The English curriculum is more of a spiral than a pyramid; kids practice the same basic processes year after year, at (we hope) increasingly sophisticated levels. But in highly structured fields like math or science, you must know arithmetic before you can do algebra; you must know some biology before you can understand genetics. Those bodies of knowledge, those big building blocks of information, need a place to live—and that's what textbooks are for, among other things.

> **How** you use your textbook may be under your own control, or it may be tightly constrained.

And by the way, wasn't there supposed to be a digital revolution happening in textbooks, right about now? After years of just-around the-corner imminence, the transformation is curiously slow in arriving. Most of the big textbook companies continue hedging their bets, adding online digital resources and supplements, but still cranking out those thousand-page tree-based volumes, too. Assumptions that "today's kids" would prefer their content digitally delivered haven't panned out either. Yes, kids love digital, but not digital *everything*. A recent study (Greenfield, 2013) showed that for school books, young people prefer paper to pixels by four to one.

Over the past couple of decades, the major textbook publishers have consolidated down to three main companies—Pearson, Houghton Mifflin Harcourt, and McGraw-Hill. The competition shrank in part because customizing the materials for each state's standards became too expensive for smaller companies—they couldn't compete with the big houses, so they were either driven out of business or acquired by the giants. However, now that the Common Core's national standards have gotten rid of the need to customize (for the most part) *and* now that digital media is becoming a realistic alternative to textbooks, there is a chance for smaller companies to spring up again.

So the world of textbook wannabes is expanding rapidly, with many new content vendors jumping into the business. Some states, like Utah, are simply writing their own textbooks, based on their own reading of the Common Core Standards and anticipation of the PARCC assessment for which their students must sit. Other newcomers include countless for-profit start-ups offering "core-ready digital solutions." A proliferation of organizations offer complete lesson and unit plans through their websites—some for free, some for steep fees. These teaching plans cover a wide range of approaches, from the grinding rigor of standards-writer David Coleman's own AchievetheCore.org, to the often lively lessons of ExpeditionaryLearning .com, which recently signed a big contract with New York City. Potentially, if teachers use these plans with Common Core exemplar texts and copyright-free public-domain readings, textbooks become unnecessary.

Additional states are taking on their own vigorous role in the textbook market. The Louisiana Department of Education got national coverage in late 2012 when it declared that *no* textbooks met the Pelican State's version of the Common Core Standards, and it would buy none of them. Other states, like Connecticut, have simply begun providing their own sample lessons directly to their teachers. In one typical middle school lesson plan, the directions for five full days of teaching are:

* Review and revise rules for classroom discussions.
* Teacher reads aloud "The Treasure of Lemon Brown."
* In small groups students discuss what makes this a "good story" (elements of literature).
* Whole-group discussion on elements of literature (How do suspense and point of view make this a good story?).
* Students independently reread "The Treasure of Lemon Brown" using note-taking strategies to cite text evidence (based on teacher-created text-dependent questions) that shows how the author creates suspense.
* Use notes to participate in a Socratic seminar (to be used formatively).

That's "the plan" for a full week of teaching. Like so many of the "core ready" lessons crowding the Web, this one is a skinny skeleton of a real curricular experience. These few hints could conceivably lead to powerful, engaging learning, or to a week of boredom and disengagement. Almost makes you wish for a textbook with at least *some* pedagogical support.

So, love 'em or hate 'em, paper or digital, textbooks are a very big part of our reality in middle and high school. They may not be perfect, they may not be the books we would choose, they may require all sorts of supplementing, working-around, and clarifying. But they are here to stay. Maybe the digital revolution will indeed arrive (when all 150 of your kids have iPads), but for now, those hefty, shiny textbooks will probably continue to be the main storage system for the content of our courses.

We think it is important for teachers to look at contemporary textbooks with a critical eye—and we'll start doing just that in a minute. But the goal of such scrutiny is not to kick educational publishers in their well-bruised shins. What we want to figure out is: How can we teach our content better, so that students learn, remember, and care about our subjects? How can we use textbooks properly and effectively, so that kids get the most out of them? Some textbooks are better than others. Way better. Some are severely afflicted by all the problems we are about to describe, while others suffer from just a few. Some defects are specific to individual books, while others are endemic to the species—built into their DNA. So, if you do use a textbook, it is very much worth the trouble to adopt the best one available.

Getting Better?

John Hubisz, a North Carolina State University physics professor who has been critiquing science textbooks for a decade, finds that many are as problematic as ever. Hubisz argues,

> Today's school science and mathematics textbooks do not lend themselves to seminars. This is not to say that they could not be so written. The great ideas of science are avoided like the plague. Facts, often distorted or irrelevant to the context, permeate these texts, predisposing the uninitiated reader to memorize without thinking or criticizing the content. Vocabulary is limited to such an extent that often the substituted word changes the meaning and a new misconception is born. (2012)

One exception is described by Barry Feierman, one of Hubisz's fellow reviewers:

> If one were to design a Physics textbook for "ALL" high-school students (8th–12th grades) what might it stress that would be different from the more traditional textbooks? First, the textbook might want to appeal to teenagers with topics that they are already interested in (Sports, Transportation, Communications, Medicine, Predictions, and Home). The text

would also set out to challenge a student's preconceptions about the way the world works, and ask them to make predictions, and then test their predictions in a lab setting by designing experiments. This is exactly the paradigm of *Active Physics* . . . For example, Activity 1 of the opening chapter asks about horizontal distances a basketball player travels while "hanging" to do a "slam dunk" during a fast break. Assuming teenagers understand the words (which they probably do) the rest of the Activity suggests ways to measure these quantities. So the strength of the book is the paradigm that students learn best by DOING, not by reading, not by listening to a lecture, not by watching a video. (2009, 00)

In preparing this new edition of *Subjects Matter*, we examined many newer textbooks, and were encouraged to see at least some improvements, especially among science texts. Steve took a closer look at three:

* Holt McDougal *Biology*
* Glencoe/McGraw-Hill *Biology*
* Pearson *Biology*

Biology

A number of features were especially worth noting. The Pearson text begins each chapter with a real-world mystery, the solution to which emerges as students learn the material in the chapter—thus encouraging students to engage with the material, think about the information as they encounter it, and actively make use of it. One mystery, for example, involves a marathon runner who grows faint, and as the first aid people give her water to address what they think is dehydration, she only gets worse, finally dying in the hospital. And so the question is: Why did this happen? What was wrong with her? (We'll leave you to investigate this yourself!)

The Holt McDougal text includes descriptions of historic biological discoveries, like DNA, which help show the subject to be a history of knowledge development, rather than just a collection of facts. This text has an identified author, with a bio about him. It emphasizes the connection of biological knowledge to personal health, environmental well-being, and biotech issues. Its online "Biozine" provides links to magazine articles and scientific updates, taking the student beyond just the textbook. So it has more of a voice and a connection with the wider world than many textbooks have had previously.

All of the texts, not surprisingly, include online materials. The Glencoe/McGraw-Hill online version includes a read-aloud facility, short webinars summarizing the material in each chapter, video illustrations of biological processes, and lab sheets. "Brain-Pops" plus a "reading coach" both repeat key information from the chapter, but in different ways.

All the books offer end-of-chapter assessments that are organized like standardized tests. However, Holt McDougal's assessments include more conceptual, critical-thinking items than the others. A review section for each chapter includes a "Write Your Own Questions" feature, plus a critical thinking page where tasks involve predicting, synthesizing, evaluating, and compare-contrast items. All of these features can potentially deepen the learning of the material—*if* they are of high enough quality and *if* the teacher can take time during the course of the year to use them.

It's interesting that the texts all take a strong stand on evolution, asserting it to be a central organizing theory of biological science. Especially important is their explanation that the term *theory* has a far different meaning in science than in everyday life. In normal speech, a *theory* usually means a guess. In science, the books point out, a guess is called a *hypothesis*. A scientific theory, on the other hand, is a larger explanation that must cover many different phenomena, each of which has been established and tested with repeated experiments and observations. Thus the books address, though in an oblique way, some of the narrow religious attacks on evolution and science in general—a fairly courageous step in this particular age.

All three texts claim to organize their material around "big ideas." And for introductory chapters on the nature of science and biology, the ideas do indeed prove to be large concepts. But as the chapters march on, the "ideas" turn out to be mere enumerations of material in the chapter—"What are the five types of . . . ," for example, or definitions of key terms—that hardly seem like ideas at all.

These are still textbooks, so they are still, at heart, reference books—huge collections of information. And the information comes at students thick and fast. The Pearson text tends to introduce terms before they are explained, which would certainly be overwhelming to many students. Glencoe/McGraw-Hill, in contrast, introduces terms promptly, in short, disconnected sentences, which makes the reading seem plodding and lifeless. The various sections of a chapter rarely connect back explicitly to the larger "big idea" that supposedly draws them together. There are plenty of bells, whistles, and activities, but they are sometimes in a disjointed jumble, and we can easily imagine that teachers who are racing to cover everything that is going to be on the next test might not believe they have the time to stop for those more interesting elements.

> *. . . we can easily imagine that teachers who are racing to cover everything that is going to be on the next test might not believe they have the time to stop for those more interesting elements.*

The Trouble with Textbooks

Notwithstanding our sincere appreciation of publishers' recent efforts, textbooks continue to be overused, and should be supplemented generously or replaced with other reading materials where possible.

As we list our concerns, we're mindful that either the Common Core or your state (or both) require you to cover eighty thousand tons of material, all of it conveniently located in a big commercial textbook. We've met the textbook reps, too, and they talk a great game. They'll show you a list (a concordance, almost) detailing exactly how their product matches, standard by standard, with all those requirements and their accompanying tests. Still, this doesn't prove that this salesman's book will actually teach your content better than another textbook or, for that matter, that a completely different set of readings, materials, and experiences might meet the standards better than any textbook. The big problem is: to pass the statewide test, the kids have to actually remember the material. Can the textbook guy guarantee that?

So here are some reasons why textbooks are not enough to build our whole courses, our whole classroom lives around. We'll start with the biggest, most intractable problems first, and get to the minor beefs later.

Textbooks are superficial

Recently we visited a Chicago high school where we had the opportunity to look through the stack of textbooks assigned to all juniors. Man, they were massive!

> British literature—1,310 pages
> Biology—1,184 pages
> French—513 pages
> U.S. history—982 pages
> Advanced algebra/trigonometry—890 pages

Now, it may seem odd to accuse five-pound textbooks of being superficial. They certainly seem complete; they feel mighty weighty. And they undeniably provide an avalanche of data, a staggering amount of detail. They are jammed with facts, figures, charts, tables, and graphs.

But strange as it seems, these books just scratch the surface, and that's because they contain *too much* material. Often, the really key concepts, the big ideas of the field, don't stand out clearly, aren't given enough time and depth for students to grasp them. Two pages on Walt

Whitman, a paragraph on Hiroshima, or a sidebar about Einstein's theory of relativity just doesn't get the job done. In the drive to mention everything, key ideas fade into the background, are never successfully communicated, or simply don't stick with students.

You may have been a victim of this textbook superficiality when you were a student. If the science teachers will play along for just a minute, we can try an experiment. Probably, somewhere in school, you studied a little about plants, including photosynthesis and related topics, right? You might even recall that little molecular label $C_6H_{12}O_6$, the key roles of chlorophyll, the phloem cells, the cambium layer, and so forth. OK, here's the question: As an acorn grows from a slender seedling into a fifty-foot oak, where does all that mass come from? Think of yourself hefting even a small log cut from such an enormous life-form. Where did all that stuff come from?

. . . textbooks continue to be overused, and should be supplemented generously or replaced with other reading materials where possible.

If your education depended too much on textbooks, you might have answered that all that mass came from nutrients in the ground, or from sunlight, or from water drawn up through the tree's roots. In fact, the great majority of the grown-up oak tree's mass came from the *air*. Remember, trees take in air, extract the CO_2, give off oxygen, and break down the CO_2 to make carbon, the building block of life. And CO_2, like all gases, no matter how invisible, has mass—plenty of it—which is conserved even when it is changed by chemical processes.

If you got this wrong, don't feel too bad. A team of researchers from the Harvard-Smithsonian Astrophysical Observatory filmed both fourth graders and seniors at MIT trying to answer the same question (Budiansky, 2001). Most of the students, both the engineering majors and the ten-year-olds on the playground, gave similar wrong answers, though both had studied photosynthesis and even knew some of the terminology.

This misconception is an example of students (maybe including us) not learning the big, key ideas in a field even while being bombarded by masses of facts and terminology. In this case, the students never got the basic idea of what *matter* is, how it can be transformed by chemical reactions, and that it is conserved. This misunderstanding, typical of so many that are spawned by our "coverage" model of curriculum and enshrined in textbooks, has real consequences. How can we expect our future citizens to understand (and maybe even protect) the environment they live in, if they don't know basic scientific principles? How are they going to grasp the importance of facts like this: driving an average American automobile for a year puts 11,450 *pounds* of invisible but very consequential CO_2 into the atmosphere? (Environmental Protection Agency, 2013).

Textbooks are exceedingly hard to read

Ever wonder why *Algebra II* has never topped the *New York Times* best-seller list? Or why no one ever buys a chemistry textbook and stays up all night reading it straight through? ("I just couldn't put it down!") Maybe that's because textbooks are reference books, not novels or nonfiction trade books. School textbooks belong in the same category as encyclopedias, dictionaries, and thesauruses. They don't attempt to provide the kind of coherent narrative you get in a *Time* magazine article or a good popular biography or expose. It is not their primary job to tell you a story, or even pay much attention to your readerly morale. Instead, textbooks are designed to inventory huge amounts of information that can be looked up when needed.

> *Instead of inviting kids into the material, many of today's textbooks are a graphic maelstrom.*

In the field of reading research, school textbooks exemplify what is called "inconsiderate" or "unfriendly" text. They are giant storage systems for information. They are intentionally "content-overloaded" with facts, dates, formulas, taxonomies. They introduce vocabulary and concepts at a blinding rate. They are overtly structured and highly orderly, packing information into labeled slots, as densely as possible. But thinking back on how smart readers actually think in Chapter 2, we realize that just being highly organized does not make a textbook any easier to read than a similarly "well-organized" home theater installation manual.

There is nothing wrong with reference books. Personally, we love them, we use them, we cannot live without them. The problem lies in the way textbooks get used in school. In the civilian world, people use reference books mainly when they have an immediate personal need to find a certain chunk of information—what the Third Amendment really says, how the colon works, or how to compute the surface area of a sphere. But in school, we often act as if textbooks were novels that kids should plow right through, from cover to cover, remembering and caring about what they read. We virtually pretend that textbooks aren't reference books at all, but rather some strange hybrid text form: long, fact-packed stories that a person can read day in day out, memorize with fascination, and pass statewide tests on.

No wonder kids "can't read" their textbooks! We start with the content overload, the inherent readability problems of the genre. Add to this the lack of narrative structures that sustain readers in most real-world nonfiction. Then throw in the expectation that kids should read textbooks cover to cover—and remember everything, even if they are reading other textbooks in three or four different courses. Then there's the strategies problem, which we just described in Chapter 2—our habitual failure to teach kids specific cognitive operations for dealing with text, especially needed for tough-going material like textbooks. Already we have a perfect recipe for ineffective and unpleasant reading experiences—and there are still more problems to consider.

Textbooks are badly designed

In recent years, publishers have worked hard to make textbooks more visually interesting and engaging to students. They are well aware that the look of real-world nonfiction has changed dramatically in recent years—think of the evolution of magazines from endless blocks of gray to today's lively columns, graphics, and features in a magazine like *Wired*. Even more urgently, the publishers of school textbooks feel they must compete with the hyper-world of the Internet and video games, where kids spend much of their time. After all, how you gonna keep their noses in the chemistry textbook after they've played "*Call of Duty: Black Ops II*"?

The problem is that these postmodern designs mostly don't work. Instead of inviting kids into the material, many of today's textbooks are a graphic maelstrom. As one teacher lamented: "The publishers try to make these books attractive to kids, to make them look jazzy and up to date. And I understand, with all the boxes and gimmicks, they are trying to give kids multiple points of entry into the text. They're trying to make it feel like a tablet or a video game where the kids feel some control. But those pages end up just being confusing and overwhelming. And it's worst for my struggling readers. They can't make any sense of those pages at all."

Textbooks are authoritarian

In many schools and subjects, a single commercial textbook constitutes the entire curriculum. At P. T. Barnum High, the entire subject matter for the United States History course might simply be *The Americans* by Danzer et al. (McDougal Littell); the Algebra II class might be based on nothing but *Advanced Algebra* by Senk et al. (Scott Foresman–Addison Wesley); the content of Spanish 3 can come exclusively from *Ven Comingo!* by Humback and Ozete (Holt, Rinehart and Winston), and so forth. For these courses, there may be no other readings, with the possible exception of a companion workbook (called a "consumable" in the business and prized for its profitability). Then, to make this exclusive franchise official, someone types up the textbook's table of contents and slaps a cover on it emblazoned: "P.T. Barnum High School Curriculum Guide: Spanish 3." Or, more often these days, the textbook sales rep does that copying job, supplying matches between his company's book and every single standard the school labors under.

For a country espousing democracy as its nominal form of governance, this sanctification of The Textbook provides a strangely incongruous apprenticeship. When we rely on a single source for all of a course's content, we are teaching kids to accept one view, one authority; we are saying that it is fine to depend on a single voice, even on complicated, value-driven questions. But what if the history textbook fails to mention that generals Eisenhower and MacArthur argued with Truman against using the atom bomb against Japan? What if the required book labels Rosa Parks "a tired maid who didn't want to move to the back of the bus," instead of a longtime civil rights activist?

Single sourcing is not the way smart and free people read. Instead, they recognize that most of life's biggest questions are hugely complex, have not yet been settled, and that science, technology, and even culture proceed on the "best theory to date." They know that every author, no matter how hard she may strive for fairness and neutrality, comes to the work with deep and often unconscious values, tastes, and preferences. That's why mature readers use multiple sources to get all the information, develop a balanced view, hear the alternative theories, and make up their own minds. Whether it is intentional or not, it is unacceptable for schools in a democracy to teach young people that only one view is sufficient—of science, of mathematics, of literature, of history, or any subject. We might think that students just need to learn the basics first and save the controversies for later—but too often, later never arrives.

Textbooks are often inaccurate

Textbook companies work very hard to make sure their products are both timely and accurate. They have teams of fact checkers scrupulously verifying information, and writers constantly creating updated editions every few years, to make sure that new findings, breakthroughs, and emerging theories are included. But it simply is not humanly possible to keep current—or to keep correct.

Math A few years ago, the Texas State Department of Education undertook a study of errors and factual inaccuracies in the mathematics textbooks that had been submitted by major publishers for use in its schools. They found a total of 109,263 errors in the math texts being considered for purchase. According to a report in the *Dallas News* (2008):

> The Board went back to the publishers and told them that they had until spring to fix the errors, after which point each publisher would be susceptible to a fine of up to $5,000 per error found. Of course, not all of the errors were in the arithmetic; some textbooks had accidentally printed the answers to the quizzes at the end of each chapter, while others

had incorrect translations from the English to the Spanish versions. But, a hefty number of the errors were in the numbers themselves. All of the publishers' books had errors, but leading textbook publisher Houghton Mifflin took the cake: 86,026 errors across its series of books, accounting for 79% of the total discovered by the Board.

"It looks like one publisher won the sweepstakes," said Board member, Bob Craig. "How can you make 86,000 errors in your textbooks? How do you do that?"

But smart teachers can even make textbook errors useful. We were lucky to visit the wonderful integrated studies program at Addison Trail High School in suburban Chicago. The kids and teachers were in the middle of one of the kids' favorite topics of the year—the "Plagues" unit. The ultimate goal was for each student to select and explore one of the many plagues that has or could afflict the world, from AIDS to bird flu to biological warfare. On the day we visited, science teacher Don Grossnickle started his biology class by saying: "Remember last week how we read in the textbook about the bubonic plague? How it was caused by a bacteria spread by rats and fleas? And we studied that cycle of disease transmission? Well, guess what, guys? It looks like the textbook might have been wrong."

Biology

Don smiled as the kids looked back curiously. "I thought about keeping this a secret from you, but I knew I had to tell you." And with that, Don handed out the just-arrived issue of *Science News* (published by the Weekly Reader group) to each student. In an article entitled "The Black Plague: Not a Bacteria After All?," kids read about a recently published book in England that argued, quite convincingly, that the bubonic plague was not a bacteria spread by rats but, in fact, a viral hemorrhagic fever—akin to what we now know as Ebola. A great discussion ensued about how fast science moves, how long-standing theories can get overturned by a single study, and why, as Don put it, "We can't always rely on a textbook that's three or four years old." As if to put a cap on Don's warning, the bacteria believers mounted a ferocious counterattack upon the virus theorists, and the Black Plague controversy rages on among historical epidemiologists to this day.

> ... smart teachers can even make textbook errors useful.

Textbooks are not written for students

Remember that old expression, "You never want to see either sausages or laws being made?" Well, the same thing applies to textbooks. It is an unsightly assembly line, guaranteed to crush the idealism of the innocent. What is your picture of the process? Maybe the recognized experts in the field sit down around a big seminar table to determine the essence of the subject and how it can best be taught to young people? Maybe they bring some actual students in and talk to them about biology or literature? Nah. There are a lot more people at the table than subject-matter experts, and their concerns are not mainly about the integrity of the discipline. And students? They may be the end users of textbooks, but they are not the "market," and certainly not the decision makers.

Obviously, textbook publishing is a business, and the overriding concern for publishers, the consideration that trumps all others, is sales and profits. This is no shock, right? Publishers need to create a product that sells, that beats the competition, that rakes in some cash. And in the high-limit casino of educational publishing, to score big you have to please a wide array of people, groups, and agencies who often disagree with each other. And today, the cross-pressures are even more complex and the stakes higher. The Common Core Standards are driving a multimillion-dollar redo of virtually all mathematics, reading, and English language arts textbooks over the next few years. But some big states, including Texas, Minnesota, Nebraska, and Massachusetts, have opted out of CCSS and have their own standards. As this book goes to press, fourteen other states are considering full or partial withdrawal from the whole Race to the Top/Common Core world. How will the textbook companies play this iffy hand? We'll see where the chips fall.

OK, so now we are watching textbooks being made, just like sausages, and it's not such a pretty picture.

OK, so now we are watching textbooks being made, just like sausages, and it's not such a pretty picture. The analogy to the meat-packing houses in *Fast Food Nation* is quite fitting. Still, in light of the strong criticisms we have laid out so far, it is amazing how thorough and cohesive many textbooks still manage to be.

Textbooks cost too much

It is not uncommon for today's school textbooks to be priced at $50, $100, or more. Take five "solids" and you're looking at a $300 bill. This can cause sticker shock in communities where parents have to foot the book bill, over and above paying their taxes. And in some city high schools where we work, the idea of affording current textbooks is simply a joke. Hey, we just got our funding cut again. We're going to be losing a teacher as a result, not buying any textbooks.

But even so, we wouldn't claim that contemporary textbooks are overpriced; after all, with their customary weight, thickness, and color, it would be hard to produce these kinds of books for much less. The problem is that buying these $70 textbooks for every kid gobbles up the whole instructional materials budget, and squeezes out the possibility of buying anything else. How can we pay for *Chew on This*, subscribe to the newspaper, sign up for *Science News*, buy site licenses for great databases, or build classroom libraries when all the dough goes for textbooks?

What Can We Do?

To free up some money for supplementary materials, one solution is to switch from one textbook per student (which might mean buying 150 copies) to one classroom set (more like thirty copies). This has a wholesome side effect—since the kids now cannot take the textbooks home, you'll get a chance to experiment with more engaging homework assignments. Another tactic is to delay adopting a new text as long as possible, pushing that big expense as far down the road as you responsibly can. This depends on the subject area, of course. At most high schools, the juniors can get along just fine with a 2001 textbook in British literature, a field where revolutionary breakthroughs are rare. But now, when the "Common Core editions" of British literature become available, and we are all worrying about the PARCC or Smarter Balanced Test, we may be tempted to forsake real books and spend tens of thousands of dollars on those foot-breakers once again.

If you must buy a textbook, think seriously about forswearing the extras, goodies, and dealer-installed upgrades (although some may be offered for free to sweeten the deal with your district). Publishers claim that teachers ask for programs with lots of activity kits, workbooks, blackline masters, practice tests, and other such "ancillaries." If that's true, shame on us. Chances are we can live without the transparencies, handouts, posters, videos, CD-ROMs, audiotapes, activity cards, and banks of test questions. Jo Ellen Roseman of the American Association for the Advancement of Science Project 2061 says, "Our reviewers went through all of this material and can say authoritatively: It's not worth it" (Roseman et al., 2001).

And, if you're feeling really adventurous, you could stop having textbook-centered courses altogether, for a few weeks or months at a time. One morning, we saw senior English teacher Matt Feldman working the one unbroken risograph (Chicago jargon for copying machine) really hard. He was creating a collection of poems for his afternoon class, but between the machine jamming and the colleagues waiting impatiently behind him, Matt was getting frustrated. "Now I get it!" he blurted out. "This is why people have textbooks, so they don't have to go through all this bullshit!"

But when we looked at Matt's handmade collection, we realized how good it was that there is no senior English textbook at this school. From the Library of Congress website, Poetry 180, and a few other selected sources, Matt had created a gorgeous and distinctive set of poems, all by and about African Americans, perfectly suited to his class, matched to their age and experience, attuned to their previous literary diet, and aimed at their interests, today. No textbook could ever do that. Now, that's what we call *teaching*.

Now, in the schools where we work, the faculty does not spend the whole year risographing supplementary materials and reading trade books. We too have mandates, subjects to teach, and tests to pass. But when we use the textbooks now, we use them much more strategically and sparingly. We focus in on smaller sections of text, taking time (and other materials) to highlight and flesh out the most important concepts. We teach kids specific strategies (to be described in Chapters 5 and 6) that involve them in thinking about, discussing, critiquing, and applying the ideas they've read. We show them how to monitor their understanding and to actively seek help and clarification when they are confused or lost. We do the good teaching it takes to convert a passive review-and-quiz approach to richer, more engaging experiences that students will remember and maybe even enjoy.

> *We focus in on smaller sections of text, taking time to highlight and flesh out the most important concepts.*

Perhaps now it is clearer than ever why we must change not just *how* we teach reading, but *what* we ask kids to read. We need to use textbooks more appropriately (and sparingly), as the reference books that they are, and also infuse the curriculum with authentic, real-world nonfiction—the kind of informational, expository, persuasive texts that adults really read. Luckily, textbooks are just the foam on the ocean of nonfiction. The world is full of fascinating, important, debatable, and sometimes inflammatory nonfiction, from partisan magazines to primary source materials to revisionist histories to amazing science discoveries—for readers of all ages. Let's go shopping for some great, kid-friendly text.

DISCOVERING

THE TRUTH

IN SCIENCE

einstein who?

TAMLYN MITCHELL

Toward a Balanced Diet of Reading

W e've argued that teachers should use textbooks more sparingly, more carefully, and with explicit scaffolding strategies—which we'll detail in Chapters 5 and 6. But the corollary is that young people should be reading content material *in other genres*: newspaper articles, magazines, research reports, websites, primary sources, biographies, and full-length trade nonfiction books. And the Common Core Standards essentially require this. But why? What is to be found in the wider world of reading that students miss when they read only textbooks? Why is it urgent that we change their reading diets? Here is an example of how "real" nonfiction text can be important to the curriculum.

Let's talk about Einstein. A typical physics textbook might give one or two pages to his world-changing equation, $E = mc^2$. So we can say that the concept is "covered," at least for the students who brave a physics class at all. Trouble is, if you go out on Main Street America today and ask a hundred textbook-educated high school graduates what each symbol in the equation means, ninety-nine of them will not be able to tell you. And the knowledge gap does not just afflict nonscience majors like Smokey (Steve studied physics in college—no fair!). Now, if you further inquire of your random citizens, or even those who took that high school physics course, what the equation *means*, most cannot say much at all. Sometimes people, shown the equation, just shrug their shoulders and say "Boom!" This is not what we could properly call "deep understanding."

The noted science writer David Bodanis was worried about the ignorance of this central fact affecting modern life. "There are plenty of books that try to explain it," he says, "but who can honestly say they understand them?" So Bodanis took a distinctly non-textbook approach in his book *E = mc²: A Biography of the World's Most Famous Equation*. "Everyone knows that a biography entails stories of the ancestors, childhood, adolescence, and adulthood of your subject," he reasoned. Bodanis takes each symbol in the equation and tells the story of the people who developed the big idea from its infancy. Believe it or not, his book is a page-turner, a stay-up-all-night-and-finish-it yarn. It takes 113 pages, but by the time you've heard all the stories, you feel that the equation, and indeed the theory of relativity itself, has entered your bones forever. How is this different from the textbook treatment? How does Bodanis provide readers both depth of understanding and page-by-page entertainment? Here's what it sounds like.

These are the elements of engagement that you'll find in any successful nonfiction book, in any content area, be it mathematics, science, history, economics, or art.

Toward the end of the book, Bodanis describes a 1938 breakthrough by Lise Meitner, a brilliant Jewish scientist who had been banned from Germany and was exiled to Sweden (2001, 109–111). Her nephew, Robert Frisch, also a physicist, came to visit her at a friend's country home. The two went out in the snow with Frisch on cross-country skis and his aunt marching briskly beside him on foot. Along the way, the two talked about the uranium atom and its peculiar properties. As an idea started to dawn, they slowed down.

Meitner and her nephew weren't physicists for nothing. They had paper with them, and pencils, and in the cold of the Swedish forest, this Christmas Eve, they took them out and began calculating. What if it turned out that the uranium nucleus was so big, and so crammed with extra neutrons in there, that even before you started artificially pushing extra neutrons in, it was already in a pretty precarious state? That would be as if the uranium were a water droplet that already was stretched apart as far as it could go before bursting. Into that overstuffed nucleus, one more plump neutron was then inserted.

Meitner started to draw the wobbles . . . Frisch took the pencil from her politely and did the sketches. It was like taking a water balloon and squeezing it in the middle. The two ends bulge out. If you're lucky, the rubber of the balloon will hold, and the water won't burst out. But keep on with it. Squeeze in some more, and when the balloon spreads sideways, let go until it rebounds toward the center, then squeeze in the opposite way. Keep on repeating. Eventually the balloon will burst. Get your timing right, and you won't even have to squeeze very hard.

By the time their walk in the snow had ended, Meitner and Frisch had developed a hypothesis that would change the world.

> The atom was open. Everyone had been wrong before. The way in wasn't by blasting harder and harder fragments at it. One woman and her nephew, quiet in the midday snow, had now seen that. You didn't even have to supply the power for a uranium atom to explode. Just get enough extra neutrons in there to start it off. Then it would start jiggling more and more wildly, until the strong forces that held it together gave way, and the electricity inside made the fragments fall apart. This explosion powered itself.

What's the difference between textbook talk and this best-selling trade book? Of course Bodanis, like all good nonfiction writers (including the more skillful textbook authors), uses solid organizational patterns. But he gives much more to make the information readable and memorable:

* content that is important or engaging
* people we can care about
* a narrative structure or chronological line
* places we can visualize
* danger, conflicts, risks, or choices
* value, moral, ethical, or political dimensions
* ideas that reasonable people can debate, dispute, or disagree about

These are the elements of engagement that you'll find in any successful nonfiction book, in any content area, be it mathematics, science, history, economics, or art. In this example, using letters, diaries, conversations, and photographs (but no other formulas or equations), Bodanis brings to life some of the most complex and consequential ideas in scientific—indeed, in human—history.

Now, about this time, any science teacher might interject: "Hey, this $E = mc^2$ stuff may be readable and maybe my kids would enjoy it. But it is 113 pages long, not three! I'll grant you that students might understand the equation better if they read this book. Maybe they'd be more able to think through issues like nuclear energy, radiation, and all that. But I don't have that kind of time! I have scores of mandated topics—and the new standardized test covers everything. What am I supposed to do?"

Fair question. Do we make time for the real book or not? And if so, how? Well, some help comes from the Common Core Standards, even if at first it seems like they ask us to do a lot. Those standards under "Integration of Knowledge and Ideas" that call for students to analyze ideas in various texts and compare approaches across texts—those thinking tasks can't be carried out on textbooks. The only way to address them is by taking time to *go deeper into a smaller number of topics*. This is exactly what 26 states are officially moving toward as they develop the Next Generation Science Standards—depth versus coverage. All this means yes, we should step outside our content area textbooks for a while—not the entire school year,

FORTY books a year?

Back in the 1990s, it seemed like everyone in the field of education was issuing a "standards report." One we admired in many ways was issued by the New Standards Project. Headed by Linda Darling-Hammond and funded by the National Commission on Education and the Economy, the NSP among other things made this declaration as their number one educational standard: all students in American schools should read at least twenty-five books per year. Huh? In middle and high school, we can never accomplish this with just one textbook for each of five or six courses! I mean, if you hang on to the regular textbook in every class, that gives you only five or six—plus students would have spent a huge amount of time on this handful of tough, thousand-page books. Then what? Where do the other books come in? Maybe a couple of novels in English, but . . .

Now, however, a surprising number of teachers have gone even further and adopted Donalyn Miller's forty-book challenge (in *The Book Whisperer*, 2009). Donalyn does not simply post a number on the wall, however. She supports students in reaching that goal—carving out in-class reading time, providing reading role models and access to books, supporting students' reading choices, streamlining work where she can. OK, you might not tackle the whole job in your math classes. But what if teachers organized to do this across the subject areas in your building? Maybe this forty books a year standard is a little *too* radical for most would-be school reformers, and a little too threatening to the textbook publishers, with their stranglehold on instructional materials budgets. But do a Web search for the forty-book challenge and you'll see that maybe it's catching on anyway!

but a while—and have students read $E = mc^2$, or *Material World*, or *The Joy of Pi*, or *No Easy Day: The Firsthand Account of the Mission That Killed Osama Bin Laden*, or *Genome*, or *Letters to a Young Scientist*, or *Postville*, or *The Relentless Revolution: The History of Capitalism*.

Now, while we noted in Chapter 3 that newer textbooks have incorporated "big ideas" for their chapters to promote deeper thinking, these are often just labels covering the same overstuffed and authoritative but sketchy summaries of material. And though the best of the textbooks do provide online links to additional articles, it's challenging for a teacher to make time to use them—and the publishers don't always keep them updated.

It is hard to make yourself put that textbook down and "teach less," giving up so much time for one book, covering just one big idea. One way to do this is to identify a few key concepts and link all of your teaching to these across the year, rather than lightly covering an endless list of facts and factoids. Our friends in the history department at Deerfield High School have made this possible by focusing on a set of overarching themes for each course. For U.S. history the list looks like this:

> **History**

* what it means to be an American
* the individual and the state
* the role and evolution of the rule of law
* popular sovereignty and states' rights
* reform/resistance
* sectionalism and sectional conflict
* war and its impact on soldiers and the civilian population
* isolation, intervention, and engagement in world affairs
* executive power in a time of crisis
* the challenges of diversity and conformity (assimilation)
* race and American society
* gender and American society
* the movement from a predominantly rural to a predominantly urban society
* the role of markets and government in the economy

At Clissold School, on the far South Side in Chicago, the junior high grades use the International Baccalaureate Middle Grades program, in which the curriculum is infused in all subjects with the following principles:

* three fundamental concepts: holistic learning, intercultural awareness, communication

* five areas of interaction: approaches to learning, community and service, environments, health and social education, human ingenuity (though we understand that these are being changed as we speak)
* seven approaches to learning skills: communication, collaboration, information literacy, organization, reflection, thinking, transfer
* ten learner profiles: balanced, caring, communicator, inquirer, knowledgeable, open-minded, principled, reflective, risk taker, thinker

In Debra Henderson's seventh-grade humanities class, for example, you'll see her students working in collaborative groups, each exploring the culture in a specific country. Once their research is done, the students reorganize in "jigsawed" groups to compare information about the various countries, and finally circulate around the room to place sticky-note comments on each other's country posters. It won't be difficult for the reader to identify the many IB principles addressed in this activity. And Debra makes sure students are reminded about the connections regularly, to understand what's behind their learning.

A simpler strategy can just be to pause frequently from the usual curriculum to explore a short, relevant article and think through the implications together. A great resource for this is Smokey and Nancy Steineke's *Texts and Lessons for Content-Area Reading* (2011). And we'll have more to say about short readings just ahead.

A Balance of What?

If textbooks aren't enough, then exactly what must be added to achieve a balance? What else should kids, adolescents, teenagers be reading? What range of genres, styles, length of texts, and so forth are we looking for? One way to answer this question is to notice what the thoughtful, curious members of the surrounding adult community are reading. Among your local lifelong learners, what's in the literacy diet? Probably you'd find that these thinking grown-ups read from a wide range of genres, in assorted situations and for various purposes. They probably read some "required" material for work, some other texts to stay informed as citizens and consumers, still more materials to get practical information, and some stuff just for fun. And that's just how we should work it in school for kids, creating a balance along a number of continua, including the following.

Textbooks versus other genres

Here's a list of some text genres that exist in our culture, roughly arranged from the most dryly factual to the most "made up."

Reference books
Textbooks
Manuals/instructions
Contracts/legal documents
News stories
Feature stories
Historical accounts
Profiles
Editorials
Essays

Reviews
Biographies
Narrated nonfiction
Memoirs
Travelogues/adventure
Historical novels
Novels
Plays
Poetry

You might debate these classifications, but we'd still argue that a well-educated middle or high school student should be regularly sampling many genres. And we can't think of a single school subject that doesn't have its own published materials in many of these slots. There are memoirs of historical figures, biographies of mathematicians, profiles of artists, reviews of literature, reference books on artists—heck, we could probably even find a contract with a scientist (a patent, for example, or a government grant contract).

Most of these genres are familiar. Perhaps the only unusual term is "narrated nonfiction," which refers to informational texts where content is delivered through a personal voice like this: "Imagine standing at the edge of an ice field, looking up at your first glacier." It's a trusty tool of magazine writers everywhere: "Beyonce sits at a back table in Starbucks, absently stirring her coffee and talking about her charity work. She looks much more fragile and thoughtful than the swaggering sex object in her videos." You know the drill.

Choice versus assigned

Usually, all school reading is assigned by a teacher. But real readers, lifelong readers, assign themselves. Sure, they may have jobs that provide some "required" reading. But in their wider lives, deciding what to read is a definitive act of literacy. Will it be the *New York Times* or the *Chicago Tribune*? *Vanity Fair* or *Wired*? A novel or a biography?

It should be just the same for adolescent students in school. In every subject area, some reading materials should be chosen by the young people themselves, reflecting their own view of the topic, their own connections and interests. Of course, students will need practice and guidance in choosing books, articles, and Internet resources—after all, they may have experienced nothing but dependence in school. So we'll help with a gentle hand, keeping in mind that giving kids choices is not a matter of "letting" them decide a few things: on the contrary, the flip side of choice is responsibility. When we invite students to find valuable reading materials for themselves, we are "requiring" them to do the jobs real readers do. We're refusing to spoon-feed every piece of text they need to understand the Civil War. We're also saying, "You cannot choose to read nothing," and forthrightly enforcing that rule. With choice, students shoulder some work—but we'll explicitly show them how. The Common Core Standards focus heavily on building students' independence as readers. Choice is an essential part of that.

History

For his U.S. history course, Ken Kramer has students read interviews from *The Studs Terkel Reader: My American Century*, using in-class reading time about once every two weeks. Sometimes he assigns a passage for everyone to discuss. But often, students make their own choice of an interview to read within a particular section. Using a single book of short pieces obviates the challenge of constantly photocopying materials, which is an issue across the school. Ken finds, too, that readings like this are essential for achieving the engagement and depth that the history text lacks.

Fiction versus nonfiction

In the content areas (English being the supposedly "content-free" exception) we are mostly concerned with a more balanced diet of nonfiction, and especially a wider range of genres. This is a realistic adjustment in many ways: after all, 84 percent of what American adults actually read is nonfiction. And the Common Core Standards call for a strong diet of nonfiction in students' reading. For some, this has been quite controversial, as English teachers fear losing their most cherished novels and plays. But much nonfiction reading can naturally take place in content-area courses, as the standards documents assert.

History

However, there are times when fiction also has a very special place in science, math, history, and other fields. Students might grow interested in a deadly historical quarrel like the Hamilton-Burr duel. What was it actually about? Well, *Burr* by Gore Vidal is one of a thousand historical novels that includes tons of factual background information, and makes both a person and a period come alive. Lawrence Hill's award-winning *Someone Knows My Name* traces the journey of a young African woman who is kidnapped and made a slave in nineteenth-century South Carolina, but escapes to make her way back home. And for a page-turner about the development of the atomic bomb, including personal peccadilloes of Robert

Oppenheimer and his band of ego-driven physicists at Los Alamos, you can't top *Stallions' Gate* by best-selling novelist Martin Cruz Smith. But we don't always need to match novels with a course topic; we can also use fiction simply to set the stage, to entice curiosity. If you're a science teacher trying to prime students for a unit on time, space, or astronomy, an Arthur C. Clarke short story could provide a great sci-fi blastoff.

English class is where kids get their official doses of fiction and poetry. But perhaps in light of the Common Core recognition of the importance of nonfiction reading, we should rebalance the diet a bit here, too. After all, some of today's most celebrated, cutting-edge writing is nonfiction appearing in progressive magazines and edgy websites. And the hot book-length genre for a number of years has been memoir—dare we suggest a little Dave Eggers in place of Jonathan Edwards?

Classics versus contemporary works

There are always steamy debates about whether kids should read "classic" works or dig into contemporary young adult literature instead—and the Common Core Standards have only intensified the discussion. In this endless and tiresome controversy, authoritative prescriptions abound. Unfortunately, the Common Core exemplar texts are surprisingly skewed. Not one African American novelist or dramatist for freshman or sophomore English? Nothing for history/social studies reflecting contemporary urban poverty, or Americans' experience with war in the twentieth century? And though the lists are only offered as "examples," some schools have simply adopted them uncritically.

> Some of what kids read in school should hold up a mirror to them by including their story, their culture, their experience.

So for an appropriate and balanced reading experience for contemporary American teenagers, we are big subscribers to the "windows and mirrors" theory of book selection. Some of what kids read in school should hold up a mirror to them by including their story, their culture, their experience. This is a way of saying, you and your family are important, you are part of us, part of our country and culture. But other books should act as windows, where kids look out not at their own reflection, but upon other peoples, other time periods, other stories, values, and ways of life.

We sure don't see many mirrors in the Common Core recommendations, especially for the African American and Hispanic and, come to think of it, the white students we teach. Once again, it's all about balance. To bind young people to school and to reading, we need to invite them in, make them welcome, honor their heritage, and address their current interests. Fortunately, the Common Core lists are just recommendations, and schools and districts can develop more-inclusive reading options. Of course, as educators we know we also need to stretch our students, to broaden their knowledge, enrich their experience, widen their worldview, and grow their fund of information. Yes, contemporary kids can identify deeply with protagonists in way-back times and far-off places. Look at Harry Potter and Bilbo Baggins. But if the school mainly assigns distant, alien, and anachronistic books, you are pushing many kids away. You are saying, in effect and not by accident, "Hey buddy, this ain't your place." And as revealed by recent research, students' success is heavily affected by whether they see school as a place where they belong.

Hard versus easy

While some reading should be challenging, students can learn plenty of content (and as research shows, actually increase their reading ability) when the text itself doesn't constantly trip them up. Too many students (some labeled "special ed" and others not) spend their entire school day staring at text they *cannot read*—and many times it's a textbook. Now if a student spends six hours a day not being able to read what we put in front of him, what is the most likely consequence? That the kid rededicates himself to reading and school? Or that he feels kicked out of a club he doesn't want to join anyway?

> *. . . kids need to read stuff they can read. This is nonnegotiable.*

We'll say it loud and clear, and research strongly supports us: kids need to read stuff they *can* read. This is nonnegotiable. Some time during every school day, students should read comfortable, fun, interesting text they can zoom through fluently without hesitation. If this means bringing third-grade materials into a ninth-grade room, fine.

If you are worried about pandering or underchallenging, think about it this way. Scratch a lifelong reader, someone who has grown up to be a sophisticated consumer of text, and you'll almost always find some Nancy Drew, Hardy Boys, or even—yikes!—comic books in their background. Maybe this even describes us. But like most grown-ups, we tend to forget parts of our own history, like the fact that young readers often grow by reading lots of really easy, sometimes formulaic materials. So have faith. If we spend part of every school day helping kids enjoy some reading, whether inside our content areas or out, we are giving a great and lasting gift. As Richard Allington's extensive review of research shows (*What Really Matters for Struggling Readers*, 2011), lots of easy reading builds the stamina that moves kids forward.

The Common Core Standards, meanwhile, argue intensely for moving students to more complex texts, and we know that to do well when they go off to college, young people will need to be able to handle these. The question, though, is how to help them get there—and simply plunging them into the deep water without any life preserver doesn't accomplish that at all. Instead, when our students are tackling more challenging materials, it's our job to provide the supports, the "scaffolding," as reading experts call it, that helps them navigate—finding engaging topics, building academic vocabulary, developing background knowledge, providing comprehension strategies, promoting lots of discussion.

Prosser High School in Chicago serves a largely Mexican American student body, and Prosser biology teacher Marnie Ware knows that difficult technical words make her second language learners feel excluded from the "learning club." So she helps them learn prefixes and suffixes that make the language more recognizable. She uses call and response for biology vocabulary to familiarize the kids with it. And she discusses the cultural issues that scientific language can bring up—perhaps inadvertently. She discusses the social justice connections in biology, including the location of polluting industry in their neighborhoods and global and local food availability. "People who don't know about these things get taken advantage of," she reminds them.

Biology

In his Deerfield High School U.S. history class, Ken Kramer helps students comprehend and appreciate historic documents by reading them aloud. He finds this brings older writing styles and challenging vocabulary to life, and students actually get better at reading such documents as a result. Reading aloud is not just entertainment, but a scaffold to stronger comprehension of subject matter Ken is teaching. For more on reading aloud, see our fuller treatment on pages 98–99.

History

Short versus long

Kids' school experience already features plenty of *long* selections, as evidenced by the subject-matter textbooks and novels we typically assign. But among real readers, a lot of important information comes from short clips, articles, reports, web pages, charts, tables, and pamphlets, too. The Common Core also recognizes the value of short texts, emphasizing the close reading of selected *excerpts* and *passages*. Whatever our teaching field, we need to build a collection of these small-is-beautiful reads. That means scouring newspapers, magazines, and websites, realizing that every school subject gets "covered" in the popular press, if we know where to look. Then we can feed class discussions with articles about air pollution in the community, the role of serotonin in brain function, the latest genetic engineering breakthrough, racial quotas in police department hiring, or a controversial art exhibit.

The Internet can really help you build this kind of collection. Obviously, if you have a hot topic at hand, you can start by Googling it or checking Google News for many articles to choose from. Most major city newspapers now have free electronic editions, with printer-friendly articles ready to be used in class two minutes from now. Many teachers we work with prefer www.nytimes.com for this service, giving kids access to "America's newspaper of record." Some also use the well-designed, mostly higher-order discussion questions that accompany articles on the *Times* educational website, "The Learning Network" (http://learning.blogs.nytimes.com/). You may prefer your home-town newspaper for local news—including events that kids can experience or investigate firsthand.

We asked middle school literacy coach Mindi Rench to share her favorite Web strategies for finding articles on content-area topics, with an eye to saving time for busy teachers. She especially likes the Learning Network because it provides links to articles by topic. She explains, however, that "Twitter is actually the place where I find most of the material I send to the content teachers in my building." She finds that if she puts out a request for reading on a specific topic she usually gets responses in half an hour. The Twitter discussion #edchat is very useful. And she uses an app, Tweetdeck, to follow specific chats.

Short articles allow for a quick in-class read and immediate discussion that leaves no one out.

The Library of Congress website www.loc.gov/teachers/classroommaterials/lessons/ enables people to search for writings by topic. The site http://longreads.com allows searches of many of the standard circulation magazines, and even reports the length of each piece. Last on Mindi's list of favorites is Pinterest, where many teachers post collections of articles by topic.

Building a collection of short articles about your subject is helpful in many ways. To begin with, you'll want to use subject-related short selections when you teach students the specific reading strategies outlined in Chapters 5. Obviously, your newfound inventory of "shorties" allows you to dip your toe into the water and step away from the textbook for brief experiments. You can add some "real" reading to the subject without committing large chunks of class time, and see how you like it. Short articles allow for a quick in-class read and immediate discussion that leaves no one out. This can bring reluctant readers (or kids who haven't done the homework) into the conversation. One warning, though: we've seen materials that are so boiled down and dumbed down that they hardly say anything at all. We just need to be judicious about the pieces we choose.

At Prosser High School in Chicago, the teachers decided to increase students' reading by scheduling ten minutes of sustained silent reading (SSR) once a week in the classrooms of all key subjects—English, social studies, science, math, and foreign languages. The reading in each subject occurs on a separate day of the week, so that some reading outside textbooks occurs *every day*. To share the searching, the math and science departments have set up hanging files to store articles that teachers dig up. The teachers use SSR in a variety of ways. Biology teacher Marnie Ware likes to introduce articles that express differing points of view, such as pro and con positions on the use of genetically modified foods. Many of the teachers have students write brief exit slips on their reading to maintain accountability. At first kids groaned about the reading, and some students wondered, "Why are we doing this reading when it's math class?" But then they found it was highly interesting and would help prepare them for the reading on standardized tests. And as English teacher Molly Rankin remarks, "There's something liberating about having the students do the work, instead of us."

Social Studies

Readings in Ken Kramer's Issues in Modern America course, an elective for Deerfield High School seniors, consist entirely of short contemporary news articles and informative pieces on the Web, organized around topical units. Some of the topics, such as high school hazing, student free speech, and student privacy, are especially relevant for the kids. Others are larger national issues such as affirmative action or wrongful crime convictions. Students read and then blog about these topics, and comment on each other's blogs to extend the conversation. Naturally, we asked whether collecting and updating the readings consumed large amounts of Ken's time; but he insists that simply reading the newspaper every day gives him plenty of material to choose from. Linking back to our discussion of chosen versus assigned readings, Ken explained that during the final four weeks of the year, students in the course study an issue of their own choice, finding readings (often on the Web, of course) and creating displays that present both sides of the issue. For a social studies fair, students conduct a "Marketplace of Ideas," standing by their displays to explain their issue to student and adult visitors—and expounding on their own point of view, as we would expect. One lovely consequence: students report that they often discuss the issues over the dinner table at home and with friends at lunch. Just how often do we think high schoolers launch into passionate dinner table conversation about textbook sections, dates, and facts they are supposed to memorize?

> "There's something liberating about having the students do the work, instead of us."
> —Molly Rankin

Math

"But what about sources for short real-world readings in a subject like math?" you may ask. OK, we accept the challenge. For a start, we suggest taking a look at *A Mathematician Plays the Stock Market*, by John Paulos. Or visit Guarav Tiwari's December 27, 2011, blog post that lists interesting articles about math (at http://gauravtiwari.org/2011/12/27/imrp/). Many are quite accessible for high school students. Or visit the "Easy Calculation" website (at http://easycalculation.com/funny/funny.php) for fascinating math facts and tricks. And for articles on statistics and data, subscribe to *Chance* magazine in hard copy or online.

Primary versus secondary sources

Many school textbooks are "secondary" sources, which means their content has been gathered from other materials (too often other textbooks), and then combined, reshaped, interpreted, and served up by the authors. Sometimes these texts are published as anthologies, where the original source of each section is cited directly in the text; more often, information is simply delivered with assorted sources combined and no way to tell where specific information came from.

Further, suffusing any textbook, however obscured by their mostly faceless presentational style, is the authors' underlying subjectivity. There is no such thing as "just the facts."

> Consciously or not, willfully or not, secondary-source authors infuse the books they create with their publishers' required attitudes, views, and cultural stances.

Consciously or not, willfully or not, secondary-source authors infuse the books they create with their publishers' required attitudes, views, and cultural stances. Often this means that important but "controversial" information is simply left out. This doesn't mean there is anything wrong with secondary sources. We all depend on them daily, from the spell-checkers on our computers to the "pill book" we consult to see which of our prescriptions might be interacting. Nevertheless, the implicit assumptions are rarely made obvious for the student readers. At least the newer textbooks in areas like biology are up front about the authors' specific attitudes toward environmental protection, the core role of evolution, and other topics that have social implications.

Primary sources are something else; they are the "raw material" of knowledge. Though we most easily see the importance of primary source materials in the humanities, especially history, they can be just as valuable in science and mathematics. Think of looking at the actual lab notes from a famous experiment, or reading the journal of a path-finding mathematician. Whatever the subject, when students go back to these uninterpreted materials they have a rare chance to really construct knowledge, build theories, develop conclusions, and see how great investigators did these things. Working with primary sources puts kids more in the role of a real scholar or sci-entist, "doing" the subject, not just hearing the summaries and conclusions of intermediaries.

The University of California Library provides this list of key primary sources, many of ￼n be gathered and put to use in your classes:

￼diaries, journals, speeches, interviews, letters, memos, manuscripts,
' other papers by participants or observers

'rs and autobiographies

' or information collected by, government agencies

* records of organizations
* published materials—books, magazine and journal articles, newspaper articles
* photographs, audio recordings, and moving pictures or video recordings
* ideas and images conveyed in the media, literature, film, popular fiction, or older textbooks
* research data such as anthropological field notes, the results of scientific experiments, and other scholarly activity
* artifacts of all kinds: physical objects, buildings, furniture, tools, appliances and household items, clothing, toys

While collecting such materials may be more work than adopting a single textbook, help is available through the websites and Internet tools we have described. Your friendly school librarian or museum administrator can also be of great support. To their credit, some of the better science and history textbooks now include sidebars and samples of primary text materials alongside their secondary-source backbone, even though many have been overstuffed with suggested questions and "thinking" activities.

A great boon for history teachers now is the Document-Based Question Project (www.dbqproject.com). Students explore a big idea by reading original documents and viewing images to explore a significant question. In American history, project materials address questions such as "What caused the Salem witch trial hysteria?" and "How revolutionary was the American Revolution?" The DBQ Project offers two books, one on American and one on world history. Each unit starts with a background introduction, and documents may include maps, informational charts, original writings from the period, illustrations, and modern articles. Materials for a series of "mini-Qs" are also available. Some of the DBQ assignments are quite teacher-centered and focused on "correct" interpretations of historic events. But, of course, once teachers get the knack, they can assemble projects and materials on such questions themselves. A favorite for history teacher Bryan McKay at Prosser High School in Chicago is the unit "Robber Barons vs. Titans of Industry," developed by a group of teachers in Huntsville, Alabama.

History

Multiple texts versus single sources

As we move away from dependence on a single textbook, one of the wonderful possibilities is to show students the range of views, the variety of ideas, and the different schools of thought that make intellectual life in our subjects interesting, controversial—and dare we say exciting. The Common Core Standards emphasize the academic importance of cross-text comparisons and integration by making these the focus of Anchor Standard 9. Is global warming a real threat or does it just represent normal variations in the temperature of the earth's atmosphere? Does evolution proceed through its own complex mechanisms or by a higher design? Has racial discrimination been eliminated from American society or does it still affect large numbers of people and institutions? How reliable are the statistics about various social attitudes in this country? Which is the most relevant of Shakespeare's tragedies to today's society and why? None of these questions can be intelligently addressed unless we consult multiple authorities. It is especially useful to gradually create sets of pieces that take different angles on the same topic.

Even when one point of view appears to students to be the correct one, it's important for them to understand and respond to the counterarguments, as the Common Core writing standard for argument recognizes. Getting both sides (or the many sides) of the story is an adult-life skill that cannot be learned and practiced too early. Obviously the DBQ materials we've mentioned enable history teachers to access ready-made collections of documents for students to compare points of view about major historical events. And in Ken Kramer's "Marketplace of Ideas" projects, students are required to find and include materials that present both sides of an issue. Even though the students themselves usually advocate for one position, they come to realize that they must also provide answers to the arguments of the opposing side.

History
History teacher Bryan McKay ramps this up with an activity he calls "speed dating with articles." He lines up short readings in pairs, with each pair presenting two sides of a question or issue. The students then form two lines, one on each side of the pairs. Students quickly read the article in front of them, discuss or debate with the student opposite, and when he calls time, the lines rotate in opposite directions so that every student has a new article and a new partner, to repeat the read-and-discuss process. Do adolescents enjoy this social/academic reading event? You bet.

Building a Classroom Library

The outward manifestation of our break with the one-textbook curriculum is the classroom library, a growing assortment of interesting reading materials collected and offered to our students. What we are trying to create is something like the living room of a big, eclectically literate family, a place where all manner of books, magazines, clippings, articles, brochures, and newspapers surround us, along with a laptop computer where the browser bookmarks websites with interesting reading. Some material will pertain directly to the subject at hand (algebra, history, etc.) while other parts of the collection can be deliciously random, chosen merely because they interest some teenagers.

So where do you get all this stuff? First of all: take your time and don't spend lots of your own money. A good start is to go through old magazines, save newspaper articles, and search some of the key websites and Web tools on the Internet that we've described. Hearing this, you may want to smack your forehead, thinking of all the years you've thrown away all those magazines, AKA valuable teaching materials. Well, don't grieve—it's all archived on Internet sites now. And trust us, you can get kids going with even a small number of items. Later on, you'll be glad you got started when you did.

If your school or department has a budget line for supplementary materials—and even in lean times it's surprising what funds can be lurking in the corners—you'd better claim the money before we do. For the rest of us, it's beg, borrow, steal, or write grant proposals—not necessarily an arduous or unpleasant process. Scholastic book club gives the teacher points for everything kids order, which you can then use to build your classroom library. In one school we've worked with, kids donate the

> *Getting both sides (or the many sides) of the story is an adult-life skill that cannot be learned and practiced too early.*

books they've finished (along with their name on the inside of the cover and a review to guide future readers). Some of our teacher buddies give a tear-jerking appeal for cast-off books and magazines at every fall parents' night, and kids schlep them in for days afterward.

Now, before you start placing an order, spending hours on the Web, or rummaging around your basement, here are a couple of quick considerations about *what* to get. No matter what grade your classes may officially represent, almost any group of students includes a very wide range of reading levels. So you'll need to find not just books for different interests but for different difficulty levels as well. While many high school kids can simply read adult trade books (David Bodanis' $E = mc^2$ is written at a much easier reading level than a science textbook), we also need plenty of books that are just right for younger middle schoolers, for kids who struggle with reading generally, or for anybody who's just seeking an informative "easy read."

Starting at the easier, general-interest end of the spectrum are many nonfiction collections that feature shorter, engaging pieces. The National Geographic's *Reading Expeditions* is a set of 177 colorful, engaging forty-page booklets on science and social studies topics; among the most discussable titles are *Feeding the World*, *The Human Machine*, *The Great Migration*, and *Kids Care for the Earth*. DK Books offers a huge line of gorgeously illustrated, browse-worthy nonfiction books that are updated or recently published, on fascinating topics including architecture, cavemen, government, crime scenes, dinosaurs, religions, fishing, and Batman.

KEY ingredients of
a classroom library

1. Interesting trade books, histories, and biographies of people in your field—and if you collect some titles in sets of three to five copies each, students can read and discuss them in groups.

2. Current articles clipped from magazines and newspapers or printed out from their online versions. For example, a recent story covered the growth of Burmese pythons in the Florida Everglades and how they are wiping out the populations of all the small animals—a typical example of the problems that occur when alien species invade an ecological system.

3. General-interest magazines like *Time*, *Scientific American*, *Harper's*, *The Atlantic*, *Wired*, *Utne Reader*, *Popular Science*, and *Popular Mechanics*, which carry stories about many of the topics covered in secondary schools—either in hard copy or bookmarked on tablets or laptops. Magazines on any hobbies the teacher has should be included also—photography, travel, fishing, whatever. Don't forget the "easy reading" dictum; this means celebrity, fashion, sports, gamer, motorcycle, car, and punk rock magazines should all be welcome. We know, we know; just lower your standards and bring it all in.

4. Educational magazines on school topics, like *ChemMatters*, *Science News*, *Discover* magazine, *Chance* magazine (on statistics), *America's Civil War*, and *American History*, are all available in both print and online versions. And go to www.historynet.com for a list of another dozen magazines focused on particular historical periods or events.

5. Website lists, like those on Pinterest, that you've bookmarked on your classroom computers and keyed to various major topics in your course. Some additional examples in one field, physics: topical pages within the *ScienceNews* website (for instance, at www.sciencenews.org/view/interest/id/2366/topic/Matter_+_Energy) cover a wide variety of recent physics-related developments. At www.aip.org/history/acap/ you'll find links to biographies of contemporary physicists and their experiments. Math teachers can find excellent news articles at *+Plus Magazine* on the web (http://plus.maths.org/content/) and instructions for making and learning about a wide variety of fascinating polyhedra at www.georgehart.com/virtual-polyhedra/vp.html.

Still shorter pieces than the book sets are found in the book-length collections of very short nonfiction. If you can get past its unfortunate name, seek out the *Uncle John's Bathroom Reader* series, which provides hundreds of one-paragraph to three-page pieces on a wide array of fascinating topics: Why does popcorn pop? Who planned the White House? Where did the Miss America pageant come from? Why do wintergreen Life Savers make sparks when you bite them in the dark? Was Henry Ford really an anti-Semite? The *Uncle John* series is now up to at least the twenty-third version, plus numerous special-topics editions, all of which ought to sit right beside the encyclopedias in every middle-school classroom. While there is now an online sampler at www.bathroomreader.com, one great advantage of hard copy is that the puzzling questions and concise answers are right there to pique a reluctant student's interest.

The annual *Guinness World Records* books deserve a place in every classroom. Many listings, from world-changing events to goofy stunts, are filled with math and science content—after all, every record requires some measurement. The annual editions of *The World Almanac* and *Ripley's Believe It or Not* feed the same curiosity about numbers and statistics. In a more applied-technology vein, our colleague Dagny Bloland says that among the most popular books in her eighth-grade gifted classroom are the *Chilton's Auto Repair Manuals* collected from gas stations and other donors. While you can choose among these based on your content area, be sure to include plenty of variety so you have more chances to hook reluctant readers with something that grabs their attention.

More grown-up in content and reading level (which we know the Common Core Standards aim to have students reach) is the collection *Short Takes*, edited by Judith Kitchen, which includes fine writers reflecting on assorted topics: parents, childhood, sports, weather, war, solitude, nature, loss—and, of course, love. A collection of longer pieces, *The Best American Magazine Writing*, comes out annually. Readers love the *2012 Best American Science Writing*, with pieces about advances in organ transplants, understanding the teenage brain, our increasingly violent weather, and the realization that there are more planets circling the stars in our galaxy than grains of sand on earth. Dave Eggers, author of the best-selling memoir *A Heartbreaking Work of Staggering Genius*, assembles a collection every year called *The Best American Nonrequired Reading*, with short and often funny pieces skillfully addressing a youthful audience.

Online sources

Then there's the endless and growing range of resources on the Internet. We've mentioned a number of tools and websites already. But here are some specific Web sources for interesting articles on science and math:

Science

Math

* Science News for Students at student.societyforscience.org/sciencenews-students
  • Science Daily at www.sciencedaily.com/

- Girls Angle: A Math Club for Girls at www.girlsangle.org/index.html
* *Math in the Media* at www.ams.org/news /math-in-the-media/math-in-the-media (some articles easier to read than others)

Also on the Web, lots of teachers use Pinterest to share their collections of valuable books and resources. A couple of our favorites:

* a collection of recommendations for historical fiction, at http://pinterest.com /librarianarnold/historical-fiction
* a list of books about math, at various grade levels, at http://pinterest.com /carlahab/math-books
* various teachers' suggestions of books for boys, at http://pinterest.com/mrsorman /books-for-boys/

Book-length nonfiction

For book-length reading, Rebecca Allen in the journal *Teacher Librarian* (February 2013) provides an excellent annotated list of books on topics that will fascinate older students in science and math classes. Typical from her list are Steven Pinker's *How the Mind Works*; *Spillover: Animal Infections and the Next Human Pandemic*, by David Quammen; *The Joy of Pi*, by David Blatner; *How to Survive a Robot Uprising: Tips on Defending Yourself Against the Coming Rebellion*, by Daniel Wilson; and the Climate Central group's *Global Weirdness: Severe Storms, Deadly Heat Waves, Relentless Drought, Rising Seas and the Weather of the Future*. What adolescent could resist? And what teacher would want to stop them?

Science

Math

Great Books for Middle and High School Content-Area Reading

Check out our annotated bibliographies of genuinely interesting, content-area-related books on Pinterest.

Twenty Great Trade Books
http://bit.ly/20TradeBooks

Great Current Issue Books
http://bit.ly/CurrentIssueBooks

Great Science & Technology Books
http://bit.ly/TechandSciBooks

Great Mathematics Books
http://bit.ly/GreatMathBooks

Great History Books
http://bit.ly/HistoryBooks

Great Novels
http://bit.ly/GreatNovels

Great Biography/Memoir
http://bit.ly/BiographyMemoir

Great Personal Growth Books
http://bit.ly/PersonalGrowthBooks

Great Adventure/Sports Books
http://bit.ly/SportsAdventureBooks

As young readers grow stronger, the whole world of adult nonfiction opens up. Some of our partner schools in Chicago have used selections from *Remembering Slavery* by Ira Berlin, Marc Favreau, and Steven Miller, a compilation of interviews from former slaves. The autobiographical accounts, which were transcribed by the Federal Writers Project in the 1930s, provide first-person testimony, sometimes harrowing, sometimes puzzling, from the era of American slavery. The students we work with have also had lively conversations about *There Are No Children Here* by Alex Kotlowitz, the all-too-real account of two brothers growing up in a Chicago housing project. *The Big Test* by Nicholas Lemann gives kids a chance to learn about the peculiar origins of the standardized tests they increasingly face. Dava Sobel's books *Longitude* and *Galileo's Daughter* both dramatically recount world-changing inventions. Jared Diamond's *Guns, Germs, and Steel* offers a chilling and persuasive theory of Caucasians domination.

Other favorites for both history and science classes are two books by Charles Mann, *1491* and *1493*. The first is a groundbreaking study of the different civilizations in North America before Columbus. Its main finding: the peoples and cultures of the continent were far more complex, accomplished, and remarkable than previous accounts had allowed for. A few years later, Mann followed up with *1493*, outlining what he calls "the most momentous biological event since the death of the dinosaurs." Turns out that the eastern and western hemispheres had been almost completely isolated biologically—and when the Europeans arrived, they brought completely novel plants, animals, and bacteria to the ecosystem. Some of those organisms decimated the native populations, facilitating their conquest, while others added to the biodiversity of the Americas.

Science

History

Don't forget novels

So far we've listed mainly nonfiction, but options for novels should be available as well. There are tons of historical novels aimed at younger readers, and there's no better core for a thematic unit than a book like *Morning Girl* (on exploration and conquest) or *Out of the Dust* (about the Dust Bowl and the Great Depression). The literature on the Holocaust, immigration, and the history of various American ethnic groups is especially well recognized and available. Amid the continuing news on Islamic fundamentalism, our colleague Nancy Steineke was able to quickly build a collection of four illuminating YA novels with Islamic protagonists and settings.

Diversity

Missing diversity in your collection? Find blogs and writings by African American scientists on *Scientific American*'s *Urban Scientist* blog: http://blogs.scientificamerican.com/urban-scientist/2012/06/12/african-american-science-bloggers-writers-and-tweeters/. Or go to the website of the Society of Hispanic Professional Engineers, www.national.shpe.org/. And for your fiction collection, consult some of the following online lists of essential multicultural titles (though we wish more of the books were more recent):

* http://wps.ablongman.com/wps/media/objects/133/136287/multilit.pdf
* www.berkeleypubliclibrary.org/children/good-books/looking-in/
* www.goodreads.com/shelf/show/middle-school-multicultural
* www.goodreads.com/shelf/show/middle-grade-multicultural-books
* ccbc.education.wisc.edu/books/multicultural.asp
* www.ric.edu/astal/multicultural/books.html

For reluctant readers

As we create our classroom libraries, we are serious about having something for everyone, especially our "reluctant readers." To be sure we hook boys, we're quick to stock Gary Paulsen's fiction and nonfiction; *Into Thin Air* and *Into the Wild*, both by Jon Krakauer; *The Perfect Storm* and *Fire* by Sebastian Junger; and *The Last River* by Todd Balf. All are adventure stories with tons of science information and strong narrative lines. For girls, www.goodreads.com/list/show/1816. Best_Teen_Girl-Books provides a long list, mainly of YA novels. We also looked for nonfiction for girls, and while there were no separate lists for this (interesting!), a few caught our eye in the more general Goodreads teens' nonfiction list:

* *The Year We Disappeared: A Father-Daughter Memoir* By Cylin and John Busby
* *Almost Astronauts: 13 Women Who Dared to Dream* by Tanya Lee Stone
* *The Pregnancy Project* by Gaby Rodriguez
* *Ana's Story* by Jenna Bush

 But we also go back to Nancy Drew, pile up the Babysitter's Club, stock plenty of Judy Blume and Sharon Draper, and even a few romances, if they want 'em.

   There's hardly any point in listing more, since new sources appear all the time. We'd just advise that you provide your classes with a list of interesting and trustworthy websites, rather than leaving students to search randomly on their own.

Using and Managing Your Classroom Library

Keep in mind that when it comes to books, kids don't always have to read the whole thing. Dipping in for a chapter or two works just fine with many nonfiction titles. Many books are promising candidates for jigsawing, where kids read just one section and then combine their learning in small groups (see page 186–189.) As you build your classroom library, gradually read the books yourself and talk with kids and colleagues, you'll become increasingly skillful at steering individual students toward interesting, readable books—or selections thereof.

On the other hand, do you, the teacher, have to read each of these books before your students do? Absolutely not. If we limit kids to books we have read ourselves, we leave them an unnecessarily narrow choice, limited by our own reading habits or special interests. Besides, there are a million great books for kids, and no full-time teacher has time to read them all. Just build your reading list from trustworthy sources: the suggestions of colleagues, friends, family, and former students; the scoop from magazine and newspaper reviews; blurbs on book-related websites; award sponsors like the American Library Association; and even our professional organizations like the National Council for the Social Studies, which recognize worthy books for young people.

A quick note on censorship. When we invite teenage students to graduate from controlled school books to real grown-up books, we add challenge, rigor, and reality to the curriculum. We also incur some risks. Adult books, even when mainly about historical or scientific matters, sometimes contain adult themes or behavior. In her powerful minimum-wage expose, *Nickel and Dimed*, Barbara Ehrenreich admits to smoking marijuana and then facing a corporate drug test at Wal-Mart, where she was earning $6.50 per hour. *Stupid White Men* uses some bad words, and *God's Fool* has brief but explicit sex scenes, and so forth. These books are meritorious, thoughtful, and important—and none of their risque words or deeds will shock the sensibilities of most contemporary teens.

But if book censorship is a big issue where you teach, then of course you don't *assign* anything questionable. Rather, let kids choose the books they wish to read. If needed, send a copy of any chosen book home with a note to parents saying, "Your student has chosen this book for chemistry class. Let me know if you have any questions or concerns." Most of our colleagues don't explicitly ask for a signature, feeling this notification process is enough to offer parents a chance to object if they must. Parents have heartfelt reasons for protecting their kids from certain ideas. The kid can pick another book.

A few final management tips: it will take classroom organization to keep your library from being permanently borrowed out of existence. Appoint a student as librarian in each class to keep track of everything. Organize storage space so books and articles can be returned to easily identified locations. And remind students how important it is to maintain materials in good condition for their classmates. Finally, try to accept the notion that a "stolen" book may be the highest possible compliment, and keep on collecting.

Tools for Thinking
Reading Strategies Across the Curriculum

W e've explained how kids need more engaging real-world reading beyond just the textbook in order to learn their school subjects. We've also explored the active mental work kids must do to make sense of all this rich material. Now, how do we make sure students actually *do* that mental work in our classrooms? And how can we accomplish this within the time constraints we face and still teach the subjects we're hired to teach?

The strategies described in this chapter are simple, quick, easy-to-use tools and activities to help students engage in, grapple with, and remember concepts in chemistry, math, history, or any other subject. The writing or jotting or sketching required for these activities need not be corrected and graded—though you may briefly check to see what students need help with or to confirm that they are actually using the strategies. The activities won't create more work for you as a teacher, but will actually make your job easier by helping students think as they read. If you decide to use them as starters for more extensive projects and writing activities—"upgrades," so to speak—that's fine, but it's not a requirement for their success.

Before we go further, however, let's make clear what we mean by "strategies." Reading experts often refer to *cognitive strategies that readers use* to understand what they are reading. But they also talk about *instructional strategies that teachers use in the classroom* to help students learn those mental strategies. Or perhaps they talk about *whole-class or individual student activities* that combine both types of strategies. What follows is really a collection of the latter. These activities involve discussion, writing, drawing, and even having kids get up and move around the room—activities that help students engage with, understand, and apply the reading they do and in the process, learn to use their minds more effectively as they read. And of course as these classroom activities take place, they activate a number of the mental strategies good readers use to understand a text.

Our teaching strategies are correlated to three key stages in reading:

* **Before:** preparing students before they read
* **During:** helping students construct, process, and question ideas while they read
* **After:** guiding students to reflect on, integrate, and share ideas after they're finished

For each stage, we begin with the simplest and easiest-to-use strategies, and then advance to some that are more complex. You'll notice that some of the strategies can be used or adapted for more than one phase of reading. They may serve different purposes depending on the stage at which you use them. The following chart shows when each of the strategies could be effective and also explains its focus so you can see what each lesson teaches.

A quick but important note: the very first strategy, Think-Alouds, is about demonstrating for kids how smart readers think. We believe this is an overarching strategy, one that goes to the very heart of good reading and that should be every teacher's starting point when teaching content-area reading.

The chart on pages 91–92 shows you some of the main reading skills that are addressed by the strategies in this chapter. For each of the twenty-six strategies, we have placed bold stars corresponding to the skills that strategy most heavily focuses on, and lighter weight check marks for those that it addresses secondarily.

Now, let's think back to Chapter 2, about how good readers think, and recall the mental processes skillful readers use, and the three stages of the work that are involved, in order to consider what exactly these strategies achieve for us as teachers of various subjects.

Before—preparing students before they read. These activities include getting students focused on and excited about the selection; activating or building connections with their prior knowledge; developing meaningful purposes for reading; and evoking students' questions, beliefs, and predictions about issues in the text.

During—helping students construct, process, and question ideas as they read. As effective readers work through text, they *visualize* what is happening in a story or historical situation or science experiment. They may notice they have *questions* about the topic. They make *connections* between various parts of the piece, with other material they are studying, and with their own lives or the larger world around them. They make *inferences*, combining clues in the text with their own background knowledge to see deeper implications. They *distinguish important ideas* as compared to minor elements or digressions. And they *monitor their comprehension*, noticing when they've lost the thread and taking prompt action to restore meaning. The mind of a good reader is extremely active, quite unlike a passive sponge.

After—guiding students to reflect on, integrate, and share the ideas after they're finished. This is when readers *synthesize* ideas within their reading and between what they've read and what they already know about a topic, to make larger *inferences* and *connections* with other information and concepts they are studying. They *follow up on the questions and purposes* they had and consider whether they've learned answers, found surprises, developed a new perspective on the topic, or as is often the case, realize they have new questions. And they share their thoughts with others to deepen this process.

Students in content-area classes always need support in acquiring the *academic vocabulary* required to understand and remember concepts, and that's why you'll find explicit vocabulary-building strategies for every stage of reading.

The Key to Teaching the Strategies: Gradual Release of Responsibility

An essential step in ensuring that the reading strategies in this chapter truly help students to comprehend and make use of what they read is the teaching process widely called "gradual release of responsibility" (Pearson and Gallagher, 1983; Routman, 2003). Many teachers know the model as "I do it, you watch; we do it together; you do it with my help; you do it alone." The steps are actually quite simple, but we must use plenty of repetition, demonstration, and practice to help students internalize a reading/thinking strategy until it becomes a mental habit that makes a difference in their reading.

Step 1: "I do it, you watch." The teacher models a particular reading or thinking strategy (making connections, determining importance, visualizing) to show students what it looks like when a competent adult does it. Keep in mind, when you offer such a demonstration, you are using important text from your subject area, so you are not "wasting time." Indeed, you are showing students exactly how an expert thinks about some information in your field. And the demonstration is short, so it shouldn't eat up a lot of time.

Lesson	Before Reading	During Reading	After Reading	Reading as Thinking	Building Enjoyment of Reading	Sharing Ideas, Discussing, Debating	Setting Purposes for Reading	Connecting to & Building Background Knowledge	Self-Monitoring Comprehension	Visualizing Meaning	Questioning, Wondering, Interrogating Text	Identifying Important Information/Evidence	Recalling and Summarizing	Making Connections to Other Texts, Info & Self	Inferring, Interpreting, Drawing Conclusions	Analyzing Author's Purpose, Theme, Point of View	Taking and Supporting a Position	Building Academic Vocabulary
Think-Alouds p. 94 *(Use this strategy first)*			✱			✓		✓	✓	✓	✓			✓	✓			
Reading Aloud p. 98	✱			✱			✓		✓									
Frontloading with Images p. 100	✱			✓	✓		✓	✱	✓	✓					✓			
KWL p. 104	✱	✱	✱	✓			✱	✱		✓				✓				
Prereading Quiz p. 107	✱				✓	✓	✱											
Dramatic Role-Play p. 110	✱		✱	✓			✓		✱				✓					
Vocabulary Predictions p. 112	✱			✓	✓		✓											✱
Partner Reading p. 115		✱		✓		✱					✓							
Post-it Response Notes p. 118		✱	✱						✓	✓		✓	✓		✓	✓	✓	
Annotating Text p. 121		✱	✱						✓	✓		✓	✓	✱	✓	✓		
Coding Text p. 125		✱	✱						✓	✓		✓	✓		✓	✱	✓	
Multicolumn Notes p. 128		✱		✓					✓				✓	✓	✓	✱	✱	✓
Sketching My Way Through the Text p. 131		✱		✓					✓	✱				✓	✓			

When should I use this lesson?

Lesson	Reading as Thinking	Building Enjoyment of Reading	Sharing Ideas, Discussing, Debating	Setting Purposes for Reading	Connecting to & Building Background Knowledge	Self-Monitoring Comprehension	Visualizing Meaning	Questioning, Wondering, Interrogating Text	Identifying Important Information/Evidence	Recalling and Summarizing	Making Connections to Other Texts, Info & Self	Inferring, Interpreting, Drawing Conclusions	Analyzing Author's Purpose, Theme, Point of View	Taking and Supporting a Position	Building Academic Vocabulary
Turn and Talk p. 134	*	*	*	✓	✓	✓	✓		✓	✓	✓	✓	✓	✓	
Tweet the Text p. 138			*	✓						✓	*				
Exit Slips and Admit Slips p. 140			*	✓		✓	✓		✓	✓	*				
Word Wall p. 143	*	*	*	✓		✓		✓			✓				*
Word Meaning Graphic Organizer p. 147		*	*	✓		✓		✓	✓	✓					*
Vocabulary Tree p. 150	*	*	*	✓		✓		✓	✓	✓					*
List-Group-Label p. 153		*	*	✓				✓	✓						*
Clustering and Mapping p. 155	*		*	✓				*			✓	✓	✓		
Written Conversation p. 159		*	*	✓	✓	*	✓	✓		✓	✓	✓	✓	✓	✓
Second Helpings p. 163		*	*	✓						*					
Where Do You Stand? p. 166			*	✓	✓	✓						✓	✓	*	
RAFT Essay p. 159			*	✓	✓					✓	*	✓	✓	✓	
Password p. 173		*		✓						✓	*				*

It's wise, though, to model the strategy repeatedly until students really get it. "Model, model, model, and even when you're sick of it, model some more," says Northbrook Junior High School science teacher Pam Mendelson. She uses gradual release for a whole range of reading strategies needed for success in her classroom, including visualizing (which helps kids prepare to do the lab experiments they're reading about), questioning (a reading strategy her entire grade-level team promotes), and writing summaries (which she has found greatly helps kids with comprehending her science material).

Step 2: _"We do it together."_ Now, the teacher models her thinking with another short piece of reading (or continues with an earlier one), but this time students are invited to help out, to jump in with suggestions about what the text means, what implications lie under the surface, predictions about upcoming ideas, or questions that puzzle them. Reading professionals call this activity a _shared reading_—the teacher is still in control, doing the main read-aloud, but the kids are joining in the effort. Here, students are operating at the stage that the famous psychologist, Lev Vygotsky, described as the "zone of proximal development"—at the edge of what a learner can do, with help. They're actually thinking while helping you, the teacher.

Step 3: _"You do it with my support."_ Next, the teacher releases learners to more independence, and to a decentralized classroom setup. Typically, students now try out the strategy, working individually or in small groups, while the teacher circulates to provide any needed scaffolding. She may set up groups based on kids' reading or achievement levels, and meet with them on a regular schedule to provide just-right support. Pam Mendelson not only helps kids with the summarizing strategy, but sees whether they understand the material. So she provides feedback when they write summaries at this stage but doesn't grade them, since the students are still coming to grasp the strategy as well as the science concept.

Step 4: _"You do it alone."_ Students now use the new strategy on their own, with only occasional support from the teacher. At this stage, teachers release—and students take—full responsibility for everything a mature reader does: selecting relevant text in the content area, capturing their responses as they read, and coming to discussions ready to join actively in the exchange of ideas. This full independence can take the form of content-area book clubs or reading workshop, which we discuss in later chapters. In Pam's science class, having begun by modeling summary writing about mitosis, she is finally ready to release her kids to summarize information about another biological process—respiration, fermentation, photosynthesis, osmosis, diffusion, or active transport. "In the past when students didn't get a concept," Pam admits, "I'd get angry. But now I realize that I hadn't *shown them* what they needed to do."

Here then are twenty-six essential strategies covering all the thinking students need to do to learn effectively from what they read. Since most of these have been developed over the years by many educators, we've tried to credit the progenitors where possible, as well as cite recent updates and variations. Enjoy.

TEACHER MODELING

STRATEGY: **Think-Alouds**

FOCUS: **Explicit Demonstration of Reading as Thinking**

DESCRIPTION:

The teacher reads a passage aloud, stopping periodically to look up at students and vocalize her mental processing of the ideas she's reading. She shows how she makes sense of the material as she poses questions to herself about it, makes connections with other knowledge that she possesses, struggles with parts she doesn't understand, and rereads when she needs to, thus displaying out loud how her mind works as she reads. As she shares these comments, she will jot down words, phrases, or codes (like a question mark or exclamation point) in the margin to label her thinking. The teacher models the process first, and then students try it in pairs.

Why Use It?

We're really good at commanding kids to read—but not nearly as good at *showing* them how to read. A football coach doesn't sit on the bench and talk about how you might block an opposing lineman—he stands up, grabs your body, puts you in the correct position, and shows you how to move. Same for reading. We have to actively coach, demonstrate, and model—with material from our own subject field. And while we cannot literally open up our heads for kids to watch the neurons firing (though some of our students might enjoy the opening process), we can learn to report what is happening in our minds as we think through text.

Skillful reading is a mystery to many students, who are quite unaware of the steady, recursive mental work that happens when competent readers go to work. Because we have never shown them otherwise, they seem to think comprehension is magic, or a gift that you just have or don't have. And so they grope or pray for answers to the questions at the end of the chapter or on a pop quiz. Others mechanically read words, hoping meaning will somehow arrive. Think-alouds help students to really see how active their thinking needs to be for real understanding to develop.

Think-alouds are the most basic of all reading lessons. They are not something you just do once or twice. Recurrent lessons demonstrate to kids the whole range of mental strategies, showing very concretely how to bring the material to life, manifesting all the thinking strategies described in Chapter 2, and illustrating the kinds of thinking involved in your subject. After you demonstrate a think-aloud, students can practice orally by themselves, in whole-class discussion, or in small groups or pairs. This will help students to begin to internalize thinking processes that may at first seem awkward or artificial, and move them toward becoming a natural part of the students' reading.

How Does It Work?

1 Plan your think-aloud carefully. Select a short passage that covers material important to the topic students are studying. Try reading it and monitoring yourself to see what sorts of thinking you actually do as you read. This can be tricky, because as competent readers in our subjects, our reading processes become automatic, and we do most of our comprehending unconsciously—unless we are struggling with the meaning ourselves (as we illustrated in Chapter 2).

Decide on several points where you will stop to share your thinking aloud. While it is more authentic to select talking points where you actually noticed yourself doing some active thinking, you may also wish to spread the stops throughout the text. Sometimes you may want to illustrate just one thinking strategy at a time, so students get a good idea of how that one works and can focus on practicing it. For instance, you might prepare a think-aloud where you just make connections between the text and your own background knowledge. But even though we value having kids practice individual strategies (questioning, visualizing, determining importance) for brief periods, we always return them to orchestrating *all* of their mental strategies in normal reading. Whatever your stopping point choices, keep in mind: a little thinking aloud goes a long way—three to five stops over three minutes of reading is usually plenty.

2 Before you begin, let students know you'll be stopping to think as you read, and indicate what they should be looking for in your demonstration—"Watch how I put together various pieces of information in the passage to figure out what's really going on. We call this *inferring*." Your goal is to show students your thinking so that later, once they've seen the entire demonstration, they can notice patterns in how you read.

3 Provide students with copies of the short reading you are going to use, or display it with a document camera so they can follow along. You may want to invite kids to skim it first so they can experience their own comprehension before the "pro" steps up. When you begin, stop at your first chosen point and share your preselected prediction, connection, question, or confusion, as appropriate.

4 When you stop to think aloud, look up at the class and shift your voice to indicate that you've moved from reading the words to sharing your own thinking. Jot brief notes in the margin to emphasize what sort of thinking you were doing—like a word, a phrase, or a quick doodle for something you visualized.

5 After modeling, talk over the process with students. What did they notice about your thinking? When do they find themselves doing the same sort of thinking or wondering? (See the "Turn and Talk" strategy on pages 134–137 on how to help get such a discussion going). Then have students try a think-aloud themselves, in pairs, using copies of another short passage or, for continuity, the following sections of the document you are already reading from. If students have difficulty knowing where to stop, point out a key spot or two where they can pause, and ask them if they have questions, are reminded of something in their own lives, etc.

VARIATION: One challenge for subject-area teachers can be the level of detail to be provided in the think-aloud. Science teacher Karen Eder, at Downers Grove High School in Chicago's west suburbs, tried a think-aloud for solving a science problem with reading coach Amy Stoops observing. Karen had figured there were four main steps for thinking through the problem. Amy listened from a student's point of view because she herself was not acquainted with the material. As a result, she realized there was actually much more to the process than Karen's four steps. This enabled Karen to elaborate a more accurate explanation for how her mind worked, helping the students to better understand and learn the process. So one strategy for developing a good think-aloud is to try out your first draft on a colleague who is not in your field, to see if you've explained your thinking sufficiently.

VARIATION: When your kids sit down to take that big state or national test, they will be required to closely read and deeply understand passages, problems, charts, data, and articles that *they have never seen before.* By definition, right? This means if you want to prepare your kids for those tests, they also need to see you thinking aloud through text you have never read before. No rehearsal, no practice, just you and your repertoire of proficient-reader strategies. Have your kids bring you some fresh subject-matter text, project it, and read it cold. Now that's *teaching.*

Addressing the Common Core Standards

Every strategy in this chapter helps you to deliver on the promise of the Common Core State Standards for Historical, Scientific, and Technical Literacy. As we outlined in Chapter 1, the Common Core provides us with detailed standards for our different subjects, for each grade band of students, and for the state and national tests that assess our kids' success in meeting these targets. To show how our twenty-six lessons can help your students achieve these standards, let's take think-alouds, which we've just outlined, and look at how you can "backmap" this strategy to the Common Core Standards. We'll take some commonly taught texts and show the correlations.

History/Social Studies in Middle School: Benjamin Franklin's speech to the federal convention in 1787, in which he (successfully!) urges the delegates to adopt the Constitution "with all its faults" for a variety of reasons beyond the content of the Constitution itself, is a rich primary source for a read-aloud, with opportunities for citing textual evidence (Standard 1) and identifying aspects of a text that reveal an author's point of view (Standard 6). If you can connect this piece to other texts that students have read about the Constitution or its creation (and, frankly, Ben's opinions in this piece make it hard not to), you're analyzing relationships between primary and secondary sources (Standard 9). Finally, you're giving students exposure to the kinds of texts that the CCSS expect them to read (Standard 10).

Science and Technical Subjects in High School: News from current research could be a source of excitement in the classroom, but the tone of academic writing makes it difficult for students to see the fresh and provocative ideas in these texts. For instance, a recent research study investigates the possible link between larger and more damaging wildfires in the American West and drier, more unstable air being observed in the lower atmosphere. If you do a think-aloud with the study's abstract, you can cite evidence to support your analysis of the text and to explore any gaps or inconsistencies (Standard 1); determine and paraphrase the conclusions of the work (Standard 2); determine the meaning of domain-specific words (Standard 4); and help students to feel at home with real-world text in your discipline (Standard 10). The short version you read may even provide hints that will help you to analyze the authors' purpose (Standard 6) or give you an opportunity to synthesize ideas (Standard 9).

TO LEARN MORE

Daniels, Harvey et al. 2011. *Comprehension Going Forward: Where We Are, What's Next.* Portsmouth, NH: Heinemann.

Harvey, Stephanie, and Anne Goudvis. 2007. *Strategies That Work: Teaching Comprehension for Understanding and Engagement* (2nd ed.*).* York, ME: Stenhouse.

Keene, Ellin Oliver, and Susan Zimmerman. 2007. *Mosaic of Thought* (2nd ed.). Portsmouth, NH: Heinemann.

Routman, Regie. 2003. *Reading Essentials.* Portsmouth, NH: Heinemann.

BEFORE READING

STRATEGY: **Reading Aloud**

FOCUS: **Building Enjoyment of Reading**

WHEN TO USE: **Before Reading**   During Reading   After Reading

DESCRIPTION:

The teacher reads aloud short articles, brief passages of interesting material, or successive install-ments of a story, biography, or high-interest book in her subject area. Individual students, pairs, or small groups may also read passages aloud.

Why Use It?

We all know that the Common Core Standards require students to be engaged in complex and challenging nonfiction text. The Core also recommends that this close, deep reading be done with *excerpts* of tough text *that the teacher reads aloud* (CCSS, 2010). Indeed, lessons sponsored by stan-dards author David Coleman (Achieve the Core, 2013) depend extensively on read-alouds by the teacher "or other competent reader" as a key activity.

   But our aim in reading aloud material from our subject matter is not just to meet a standard, or even to test students' reading or listening ability, but to let the whole class experience powerful language about important ideas. Reading aloud evokes the time-honored human experience of listening to stories, telling family and cultural histories, trading "war stories," hearing lessons from elders—around a fire, at the dinner table, in family gatherings, at business conferences, wherever people meet in groups. People of all ages enjoy hearing stories, ideas, and beliefs told aloud. It helps students grasp the big ideas, fascinations, and questions that make our subjects meaningful to us as thoughtful adults. Good teachers have learned that reading strong writing aloud (and per-forming it well) draws in students who would otherwise resist engaging in school topics. And when it is students' turn to serve as "competent" read-alouders, their experience with performing text can also build their fluency and comprehension.

How Does It Work?

1 Choose the text—and we are not talking about the textbook. To achieve all the goals above, the reading selection must explore important issues, surprising facts or experiences, or fascinating, funny, or thought-provoking problems. It must be very well written, in clear, vivid language. Every content field has examples of brilliant and beautiful language that's worth savoring in the ear as well as on the page. We think of Richard Feynman on physics, Edward O. Wilson on sociobiology, Nathaniel Philbrick on U.S. history, or David Sedaris on humorous human frailty. And whether the teacher or the students do the performing, these specially valuable texts must be read with expression and understanding. As we peruse the possibilities, we can go for pretty challenging stuff because kids will be able to understand harder text when we read it aloud than they can when reading silently and alone.

2 Rehearse! Primary-grade teachers actually value, practice, and receive training on reading aloud—and they do it with fiction and nonfiction picture books every day. They know how powerful a teacher's voice can be in helping kids fall in love with reading and ideas. In secondary education, we have little tradition or training around this, so we have to build this muscle ourselves. But what a joy to get better at this particular skill, especially since most of us are would-be entertainers anyway. And the training is just one step. When we take the stage to hook our kids on a text, to engage them in deep thinking about it, we must bring our "A" game, reading with energy, drama, and vocal variety. And that means we have to practice beforehand. Our rule of thumb: read the piece aloud five times to develop the best version before you go public with kids.

3 After you have modeled read-alouds for kids a few times, invite students to do some reading aloud of their own. Provide time for individuals or small groups to practice. Groups can use "readers' theater," in which they divide up a piece of text, doing some sentences individually, some as pairs, and some as a choral group. They can practice on video to hear themselves, try out variations, and improve with practice. (This works for us, too).

TO LEARN MORE

Trelease, Jim. 2013. *The Read-Aloud Handbook* (7th ed.). New York: Penguin.

BEFORE READING

STRATEGY: **Frontloading with Images**

FOCUS: **Visualizing Meaning**

WHEN TO USE: **Before Reading**   During Reading   After Reading

DESCRIPTION:

Before students embark on a reading passage (or a unit of study), the teacher projects a series of images—photographs or artworks—that help students understand the setting, context, process, problem, or people involved in the upcoming reading. To make sure that students study an image carefully, the teacher may mask and then reveal different sections one at a time, asking learners to take notes on each segment before they see the whole.

Why Use It?

We know that today's kids live in a world of vibrant, powerful images, supplied to them by a variety of devices. Sometimes we teachers even worry about those images, especially when they illustrate some homicidal video game. But we are also in competition with those images, and if kids are in some sense our customers, it's smart for us to augment the curriculum with vital, dramatic graphics. We also know that whenever we assign almost any printed whole-class text, it immediately divides the class: too hard for some, too easy for others, and "boring" for the rest. Instead, when we introduce a series of images or photos, everyone can play. The language learners, the kids with IEPs—everyone can view and study and talk about and draw inferences from and speculate about images projected on a screen. Then, once we have built background knowledge and evoked curiosity, we can make a better transition to printed material.

It's a funny thing. Everyone, even grumpy old culture critics, tends to be captivated by images. One of the great dynamics you see with this lesson is that everyone will be manifestly paying attention—you can look at your students and see every eye in the room locked onto the same focal point. When the kids are pointing at the screen and talking animatedly to a partner, you know you've got engagement.

Oh, and the anchor standards of the Common Core say that our students should be able to "integrate and evaluate content presented in diverse media and formats, including visually and quantitatively, as well as in words" (Common Core, 2010, 10). So we are not just having fun here (perish the thought!)—we are *required* to teach kids how to read visual images.

How Does It Work?

1 Based on an upcoming chunk of reading, or even a whole unit, search out a set of related images you can project to build kids' background knowledge and introduce the subject. Among many others, we've seen teachers use:

* pictures of a variety of rooftops to illustrate the mathematical concept of "slope"
* news photos of the integration of Little Rock Central High School, 1955
* paintings depicting westward expansion and the idea of Manifest Destiny
* photos of the tools of slavery, whips, shackles, chains, auction posters
* Edward Curtis photographs of Native American tribes in the 1910s
* the moons of different planets, objects in space, the Martian surface
* illustrations and diagrams of the Globe Theater
* pictures of assorted invasive species—animals, plants, bacteria
* plans of buildings illustrating different architectural principles
* photos and life documents of mathematicians, scientists, historians, writers
* fifteenth-century and modern paintings that illustrate the "vanishing point"

Having used image sets for many years, we now believe that there is almost no school topic that doesn't have some kind of visual representation that can help hook kids.

Where do you find these images? Obviously the go-to place for photos is Google Images, which provides a vast selection. For artworks (think *Washington Crossing the Delaware*) you can go to a variety of museum websites, among which the Art Institute of Chicago excels. The National Endowment for the Humanities and Smithsonian websites have lots of school-friendly historical and cultural imagery as well. Smokey and Nancy Steineke developed this idea extensively in *Texts and Lessons for Content-Area Reading* (2011) and offer many suggestions for sources there.

Assemble a set of six to twelve slides that give kids the background you want them to have. In choosing from an abundance, lean toward the most dramatic, puzzling, or surprising choices available. Also look for one especially emblematic, visually complex "anchor" image for closer study. Then put these into a PowerPoint or Keynote slide show so you can project them big enough for all to watch. No captions, just the images. Are you worried about copyright issues? Here's the deal. Many of the images you'll find are not copyrighted and are fine to use. Others are under copyright (they may have a logo partly obscuring the image) but it is still OK to use them for the classroom, as long as you are not reselling the image or using it to make money. If you are a stickler, leave the credit on the screen so you'll feel better about this.

2 Now, you do not present these images like an illustrated lecture, where you do the narration. In this lesson, you'll have the kids do the reading and thinking; you won't be narrating or lecturing. Gather students together and proceed something like this:

"Later today, we are going to start reading about a new topic. But before we jump into that text, I want to show you some images that will help you understand it better. While I show you these slides, one at a time, I will pause for you to think and talk about them. Instead of talking to a partner you're going to just talk back at the screen, out loud, about what you are seeing. You'll get used to it. OK? Somebody get the lights."

Now go through the pictures one by one. If your kids haven't done this before, you have to coach them to really talk out loud, to the screen and to each other, about what they are seeing, what they think is happening, what it means, how the slides fit together. If you like, you can have kids jot down a word or phrase after they've viewed and talked about each picture, but don't make it a mechanical note-taking drill.

3 Just doing these activities is often plenty to prime kids for the upcoming reading. But to add depth, have kids do "close reading" of that special "anchor image" you chose. There's a little preparation here: using the cropping tool, you need to divide this image into sections—thirds or quadrants work well. When you introduce this slide to the kids, first show the whole image and let them talk as with the others. Now it's time to "reread." Start showing students the image one section at a time. Instruct them to look deeply into the image and write down every detail they notice, every thought they have, every question it raises. Give one full minute per section for viewing and note taking, challenging them to keep noticing and jotting down more thoughts until time is up. After they have seen and written about each section, then reveal the whole image again—often it will seem to jump into 3-D when you have studied the individual sections first.

Finally, invite a class discussion about what the whole set of pictures showed, what the larger theme seems to be, and how particular details contributed to this understanding. Then ask students to predict what the upcoming reading will be about. Keep a list or chart of those predictions so you can come back to it after the print reading begins.

TO LEARN MORE

Daniels, Harvey, and Nancy Steineke. 2011. *Texts and Lessons for Content-Area Reading.* Portsmouth, NH: Heinemann.

The National Gallery. 2013. "How to Read a Painting." London. http://www.nationalgallery .org.uk/learning/teachers-and-schools/teaching-english-and-drama/how-to-read-a-painting.

"Arrest and execution of Thomas More depicted in painting by Antoine Caron." Credit: Photo.com/Jupiterimages/Getty Images/HIP

STRATEGY: **KWL**

FOCI: **Setting Purposes for Reading**
Connecting to and Building Background Knowledge

WHEN TO USE: **Before Reading   During Reading   After Reading**

DESCRIPTION:

The teacher leads students to list first what they think they already **Know** about a topic, then what they **Want** to know, and later, after reading, what they've **Learned**. One can ask students to create their own lists and then share items with the whole class, or simply start with a whole-class list. Thus the activity begins before the students read, but extends into the process of reading itself, and then on to reflecting on learning after the reading is completed. Some teachers substitute a **Q** for the **W**, focusing on **Questions** students can generate rather than opening up the floor to what students may or may not say they *want* to know.

Why Use It?

This classic strategy, developed by our colleague Donna Ogle, is helpful for students of all ages and achievement levels.

First, the **K** step asks students to access their prior knowledge about a topic. Again, why is "prior knowledge" so crucial? Because even when it is partial or less than accurate, it's the material a reader uses to begin building an understanding of the words he or she is taking in. Students often feel lost and confused when they encounter a concept they've never considered before; but when they can connect it with something familiar, they have an easier time making sense of the new information. As reading researchers explain it, you can only build new knowledge on top of the schema or background knowledge that you already have. This kind of connection is an essential component of comprehension, including at those times when the new information contradicts something the student previously believed.

The **W** stage, generating questions about the topic, develops purposes for reading. Building curiosity is essential to creating self-activated learners. It enables the student to anticipate the information and ideas that lie ahead, and to realize those that will be especially important. Leading students through this stage also enables the teacher to see what students know, what their misconceptions may be, and how they are beginning to think about the topic. Teachers at Downers Grove South High School regularly have students generate questions before they read. They've found that when students are searching for answers to their own questions, they are much more attentive to the reading compared to assignments in which the students seek answers to questions supplied by a teacher or a textbook. As we'll explain, the teacher may need to employ several strategies to help get the questioning process going, particularly if students are not accustomed to participating in it.

Then, after completing a unit, chapter, or inquiry project, looking at **L**—what we've learned—enables students to appreciate and reflect on their learning. The whole class returns to examine the original **K** and **W** lists, and kids enjoy the ceremony of checking off items accomplished, questions answered, even misconceptions corrected. This public review process helps to solidify the knowledge in kids' minds, rather than just getting "work" done and forgetting about it. Students can consider how and whether they've achieved the goals they set, what helped them learn, or what obstacles they encountered and overcame.

How Does It Work?

1 For **K**, students' knowledge may be sketchy or even incorrect. What do I know about the French Revolution? Photosynthesis? Nuthin'! Kids may need encouragement at first, to locate in their minds whatever bits of information or associations may be tucked away there. Like brainstorming, no answer is "wrong" at this point. This step is simply a picture of where students' heads are at the start of a unit. So this is not the occasion for giving a lecturette to correct all misconceptions. If you hear a glaring one, you might just flag it briefly—"That's an interesting idea. When we're reading, let's watch to see what the text tells us about it." As students brainstorm what they already know, list the items on chart paper or screen so kids can look back as the unit progresses.

2 While the **K** step usually goes smoothly, students often need help getting started on the **W** questions—perhaps hesitating to show their lack of knowledge, or because they're so rarely asked what they want to learn. Or maybe, when we ask kids, "What do you want to know about the French Revolution?" the underlying answer is "Nothing, thank you!" One way to steer around this pro forma resistance is to simply rename the center column **E** for "What do you **Expect** we will learn about the French Revolution?" And develop questions (probably quite similar) that way.

A more artful approach is to use items in the **K** column to tease out the questions—"I notice that you said Iraq was a desert. So what do you wonder about how people live in such a place?" Middle school teacher Annie Combs, in New Miami, Ohio, often projects pictures to help get questioning started. Or she'll show the title of a book they're to read and asks students what it makes them wonder. She doesn't hesitate to ask a few questions herself, which she finds helps students to question further as well.

❸ After completing the **K** and **W** columns, students can group and label the items in categories they decide on, to begin building connections among the various ideas that will come up in the reading. This step is very similar to the List-Group-Label vocabulary strategy described on page 153. Take time to reflect back repeatedly—KWL is not just an exercise to rush through at the start, but a tool to support thinking as you go.

❹ When completing the **L** list at the end of the project, be sure to compare it to the **K** and **W** columns. Downers Grove High School teachers find that their students are often surprised and pleased that the textbook or article they're reading actually did provide answers to their questions. Students should not only become more aware of what they've learned and what misconceptions got clarified, but they can also see how, as is often the case in learning, some questions didn't get answered, while unexpected ideas turned up as well.

VARIATION: Filling out the **K** and **W** columns of KWL doesn't need to take place only at the start of a topic. When Annie Combs introduced her sixth graders to a science unit on erosion, she found that the students had no idea what the concept meant. Fortunately, a creek runs close by the school, and the students were used to hanging out and fishing there. Tree roots are visible at the edges, where the water has washed the soil away, so to get a KWL started, Annie took pictures of this—and of course the kids realized that they were actually familiar with the phenomenon and could begin to list things they knew about it. For the **W** step, knowing that this was still a new academic concept for the students, Annie got them thinking by introducing an article about preventing erosion. Once they read it, the students quickly realized they had questions about how to do this, how long it takes to erode a specific area, how much damage a single storm can do, and so on. For students' further reading, Annie used sections of the book *Sciencesaurus* (Martin and Needham 2009) plus news articles she'd gathered to better connect the students' learning to real-life situations. Annie repeatedly focused their reading by asking, "Is there anything in this article that helps answer one of our **W** questions?" And of course the articles led to further **W**'s as well.

TO LEARN MORE

Ogle, Donna. 1986. "The K-W-L: A Teaching Model That Develops Active Reading of Expository Text." *Reading Teacher* 39: 564–570. (This was the original introduction of this strategy to the education world.)

The KWL strategy has become so popular and so widely recognized, it now has its own substantial and fairly accurate Wikipedia entry: http://en.wikipedia.org/wiki/KWL_table (accessed 7/25/2013).

STRATEGY: **Prereading Quiz (PRQ)**

FOCUS: **Connecting to and Building Background Knowledge**

WHEN TO USE: **Before Reading**   During Reading   After Reading

DESCRIPTION:

Do you love those little quizzes that often lead off articles in popular newspapers and magazines? Ones like, "Test your Marital IQ" or "Guess the Ten Most Popular Baby Names for Last Year!"
In the reading world, these little curiosity provokers are called *anticipation guides*, brief sets of
questions (three to five items) that help kids activate their prior knowledge (including misconceptions), make predictions, engage important issues that will surface in the reading, and enter a
text thinking. You create a quick, engaging, even mock-competitive quiz or survey for students to
take before reading. The items focus on big ideas, concepts, surprising or puzzling information,
or controversial issues. Kids simply circle or jot down their answers, and may talk them over with
classmates before reading.

Why Use It?

Inviting students to think about key concepts *before they read about them* establishes a tangible
purpose for reading: namely, to raise important questions or compare what students know or
believe with what actually turns up in the text. And a PRQ does this by involving the students in the
ideas, rather than having the teacher simply state, "Here's why this reading is important"—which
may or may not get heard in any serious way by the students. Too often, when we have asked students, "Why is your teacher having you read this?" the answer comes back, "I don't know. She just
told us to do it." In fact, the teacher may well have explained the purpose, but it didn't necessarily
stick in the students' minds.

This broader process is sometimes called *frontloading* (Wilhelm 2001), a great term for investing
class time in activities that launch kids into the text with their brains switched on. Reading becomes
a support for, or a challenge to, the positions students have taken. The questions guide students to
focus on big ideas in the reading. Instead of simply an assignment, reading becomes part of an ongoing conversation students have joined—perhaps without their realizing it. Of course, some topics,
like "kinetic molecular theory," will call just for simple prediction about the content. Others, like "the
discovery of radioactivity," more readily invite controversy and consideration of important beliefs. But
even simpler prediction questions still help students think as they read.

Anticipation guides are easy to prepare and take little class time—they are a great way to dip your toe into prereading activities. A five-item guide might take no more than five minutes—two minutes for students to respond, two to compare answers in pairs, and another minute to hear what one volunteer per question says about his or her answer.

How Does It Work?

1 Create a few (three to five) short questions or statements related to the text, using true/false, yes/no, or agree/disagree formats. Effective questions pose big, open-ended issues or draw kids' attention to curious or startling information. When studying earth's biosphere in science, you might offer a statement like:

> *"Human pollution of the atmosphere is always wrong." Yes or no?*

If your students will be reading Orwell's *Animal Farm* you might ask:

> *"Is it OK to have just a few people in charge of a government or organization?"*
> *Strongly agree, somewhat agree, somewhat disagree, strongly disagree*

For an upcoming Civil War unit:

> *Suppose you were in Lincoln's cabinet deciding whether to issue the Emancipation Proclamation, and a poll showed he would lose the next election if he signed it. Would you vote to: (a) sign it anyway; (b) not sign it; (c) wait a few months and decide later?"*

In a world history class you might survey:

> *What percentage of the world's children between 5 and 17 do you think are in forced labor?*
> >   A. 1 in 1,000
> >   B. 1 in 100
> >   C. 1 in 20
> >   D. 1 in 12
> >   E. 1 in 6

What percentage of those children are girls?

A. 3%

B. 10%

C. 34%

D. 50%

E. 68%

F. 90%

These prereading questions are a good example of the kind you are looking for. The correct answers (E and D) often startle kids—and galvanize them to read about this topic (UNICEF, 2012).

2 Kids can go right into the selection after doing the prereading quiz. This is meant to be a brief get-ready activity—it's not about correct answers. What we are trying to do is activate prior knowledge, beliefs, and ideas, and send students into the text with an agenda, looking for answers to questions that provoked them.

3 If you can take a little more time, it really helps to deepen students' thinking and engagement by having them discuss their answers with a partner or small group. Then you can call the class back and discuss the quiz, share consensus predictions, or surface a core disagreement, just before reading. If kids are slow to talk, have them jot their justifications first. Students tell us that discussion and opportunities to express their own opinions and ideas are some of their most valued and meaningful activities in school. Some teachers design their PRQs to feature surprising information. For example: Q: How many earthlike planets have astronomers discovered revolving around other stars? A: Billions. This not only tantalizes kids for the reading, but also allows for friendly competition as kids pit their guesses against each other's as the correct answers are revealed.

TO LEARN MORE

IRA/NCTE. 2013. "Anticipation Guide." ReadWriteThink. www.readwritethink.org/classroom-resources/printouts/anticipation-guide-30578.html.

Wood, K. D., D. Lapp, J. Flood, and D. B. Taylor. 2008. *Guiding Readers Through Text: Strategy Guides for New Times* (2nd ed.). Newark, DE: International Reading Association.

STRATEGY: **Dramatic Role-Play**

FOCUS: **Visualizing Meaning**

WHEN TO USE: **Before Reading** During Reading **After Reading**

DESCRIPTION:

Choose a situation, process, or event that will be described in the reading students are about to do, and prepare a very brief description of it. Students work in pairs or small groups (depending on the number of characters or roles involved) and rehearse role-plays to represent the passage or element to be explored. One or more groups present their role-plays for the class.

Why Use It?

In his research comparing competent and struggling eighth-grade readers, Jeff Wilhelm found that successful students consistently visualize what they are reading about, while struggling ones do not. As he searched for ways to help students visualize, he found that just telling them to do so was generally ineffective, while short, simple role-plays were quite powerful, sometimes when nothing else would work. While many teachers use drama as a means for re-expressing ideas *after* reading, role-plays that are carried out *before* reading are especially effective because they help kids build pictures of the action in their heads, to be accessed as they get into the content.

How Does It Work?

1 When designing a role-play, keep the scene simple, focused on a single problem or challenge. Leave it open for the students to improvise. For example, before reading the illustrated book *Pink and Say* by Patricia Polacco, a true account of an African American and a white soldier in the Civil War, Steve had the students count off by twos. He instructed, "Ones, each of you is a Union soldier who has been wounded. You're lying on the ground, barely conscious. The battle is over, but you can't walk. Twos, each of you is a Union soldier who has gotten lost from his company. You're frightened, and occasional bullets whiz by. You discover the wounded man lying on the ground. What do you say to each other?" For science or math, the roles can represent inanimate objects, such as chemicals, viruses, electrons and nuclei, or numbers and variables. The teacher may specify a single situation or process for all the groups to portray, or students may be invited to choose some part of

History

the passage to represent—in which case the role-plays will explore various aspects of the reading. Be sure the students keep their performances short. The activity is not an end in itself but simply an opportunity to get students thinking about the material they are going to read.

2 After the groups have planned and very briefly rehearsed their role-plays, some of them can present to the whole class, particularly if they have developed differing takes on the same situation. Include as many of the groups as time permits. However, as long as everyone has experienced the scene in their small groups, the main purpose of the activity—helping students create mental visualizations of the elements in the reading—will be achieved.

3 If you do have students present their role-plays it's especially worthwhile to debrief the role-plays with the class as they are performed, to help students think about the concepts and ideas that are being portrayed. As each group performs, one or more students in the group can also lead the discussion about it. This helps to strengthen the students' sense of ownership in the activity.

VARIATION: If you use role-plays *after* students have read a selection, your purpose will be somewhat different—more about reflecting on the reading, or considering alternatives. For the *Pink and Say* Civil War example we described, you could invite small groups to consider alternative ways the two characters might have interacted and why these could happen. It would be important, in this case, for the class to then discuss the motives and the historical background that they think are being reflected in the various choices—so the activity is for thinking more deeply about the history being studied.

TO LEARN MORE

Steineke, Nancy. 2009. *Assessment Live: 10 Real-Time Ways for Kids to Show What They Know— and Meet the Standards.* Portsmouth, NH: Heinemann.

Wilhelm, Jeffrey. 1996. *You Gotta BE the Book.* New York: Teachers College Press.

STRATEGY: **Vocabulary Predictions**

FOCUS: **Building Academic Vocabulary**

WHEN TO USE: **Before Reading**   During Reading   After Reading

DESCRIPTION:
The teacher selects a set of eight to fifteen key words from the piece to be read. Working in small groups, students try their best to place the terms in a set of categories the teacher has established. Each group then creates a "gist statement," which they predict will summarize the reading. Finally, they list things they hope to discover as a result of words they didn't understand or questions that were inspired by the process.

Why Use It?

This activity takes some time, but addresses a number of important mental strategies for good reading. It leads students to use their prior knowledge, focuses on important academic vocabulary, and uses prediction to build active thinking about a topic before reading. Predicting helps readers become aware of their expectations and how the reading either fulfills or surprises them—an important aspect of learning. The activity gets students talking in small groups in a carefully organized way. It helps them become conscious of the structure of a story, argument, or explanation. Talking over the words in their groups helps students not only to notice these key words as they read but to go into the reading with their minds focused on the ideas expressed through them. Finally, the "to discover" step sets purposes for students' reading. Students can be observing, as they read, to see which of their own questions get answered in the text. As we discuss later, in Chapter 11, even struggling readers become more engaged when they are thinking about their own questions rather than those supplied by a teacher or a question section at the end of a textbook chapter.

How Does It Work?

1 Choose eight to fifteen key words from the upcoming passage, words that invoke main elements or ideas in the reading. To give kids a fair chance at speculating, the mix should include some words kids already know; some technical (Tier 3) words (please see p. 179 for a definition of these three-tier models) that will be a stretch (kids can use knowledge of word roots, affixes, or suffixes to make informed guesses); and some important Tier 2 academic terms that will not only help kids understand this particular text, but also serve them in the future, across the curriculum.

Similarly, the categories for labeling these words depend on the subject and kind of material to be studied. Typical categories for a fictional story or a biographical piece might be Characters, Setting, Problem, Outcomes, Unknown Words. For a nonfiction news article on the spread of flu strains, for example, the word list might include: *virus, mutation, interspecies transmission, respiratory, epidemic, genetic shift, travelers, virulence, Centers for Disease Control and Prevention, quarantine, death rate, co-evolution.* (See the great Tier 2 words in there?) Some categories for sorting these words might be Problem, Setting, Causes, People, Solutions, Unknown Words. At first you may want to provide the categories for sorting the words, but as students get accustomed to the activity, you can also ask the groups to determine their own categories (which makes this activity more like the List-Group-Label strategy (see pages 153–154).

2 Model the strategy first with a group of words on a topic in your subject, thinking aloud so the students will understand what is involved. Along with the groups of words that you arrange (on a whiteboard or projected slide), be sure to also list a few questions the words have engendered, which you hope to get answered in the reading selection.

3 Provide a few key directions: The "unknown words" category is only for terms the group does not have any inkling about. Tell students whether you want them to use all the words in their gist statement, or only a certain proportion. Explain that if their gist statement doesn't completely match the reading, there's nothing wrong—but it does show that their expectations and the reading differed, and that's important to realize. The differences can help students realize that they've learned something new, or that the information or story was more complex or surprising than it first appeared to be. And remind students to list the "to discover" questions that the words led them to ask—not just about the word's meaning but anything else that could go with it. Students might wonder not just what the Federalist Papers were, for example, but also why they were important or how they influenced the people who read them at the time they were written.

4 Group representatives briefly share with the class how they grouped their words and especially what their "to discover" questions are.

5 When the reading is completed, groups revisit the "to discover" lists to see which questions got answered and which did not. They can report these to the class, which can discuss when and how their unanswered questions might get clarified later in the unit or by some future online research.

VARIATION: If your students will be reading a narrative text like a short story, biography, or historical novel, you can do a very similar predicting activity by selecting a set of eight to fifteen *sentences* instead of single words (of course, you will pick sentences with great Tier 2 words in them as well as technical vocabulary). Each student gets one sentence on a piece of paper, and then students walk around the room, reading their different sentences to each other and predicting what the text will be about. When they go on to read the complete passage, students will implicitly be comparing the actual text to their hypotheses. Kids seem to find it fun when the sentences they worked with earlier suddenly pop up in the text. We call this activity a Quotation Mingle and Harvey and Nancy Steineke have written about it in another of our family of books (Daniels and Steineke, 2013).

TO LEARN MORE

Daniels, Harvey, and Nancy Steineke. 2013. *Texts and Lessons for Teaching Literature*. Portsmouth, NH. Heinemann.

Wood, K. 1984. "Probable Passages: A Writing Strategy." *Reading Teacher* 37: 496–499.

STRATEGY: **Partner Reading**

FOCUS: **Sharing Ideas, Discussing, Debate**

WHEN TO USE: Before Reading   **During Reading**   After Reading

DESCRIPTION:

Instead of reading silently and alone, pairs of students sit side by side and take turns reading a selection of content-area text aloud to each other. Between paragraphs, the partners stop to discuss and clarify their understanding of each section before changing readers and proceeding. While partners work, the teacher observes, confers, and coaches. After five to ten minutes of this collaborative reading "warm-up," kids can shift into individual silent reading for the rest of the text.

Why Use It?

When we think of our students at work reading, we naturally envision individual students quietly processing text, pencil in hand, in a well-lit place. And obviously, being able to fluently read in this mode, without much outside scaffolding, is our goal in every subject—and an explicit target of the Common Core Standards. But some students—and highly technical content—require more support, especially early in the year. Remember, both the standards and our curriculum call for a long, gradual ladder of experiences, maybe 180 rung-days, leading to end-of-year proficiency. We must start kids where they are today, and keep moving up, using necessary scaffolds like paired reading. What our students can do out loud with a partner today, they can do silently and singly later, as they internalize the thinking strategies of proficient readers.

How Does It Work?

1 Select an important chunk of content-area text and set aside at least five to ten minutes of classroom reading time. We know, finding that time can be hard. We have so much content to cover that we often assign most reading as homework. While this seems to save instructional time, if kids come back the next day with zero understanding, then the shortcut has failed. And further, if kids never read under our close supervision, we cannot monitor their challenges, understand what support they need, and just plain coach them through. With this strategy you provide some live, interactive reading to launch kids into a text, so they can continue reading alone with high comprehension when they tackle the rest of it.

2 Form partners, matching kids who will work well together and who are at roughly the same reading level, so one doesn't shame or dominate the other. A variation of this strategy, more popular in the elementary grades, is commonly referred to as "paired reading," in which the teacher intentionally matches up stronger with weaker readers, hoping that the more advanced student will be a good peer model. We've seen this tried in middle and high school too, but often the interpersonal issues are too tender to make this a safe choice. Instead we partner up kids at the same level.

3 Now, explain partner reading, and then demonstrate it for the class, using a student volunteer as your own partner. Show students the basic version, where partners sit close together so they can comfortably use their "indoor voices." Both people have a copy of the reading selection in front of them, and they take turns reading aloud one paragraph at a time. After each paragraph, you and your kid partner stop and discuss your thinking. You may want to show (or later, co-create) a list of possible partner discussion topics, and project it for kids to use until they internalize the process. Typical conversation starters might be:

* What did the author say?
* What were the big ideas?
* Were there some hard words?
* Is there anything we didn't understand?
* How can we figure it out?
* What questions do we have?
* What do we think will come up in the next paragraph?

These items help kids focus on clarifying meaning, confirming what was actually said in the text, and how the passage fits together with previous and upcoming paragraphs.

4 After your demonstration, set pairs to work on another chunk of text. Roam the room and sit in with several pairs to see what successes and struggles different kids are having. Don't be shy to jump in and coach or do a mini-think-aloud of your own, to show how you monitor your thinking, notice your own confusions, and demand clarity of this particular subject-area text. And when you find common problems coming up in multiple pairs, you can shape these into a whole-class mini-lesson to teach later in the day, right at the moment of use.

5 As time runs out, call for some discussion of the text so far, asking several pairs to share what understandings and questions they had. At this point, the students should be prepped to complete the reading independently, in class or at home.

VARIATION: Pairs can read the whole text out loud in unison, as long as they can synchronize their voices, have those between-paragraph chats, and not get crazy loud. Or kids can read each paragraph silently, and then discuss out loud at the same intervals; this requires partners to roughly equalize their reading rates so no one is staring into space while the other is still reading silently. If you do this frequently, we encourage you to constantly mix up the pairs, so that kids read with many different classmates, building friendliness and support in the room.

TO LEARN MORE

Daniels, Harvey, and Nancy Steineke. 2011. *Texts and Lessons for Content-Area Reading*. Portsmouth, NH: Heinemann.

Simon, Cathy Allen. 2013. "Using Paired Reading to Increase Fluency and Peer Cooperation." IRA/NCTE ReadWriteThink. www.readwritethink.org/professional-development /strategy-guides/using-paired-reading-increase-30952.html.

STRATEGY: **Post-it Response Notes**

FOCUS: **Reading as Thinking**

WHEN TO USE: Before Reading   **During Reading**   After Reading

DESCRIPTION:

As they read, students stop, think, and react to the text. They pause to jot briefly on small sticky notes, recording key aspects of the topic as well as their reactions, questions, and connections. The teacher can specify the kinds of information to focus on or the kinds of response she'd like for students to try out. Students can then use these notes to help them participate in discussions, write response pieces, or engage in other processing of ideas after they've read. If the books or articles are their own, students can leave the notes in place for later reflection. If the materials are from a class library or class set, before returning them students can transfer the sticky notes to their own notebooks, where they can serve as review material. Sticky notes can also be used to hold the codes or annotations described in our next two strategies, Annotating Text and Coding Text (pages 121–127).

Why Use It?

How did we ever function without Post-it notes, in any part of our lives, including reading challenging text? We've all had that experience of "waking up" after half an hour of reading to realize that our minds were elsewhere, mulling concerns in the rest of our life, and we have no idea what we've just read. Post-its to the rescue! Tracking and returning to important spots in our reading is something all competent readers do, particularly with material for a course or other practical purpose. Jotting and placing Post-it responses along the way makes this kind of thinking concrete for students, helping them slow down and recognize significant information or elements they encounter.

When using Post-its, instead of a separate notebook, students can attach their thinking directly to the point in the text where they had a response, question, or connection. The movability of sticky notes adds to their usefulness, too, because they can be rearranged or relocated in a variety of ways, enabling students to explore and elaborate on the material being studied. And they are just plain vital when kids are working on books or magazines that they are forbidden to mark up (which is a lot of the time). Sticky notes are thus a great tool for supporting many of the other during-reading strategies in this chapter.

How Does It Work?

1 Before students first try this thinking tool, model its use with a separate short piece of reading—just a paragraph or two—so they can watch the kinds of information or responses that you stop, jot, and stick. Then give directions about specifics kids should watch for as they read, and what to write on their sticky notes. For example: "As you read the article from the Internet, 'Radiation and Risk' [www.physics.isu.edu/radinf/risk.htm], on the effects of nuclear radiation on the human body, place a sticky note at any spots where you were confused and write a few words or phrases on it to explain your confusion or question. Also place sticky notes at points where the information surprised you and in just a few words, explain on each one how your thinking was changed."

2 Now let kids try it out with a fresh piece of content-area text. After a few minutes of posting, have students use their notes to turn and talk with a neighbor (see the Turn and Talk strategy on pages 134–137).

3 Next, call everyone together for a whole-class sharing of the Post-it notations. Seek a wide range of volunteers to get a sense of the scope of reactions to the text. If you want to be sure kids noticed certain passages that you consider critical, prime the pump by asking things like, "Did anybody have a Post-it at the bottom of page 3? Will you read it aloud for us, please?" If nobody posted in that critical spot, share your own!

Language arts teacher Annie Combs, in New Miami, Ohio, often has students jot sticky notes on a debatable issue in their reading; for example, "What do you think is the main conflict in the book *The Outsiders*?" Then after the students have compared notes in pairs, they bring their notes up to the whiteboard at the front of the room (a few at a time, of course), where they place them in specific categories. The whole class can see how the votes went and then discuss the options and why people chose specific ones.

4 As you finish your whole-class discussion, ask students to write on each note the page number where they had attached it and then transfer the notes to a separate sheet of paper with their name on it, so you can easily collect and review these. If they are reading a historical novel or nonfiction book, the series of Post-its constitutes a record of their thinking all the way through the book—who needs a quiz?

VARIATION: For many of us, Post-it note responses have become a bread-and-butter strategy, one applying to all kinds of subject-area reading, every day. And we regularly use all kinds of interactive groupings—pairs, literature circles, lab partners, inquiry teams—for kids to process their notes and their thinking. We keep it fun and fresh. The small 1½ × 2-inch notes don't take up lots of space

Physics

and actually reduce anxiety at the beginning. When we say to kids, "Just write a little bit," they can see that we really mean it with that tiny yellow square. Students enjoy using multiple colors of Post-its to distinguish between various kinds of response. And later, the larger notes come in handy when students have more to say about some question or idea. When kids are reading books, show them how to place the Post-its so that they hang slightly off the edge of a page, to make each one an easily located tab. As we have suggested, it's often useful to have kids come up to the front of the room and place their Post-its on a chart or list of responses. When you do this, be sure to have students sign them first.

VARIATION: Annie Combs often asks students to place notes to mark three important ideas in a chapter or article they are reading. On these notes they write the quotes they've chosen, or write out the ideas in their own words. They transfer these to their writer's notebooks and use them to write a summary paragraph. Annie finds that this process strengthens students' comprehension of the material and focuses on the important elements rather than random details.

Annie also uses the notes as admit slips of a sort (see this strategy on pages 140–142) for developing vocabulary—something her students need lots of help with, since most have few books in their homes. She places a Post-it on each desk, and when the students come in, she asks them to compare two words—say *biography* and *autobiography*. Each student writes a definition for one or the other and places his or her note up on the board under its category. She and the class then discuss the various definitions and what they reveal about the words as well as what the students understand about them.

TO LEARN MORE

Daniels, Harvey, and Nancy Steineke. 2011. *Texts and Lessons for Content-Area Reading*. Portsmouth, NH: Heinemann.

Harvey, Stephanie, and Anne Goudvis. 2007. *Strategies That Work: Teaching Comprehension for Understanding and Engagement* (2nd ed.). 67–80. York, ME: Stenhouse.

STRATEGY: **Annotating Text**

FOCI: **Reading as Thinking**
Making Connections to Other Texts, Information, and Self

WHEN TO USE: Before Reading   **During Reading**   After Reading

DESCRIPTION:
Annotation is the mother of all during-reading strategies. It is a practice that virtually all skillful readers apply when they seek deep understanding of text. In school, this means having students purposefully stop, think, and react when they run across important information in content-area material. Instead of rushing through the assignment, they slow down and monitor the selection for key information, relevant connections, puzzling questions, mental imagery, contradictions, and things that just make you go "What?!" And then students jot down a few words in the margin to capture and flag those reactions. Later, students draw upon these notes for a wide array of discussions and interactions.

Why Use It?

What do *you* do when you encounter a piece of "high-stakes text" in your own reading life? Something you really need to understand deeply: a required article for a graduate course, your teaching contract, a report from your doctor? If you are like many skillful adult readers, you'd probably say: "I mark it up." Meaning that, over your long reading life, you have developed a way of making notes on a piece of writing that help you to understand and remember it better. Well, if this is something that we lifelong, pro-level readers routinely do, then we'd better be teaching this strategy to kids right now. In fact, in the elementary grades, this kind of "stop, think, and react" reading is already happening, guided by excellent resources like *The Comprehension Toolkit*, from our colleagues Stephanie Harvey and Anne Goudvis (2005).

Check out the example of an annotated text on page 124. It shows the residue of one student's thinking on the way through a science article, using that active, self-monitoring "stop, think, and react" mind-set. You can see how the reader is chewing on details, connecting ideas inside the text, posing questions, making interpretations, and even doodling some ideas. Harvey and Goudvis call these marks the "tracks of a student's thinking." But this is not just for little kids. Laying down such tracks is also recommended for incoming freshmen at Harvard University: "Mark up the margins of your text with words and phrases," implores a memo from the University Library, "Get in the habit of hearing yourself ask questions" (2013).

How Does It Work?

1 First, as usual, the teacher needs to model her own annotation on a projected article. If you already taught our think-aloud on pages 94–97 , you have already done this. When you did that think-aloud and stopped to share your thinking with kids, we suggested that you jot down a couple of words in the margin to label your thinking, right? Basically the same thing here. But with annotation we want kids to focus on the content as much as the thinking process, and so we write a little bit more on the page.

2 After your demonstration, invite students to see if they can classify the different kinds of thinking you were doing as you annotated—and make a list of the categories.

questions
connections
visual images
important parts
times I got lost
wow factors: surprising, funky, weird, yuck, no way
authors' style/point of view

3 Now give students another short article—just a couple of paragraphs—and ask them to annotate it, looking at the posted list for cues on when to stop, think, and make notes. When they are done, ask several kids to share their experience: "Did anyone make a connection?" "Who had a place where they got lost or confused?" "Did anyone do some kind of thinking that we don't have on our list yet?" If someone reports making a prediction, drawing a quick cartoon, or any other kind of useful thinking, add those to the list.

4 Provide ample instruction and practice. Annotation is not something you use once; many teachers use some version of it with *every* reading assignment. Once we see how much better students comprehend when they have some purposes for reading and a pencil in hand, it just doesn't make sense to say "read this for Friday" anymore. And there are countless variations to keep it fresh. Coding Text and Post-it Note Responses are other valuable versions of annotating. In Smokey and Nancy's book *Texts and Lessons for Content-Area Reading* (2011), they lay out an iteration called Point-of-View Annotation in which kids read the text as a character or historical figure and annotate it from that point of view.

VARIATION: There is another kind of text marking that we call *conceptual annotation.* Instead of having kids mark general reactions to a text (questions, inferences), we offer a little more teacher direction. We identify three or four big ideas (obviously, the key ideas in the text) that we want kids to be on the lookout for. Let's say you are a biology teacher having kids read an article about concussions as part of your unit on the brain and the nervous system. Here's how you might set up conceptual annotation:

> *"OK, guys, while you are reading this article, there are four things I want you to annotate for:* [project these terms]
> * the *causes* of concussions
> * the *symptoms* of concussions
> * the *treatment* of concussions
> * the *prevention* of concussions

> That means, as you read though this piece, when you run across some information about what causes concussions, you're going to stop, think about what the author is saying, and make some notes in the margin to help you remember that information. And when you come across some info about the symptoms of concussions, you'll stop and think about it, and make some marginal notes about that. Same for treatment and prevention. Now here's a warning, the information will not necessarily arrive in this order, and there may be repeated, separate sections with information about each of our four targets. So be alert. When we are done reading and annotating, you'll be able to compare your notes with a buddy to see what you captured and what you might have missed. Ready? Let's read."

When setting up conceptual annotation, it is important to narrow the focus to just three or four key concepts, so kids can enter the text actively searching for those big ideas, not scrambling to memorize every detail.

TO LEARN MORE

Harvard University Library. 2013. "Interrogating Texts: 6 Reading Habits to Develop in Your First Year at Harvard." http://guides.library.harvard.edu/sixreadinghabits.

Harvey, Stephanie, and Anne Goudvis. 2005. *Comprehension Toolkit*. Portsmouth, NH: Heinemann.

Tovani, Cris. 2003. *I Read It but I Don't Get It*. York, ME: Stenhouse.

EXAMPLE

Los Alamos National Laboratory
70 YEARS OF INNOVATIONS: Creating a safer, more secure tomorrow

[handwritten: isn't this where Japan bombs were made?]
[handwritten: ? really]

Mission nuclear weapons

While the role and prominence of nuclear weapons in U.S. security policy has
diminished with the end of the Cold War, nuclear weapons continue to provide
an essential component of national security.
Nuclear weapons are used every day

[handwritten: not "used", except as a threat]

- as security hedge in very uncertain world
- to reassure allies that U.S. security guarantee remains unquestionable
- as a disincentive to adversaries from taking hostile and aggressive
  actions against the U.S. and its allies

[handwritten: what about 9/11?]

Four systems designed by Los Alamos
Los Alamos is the design agency for four systems in the stockpile, including

- B61 gravity bomb, deployed to variety of strategic and tactical aircraft
- W78, carried by U.S. Air Force's Minuteman III intercontinental ballistic
  missiles
- W76 and W88, carried by U.S. Navy's Trident missile submarines

[handwritten: no idea what "Triad" planes ships missiles ships]

This triad of launch platforms (aircraft, land-based missiles, and submarines)
provides the President with the strongest, flexible, and most survivable nuclear
deterrent.

[handwritten: for who? the enemy of us?]

Each warhead/bomb designed by Los Alamos meets a rigorous and demanding
set of requirements and conditions as outlined by either the Air Force or the
Navy.

Stockpile life extension work

The nation's investment in the advanced scientific experimental, engineering,
and computational capabilities at Los Alamos allows the Laboratory to
confidently extend the service life of the nation's nuclear deterrent without
resorting to full-scale underground testing.

[handwritten: do not get this — if we know how to build them already? why test]

Life Extension Program (LEP) activities are extending the lifetime of warheads
and bombs designed to meet Cold War requirements (high yield to weight) for an
additional 20–30 years beyond their original expected lifetimes (10–15 years).
LEPs also provide the opportunity to install enhanced safety and security features
in existing weapons to meet today's—and the future's—security environment.

[handwritten: make bombs last longer— do they wear out?]

[handwritten: funny to say safe about a nuclear bomb]

Los Alamos, in partnership with the production plants and Sandia, is performing
an LEP on the W76, which will ensure the long-term viability of the nation's sea-
based deterrent. Los Alamos also is in the very early stages of an LEP in support
of the B61. Under guidance provided by the Nuclear Weapons Council, Los
Alamos plans to deliver the first LEP B61 to the U.S. Air Force in 2019.
Components that will be refurbished as part of the B61 include new detonator
cables, main charges, foams, and polymers and a new gas transfer system.

[handwritten: must be the parts that have to be fixed]

[handwritten: I never thought atom bombs could "wear out" or need maintenance but looks like they do…]

STRATEGY: **Coding Text**

FOCI: **Reading as Thinking**
Inferring, Interpreting, and Drawing Conclusions

WHEN TO USE: Before Reading **During Reading** After Reading

DESCRIPTION:

A quick way for students to capture and record their mental responses to their reading is to use a simple coding system. While she is reading, if a student notices a connection to another unit in your course, to another subject, or to something in her life, she jots a **C** in the margin; if she has a question, she jots a **?** If she runs across something new and exciting, she'll put down a **!** Students may add brief phrases or comments to explain their thinking. If the book belongs to the school, or if the teacher wishes students to be able to spot their notations quickly during class discussion, the codes can be placed on the Post-it notes as we described previously.

Why Use It?

Coding is basically a speedier form of marking text that achieves the same goals as annotation— getting kids to stop, think, and react as they read. If students are not accustomed to thinking their way through texts, they need to make conscious efforts to do so, but the marking should not be so laborious as to totally interrupt the flow of their reading. Symbols help students remember a strategy, notice when their thinking has followed it, and then very briefly note the spot in the text where that thinking occurred. If we want students to think more deeply as they read, we need to provide explicit mechanisms for them to do this, rather than just exhort them to "really think about this material."

How Does It Work?

1 Choose some codes that would work well in your subject area. Here is one generic set called INSERT (Interactive Notation System for Effective Reading and Thinking) that many content area teachers have found useful:

✓	Confirms what you thought
X	Contradicts what you thought
?	Puzzles you
???	Confuses you
★	Strikes you as very important
!	Is new or interesting to you

You can also invent your own coding system that matches the subject matter at hand.

2 Project a short text and model your own coding process for the class. Teachers at Downers Grove South High School have students use text coding extensively in their classes. But as reading coach Amy Stoops and science department chair Karen Eder explain, without this initial modeling, the students dutifully insert the codes—without realizing their purpose. Because the teacher is usually well acquainted with the material she's teaching, it can be difficult to realize the challenge students experience when the same information is often so new to them. Without some demonstration and guidance, students can have difficulty understanding what to mark and how to think about it.

3 Have students share their coded responses with a partner as they work through the selection. Then gather the whole class by asking, "Look through the reading and see if you've put any exclamation points in there for new and exciting information. Good, who'd like to share one?" For math application problems, students in pairs can compare their coding of information provided or requests for solutions in order to learn problem-solving processes. In book or article discussion circles, the codes can help students refer back to relevant information or evidence to support the ideas they are sharing. For reading support activities like KWL, students can mark spots in the material where their questions get answered or where new questions come up. In studying for tests or performance evaluations, the codes can help students spot important information or ideas they need to remember.

VARIATION: At Downers Grove South High School, the application of text coding varies widely across various subjects. With physics problems, for example, codes can help students to identify relevant information and figure out what result they are seeking. In biology, students may be looking for evidence of a particular phenomenon or concept, or the use of a particular vocabulary term. And as the students grow expert with the strategy, teachers invite students to create their own sets of codes. These young people enjoy including colors, emoticons from the text messaging world, and symbols they make up.

TO LEARN MORE

Buehl, Doug. 2009. *Classroom Strategies for Interactive Learning* (3rd ed.). Newark, DE: IRA.

Vaughn, Joseph, and Thomas Estes. 1986. *Reading and Reasoning Beyond the Primary Grades.* New York: Allyn and Bacon.

A wide variety of websites provide explanations of the strategy—including one at www.famlit.org/free-resources/educator-resources/educator-resources-adult-learners that includes video clips showing a teacher introducing coding with an adult literacy class.

STRATEGY: **Multicolumn Notes**

FOCI: **Inferring, Interpreting, Drawing Conclusions**
     Analyzing Author's Purpose, Theme, Point of View

WHEN TO USE: Before Reading **During Reading** After Reading

DESCRIPTION:

Students take reading notes in two or more columns, with lines drawn vertically down the middle of each page. In the standard version, the left-hand column is for summarizing important ideas from the text. In the right column, students write their own thoughts and responses—questions, confusions, personal reactions, reflections on what the information means. Sometimes teachers call this base version a *double-entry journal*—and they often go on to develop more complex three- or four-column note-taking forms to suit their subject matter. This structure was originally called Cornell Notes, but whatever the name, it is a highly flexible strategy that can be tweaked to serve every subject area.

Why Use It?

Students must be able to discern the most important information in a text, rather than mechanically plodding through the reading and viewing everything as equally significant. Putting the material in one's own words—that is, taking effective notes as one reads—is one way that proficient students do this. Along with summarizing information, students need opportunities to reflect on the topic, to wonder about its significance, or to ask themselves what might be implied by the ideas presented. Thus the notes balance the two main aspects of reading that the Common Core Standards highlight—clearly comprehending information and ideas that a text conveys, and actively thinking about its meaning, significance, legitimacy, truth, and application. This is a more continuous, expansive, and self-directed response tool, compared to Post-it notes or coding.

How Does It Work?

1 As always, it's essential to model, so that students not only carry out the activity but also learn to use it in meaningful ways. Read aloud through a short selection that you project (or photocopy) for all to follow. Demonstrate for students how to distinguish between important and minor ideas in their reading, how to restate ideas in your own words in column one, and then think aloud about those ideas and jot this thinking, along with other responses, in column two.

2 Following the gradual release pattern, invite students to practice this kind of summarizing and thinking, first as a whole class together and then in pairs or individually, with additional short chunks of reading. After the pair or individual practice, be sure to have the whole class share their jottings together.

3 Once kids are skilled at the base version, feel free to develop multicolumn notes for specific content. Provide these in advance to guide and structure students' reading. Be sure to have kids debrief their notes with partners and/or come back to the whole class to share the range of thinking. This will naturally enable more students to actively participate than is often the case. And it will help make instruction more interactive so that all the work isn't being done only by you, the teacher.

4 Assess the thinking. If you require students to take these notes regularly, you'll probably want to check the notebooks periodically. Stagger the due dates for various classes so you aren't over-loaded with paperwork. Skim over and check off the entries quickly and, if you have time, comment on just one or two for each student, perhaps with sticky notes of your own. And if you see limita-tions in the kinds of summarizing or reflecting that the students are jotting, don't hesitate to model once again to help students grow increasingly effective at the practice. But we'll also warn you: students won't bring high-grade energy to this quite demanding strategy if you do it all year long. Be sure to vary these notes with the many other ways of helping kids through their reading.

VARIATION: Teachers throughout Downers Grove South High School have students employ multicol-umn notes in a wide variety of ways, depending on the material being studied and the kind of think-ing explored in each class. As reading coach Amy Stoops and science department chair Karen Eder described to us, the most frequently used are three-column versions. In the left column, the teacher may ask students to sketch a picture, jot down a key statement, or note a lab rule. The middle column is for making predictions before the student reads. The right-hand column is devoted to thinking or reflection and may be labeled "So what?" or "What if the variables were different?" or "How would you do the experiment differently next time?" The possibilities for the columns are as wide as the kinds of thinking and learning that we want students to experience. When teachers are helping students develop an argument in a current events unit in a social studies class, for example, an issue might be written in the middle column—"Do you think the government should raise taxes, cut social programs, or both?" Then supporting evidence from the reading is listed on the left and counterar-guments on the right. The student's conclusion is written at the bottom. In a math or science class, the left-hand column may feature a graph, the middle column the relevant evidence drawn from the graph, and the right-hand column the inferences or problem solutions that can be drawn. As Amy and Karen explain, "It all depends on the material and the thinking that you're teaching."

EXAMPLE

Name: _____

Directions: For each of the statements below, record evidence from the text or speeches that supports the statement **and** evidence from the text that refutes the statement. You may paraphrase or quote directly from the text. After each piece of evidence, indicate what source it was from: Taft Reading (T), Roosevelt Reading (FDR), Obama Speech (O), or Romney Speech (R).

Evidence Supporting Statement	"So What?" How does the evidence support the statement?	Anticipatory Statement	Evidence Refuting Statement	"So What?" How does the evidence refute the statement?
		A good way to revatilize our country's economy is to encourage independent business opportunities.		
		Providing too much government relief damages people's desire to work.		

Example contributed by Brennan Lazzaretto, history teacher, Downers Grove South High School.

TO LEARN MORE

"Double Entry Journal." 2013. IRA/NCTE ReadWriteThink. www.readwritethink.org/classroom-resources/printouts/double-entry-journal-30660.html.

Paukin, Walter. 2013. *How to Study in College* (11th ed.). Cengage Learning.

STRATEGY: **Sketching My Way Through the Text**

FOCUS: **Visualizing Meaning**

WHEN TO USE: Before Reading **During Reading** After Reading

DESCRIPTION:

We have already shown several ways that kids can stop, think, and react by marking up a text. Drawing simple pictures or diagrams along the way can also help students conceptualize ideas from their reading. In this strategy, they create a sequence of sketches, drawings, or cartoons to illustrate the ideas described in their reading. The sketches may show linear changes over time, a cyclical pattern, or a group of related elements such as the various parts of a plant or elements in its ecosystem. These are not highly refined drawings, but quick and simple representations, so you must emphasize that artistic ability is not the point of the exercise. For visibility and ease of sharing, these sketches are done on 8½" × 11" blank sheets of paper.

Why Use It?

We don't all think in the same way. As researchers on multiple intelligences explain it, words and numbers are just two of the many modes by which people may understand an idea. Drawing is especially powerful for many students because it helps them visualize what they are reading about, and that's one of the most effective thinking strategies that proficient readers employ. A sequence of drawings expands thinking, revealing processes of change and development, or multiple perspectives around a topic. It can be especially useful for understanding subject-area material that involves changes over time—in chemical processes, biological cycles or growth, historical events, literary plots. Students can certainly study diagrams and charts, but as plenty of research shows, they will think through and remember much more when they create their own.

How Does It Work?

1 Show kids how you create your own quick sketches as you read aloud through a piece of text. Even if you were good in art, don't get carried away. Make sure the drawings are rough diagrams and stick figures, so the kids understand they are not meant to reflect artistic merit. If you teach history, the sketches can show a series of important events—but they might also represent the attitudes or concerns of various groups of people: perspectives of various states at the Constitutional

Convention, government versus settlers versus Native Americans, and so on. In math, the drawings can represent steps in the process of solving a complex problem. The example on the next page shows a teacher's modeled sketches for a math lesson.

2 Now let kids try it out. Depending on the material being read, students can stop at various points in their reading to do their quick sketch. Emphasize that the drawings should be quick and simple, so they don't break the flow of reading for too long or consume all the reading time provided in class (and providing some reading time in class is always a smart idea). If they're working on a math word problem, students may do all the sketches at once, to illustrate their process after they've solved it—or better yet, beforehand, to help them think through *how* they'll solve it.

3 Organize for sharing. Students should make their sketch sequences big enough for classmates to easily compare them and see the many ways an idea might be represented. For physical sharing in your room, students can make their drawings on newsprint and tape them up on the walls. Then in a gallery walk, small groups move from one set of drawings to the next, noticing how people pick up on various aspects of the reading. If your students have tablets or laptops, they can take pictures of and post their series of drawings on GoogleDocs, Edmodo, Padlet, or whatever document-sharing Web tool you use. That way they can view each other's work in an electronic gallery walk. Budget time for comments, responses, and whole-class or small-group discussion. Allowing students to view each other's sketches can easily lead into prompts for discussion, means for students to compare various ways of interpreting material, and aids for review.

VARIATION: Concerned that you don't have time for this strategy along with so many others described in this chapter? Solution: don't hesitate to incorporate one into another. Sketches can go onto Post-it response notes (pages 118–120). They can be featured in mapping (pages 155–158). They can serve as entries in one of the columns in students' multicolumn journals (pages 128–130) or as part of an exit or admit slip (pages 140–142).

EXAMPLE

In the *Interactive Mathematics Program* textbook, the "Chef's Hot and Cold Cubes" activity ingeniously uses the concept of unmeltable ice cubes to represent negative numbers and ever-burning charcoal briquettes to represent positive numbers. As the chef adds or removes cubes from the cooking pot, its temperature goes up or down. The temperature of the pot can be increased one degree by either adding a hot cube (adding a positive number) or removing a cold one (subtracting a negative number). Thus, students can envision a very understandable meaning for adding and subtracting positive and negative numbers. Multiplication of positive and negative numbers simply means adding or taking out multiple "bunches" of cubes. Here is one set of drawings for several of the chef's actions:

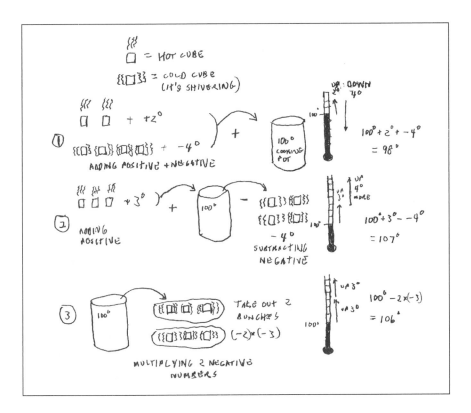

TO LEARN MORE

Harvey, Stephanie, and Anne Goudvis. 2007. *Strategies That Work: Teaching Comprehension for Understanding and Engagement* (2nd ed.). York, ME: Stenhouse.

Hoyt, Linda. 2002. *Make It Real: Strategies for Success with Informational Texts.* Portsmouth, NH: Heinemann, 139–141.

Rhode, Mike. 2011. "Sketching: The Visual Thinking Power Tool." A List Apart. http://alistapart.com/article/sketching-the-visual-thinking-power-tool/.

AFTER READING

STRATEGY: **Turn and Talk**

FOCUS: **Reading as Thinking**

WHEN TO USE: Before Reading   **During Reading   After Reading**

DESCRIPTION:

One of the simplest, briefest, yet most powerful strategies in your reading toolkit is the short minute or two when pairs of students turn and talk about a question or issue before them. Also known as "think-pair-share," this is a fundamental activity that skillful teachers might use *five or eight times in a class period* to keep kids active and engaged—and to access their thinking. Any time the teacher reads something aloud, introduces a concept, or poses a question, she can immediately ask everyone in the class to turn to someone next to them and talk over the matter being considered. A minute or two is plenty of time for this. Then the teacher solicits responses from a number of students in order to feed the ideas they've exchanged into the work of the class. If this is a brainstorming session or creation of a list of possibilities or options, then all or most of the class may contribute their answers.

Why Use It?

Many teachers find it's hard to get some students to participate in class. A few eager beavers raise their hands all the time, and everyone else tries to pretend they're out to lunch (or actually *are*). But turn and talk enables students to stop and think about a question or a challenging problem before you ask them to share with the class. It draws on social interaction to advance learning, something the Common Core explicitly recognizes in the speaking and listening standards. Turn and talk prevents students from drifting and losing focus when you need to present information, by presenting a sociable interlude during which the students digest and reflect on the ideas. And it increases the number of students who participate in class because it helps everyone gather their thoughts before raising their hands (or failing to). It ensures that all kids get to process ideas with their own words, rather than just a few students reciting an answer.

   In fact, consistent pair shares shift the dynamic significantly in the classroom. Traditionally, a single student responds while others, we fear, half listen. With turn and talk, everyone responds, and then when the teacher does ask to hear some of the answers, a variety of versions or perspectives get aired. If you want the class to generate a list of some kind—animals in a particular kind of habitat, possible causes for a historical event, practical applications for a mathematical concept—it's a great way to get a long list going. And you'll see very quickly how much the students already know about the topic, along with what they haven't yet learned.

How Does It Work?

1 How many times have we said this? Model it first. Get a student volunteer to stand beside you (choose a student who knows how to have a conversation, or whisper some coaching before you start). Have the class suggest a school-appropriate topic for a quick conversation (something in the news, a school issue), then turn to your partner and chat for a minute or two. Then ask kids what they noticed the two of you doing, while you make a list. Kids should have noticed behaviors like:

* faced each other
* made eye contact
* took turns
* asked each other questions
* stayed focused on the topic
* listened to each other
* built on each others' comments
* acted friendly

If students fail to notice or mention any key elements, by all means put them on the list yourself. This co-created chart now becomes the kids' guide for doing a turn and talk.

2 Next, have kids practice turning and talking about a short article, an image, or a poem. As always, you are using course-related material, not wasting time with irrelevant content. But before they share, you must make sure each student has a single partner. Left to their own devices, some kids will have one partner, others will have three, and some will have none. For turn and talks to work, each student must have one partner, know who it is, and be sitting right next to them from the beginning of class. You do *not* want kids scrambling for a partner after you've called for a pair share. (If numbers are uneven, you can allow a single group of three or be the leftover's partner yourself.)

When kids are set, your instructions will be very simple, along the lines of "Turn to your partner and take turns sharing what you think about our topic [article, poem]." Partners should rotate frequently (daily or weekly) so that everyone works with everyone else in the room, building more friendliness and support through the year.

3 As you use the strategy, fine-tune it with further training in ways to get conversation started, turn-taking, listening, and reporting out. Google "turn and talk anchor charts" and you'll find a large collection of handy lists for guiding effective student conversations. However, while these can inspire you, it's best to use turn and talk itself to have your students generate their own list of good conversational practices. Then be sure to refer to it frequently, and don't let it just fade into the woodwork. Just because we're dealing with older students, we shouldn't assume they've already learned the art of good conversation.

4 Use turn and talk a lot—as we said, several times per class period should be the norm. Use it to establish a rhythm between presenting, reflecting, and responding during a class. We've watched science teachers invite students to hypothesize about why an unexpected result occurred in an experiment. In Kettering, Ohio, art teacher Meghan Dillon uses turn and talk in a variety of ways, particularly at what she likes to call "checkpoints." She may show images of several paintings and ask students to take a moment to talk over and compare the two. Or she may have her students read a one-page biography of an artist like Keith Haring (available at www.haring.com) and then talk over and pick out a key word or phrase that reveals something important about him. Or she'll stop the class in the midst of a project and have pairs look at each other's work for a minute, then trade some feedback. We've seen math teachers put students to work in pairs to solve a problem or identify a particularly significant number. And you needn't worry that you're overusing it—students never seem to tire of the strategy, perhaps because they're just happy to get a moment to talk. But do be sure to elicit some responses from the whole class after the pairs have had their discussion. It's important for students to have their thinking put to good use.

5 Monitoring the conversations is always a helpful practice—both to see how students are using the process, and to get an advance sense of their thinking. This can enable you to draw out some of the shy students during later sharing—"John, I heard you explaining a great idea about . . . Could you share that with the whole class?"

VARIATION: Meghan Dillon wants to be sure students use turn and talk well and efficiently, so she starts the kids with turning *and writing* at the beginning of the year, using Post-it notes for the responses (see pages 118–120). Using a photocopier, she photocopies smiley faces plus a star onto two-inch square sticky notes by running sheets filled with them through a copy machine. The smileys are for jotting two things a student likes about his or her partner's piece and the star is for one suggested improvement (nice that the symbol for improvement is something positive and not a frown or an *X*). Meghan first models how to use these to give quick feedback to an adult friend or colleague's work. Then students swap sketches they are working on, fill in their notes, and place them on the back of their partner's sketch. Meghan finds that after just two or three rounds of this, over several weeks, the students can switch to meaningful, quick oral turn and talk moments without any trouble.

TO LEARN MORE

Harvey, Stephanie, and Harvey Daniels. 2009. *Comprehension and Collaboration: Inquiry Circles in Action*. Portsmouth, NH: Heinemann, 126.

Simon, Cathy Allen. 2013. "Using the Think-Pair-Share Technique." IRA/NCTE ReadWriteThink. www.readwritethink.org/professional-development/strategy-guides/using-think-pair-share-30626 .html#research-basis.

STRATEGY: **Tweet the Text**

FOCUS: **Reading and Summarizing**

WHEN TO USE: Before Reading   During Reading   **After Reading**

DESCRIPTION:

After they have read a passage, textbook section, or article, students work with a partner to create 140-character summaries, which are then shared and refined with the whole group. Sound goofy? Here's one for Manifest Destiny:

> In 1840, God smiled as miners, farmers, railroads, and telegraphs drove the native peoples ever further west toward extinction.

And one for trigonometry:

> Sine measures an angle. In a right triangle with that angle it = opposite side divided by hypotenuse. Its graph shows curve of a sound wave.

If cell phones are available and legal in school, kids can type their summaries on real phones. If not, we use laptops or just pretend on paper.

Why Use It?

The kids are texting anyway, so why don't we co-opt their attraction to this technology and harness it to the curriculum? And very seriously, synthesizing a text, putting it into your own words, and boiling down the ideas to a compact but accurate statement are among the most crucial of all reading skills. As the Common Core Anchor Standards (National Governors Association 2010, 10) put it, kids must be able to "determine central ideas or themes of a text and analyze their development; summarize the key supporting details and ideas." If we can make this important cognitive process fun, tactile, and interactive, let's go for it.

How Does It Work?

1   Have students read a selection of subject-matter text. Choose a chunk of material that's reasonably summarizable. The Periodic Table, maybe not. One- to three-page nonfiction articles work well for this; historical narratives, biography, or fiction can be longer. If the content density is super-high, as in a math or science textbook, use a shorter passage.

2 When kids are done reading, put them in pairs and have them get out their cell phones or jump on a laptop. (Worst case, paper.) Have them work together to create a 140-character summary of the text they have just read. This discussing out loud with a partner and co-composing a common tweet is very important—it forces students to externalize their thinking, compare it with some else's, negotiate meaning, and shape the most important ideas into a very tight space. Encourage them to hit 140 characters right on the nose for the fun and discipline of it. Doing it directly on Twitter (if that's permitted in your school) makes it easy to count the characters, or just use http://www.twitter-character-counter.com. And don't forget: spaces are included.

3 Gather the class and have many pairs share their tweets aloud, or onscreen if you can project them. Stop and talk about the different ways people found to express the underlying big ideas. As a final step, collaboratively compose the "uber tweet," the very best you can do inside the limits.

VARIATIONS: Obvious adaptations of this strategy would be to "email the text" or "post on our Edmodo page," with all sorts of possible constraints and rules. Each of these is just an example of putting a lesson we'd do anyway—like discussing an important reading—into a sociable channel that kids will enjoy, share, and remember.

TO LEARN MORE

Daniels, Harvey, and Nancy Steineke. 2013. *Texts and Lessons for Teaching Literature*. Portsmouth, NH: Heinemann.

Miller, Samantha. 2013. "50 Ways to Use Twitter in the Classroom." TeachHub.com .www.teachhub.com/50-ways-use-twitter-classroom.

FOCUS: **Reading and Summarizing**

WHEN TO USE: Before Reading   During Reading   **After Reading**

DESCRIPTION:

At the end of class, students write on index cards or slips of paper stating one important idea they learned, a question they have, a prediction about what will come next, or a thought about a character, event, or other element in the reading. Alternatively, have students turn in such a response at the start of the next class—or allow kids three minutes to jot one when they arrive. Then use these notes right away to start class conversations, having kids read theirs aloud or turn to a partner and share. Later, without even grading these, you can skim through them to observe what kids do or don't get, what they're noticing in their reading, and what ideas may need to be clarified or reinforced.

Why Use It?

Kids in middle and high schools rush from one class to the next, from math to PE to social studies. In all but a few innovative programs, the day splinters into forty-five- or fifty-five-minute pieces, followed by sports and afterschool activities, plus the socializing in between that matters more than anything else for many teenagers. This brief writing activity helps connect one day's learning to the next, and last night's reading to this morning's discussion, across all the distractions, activities, and competing schoolwork in between. It helps kids focus as they enter our classrooms, or solidify learning just before they leave. And it provides a snapshot of where the kids are, so we and they aren't taken by surprise at test time or when studying the next topic that depends on an understanding of what went before.

How Does It Work?

❶ Yes, we sound like the education version of *Groundhog Day*, but we'll say it again: modeling is the place to start. This activity invites students to reflect on what they've read or learned from a class activity, and many students are not accustomed to this mental work. They may need help putting into words what seemed most important in the reading, what they are confused about, or why some problem was difficult. They may need reassurance that writing about challenges will enable you to help them rather than just expose them to judgments of failure. They may need to hear from you that it's OK to ask a question or request that something be explained again. So yes, once again, do the modeling that will show students the possibilities for using the strategy and how it can help their learning. We can't just take their understanding of this for granted.

2 For two or three minutes at the end of class (or the start of the next one), students jot responses to their reading on note cards. Base directions on what you want to learn about their thinking. Keep it simple—"one thing I learned and one question I have," for example. If you've taught particular thinking strategies—connecting, summarizing, or inferring—you can ask students to use them.

3 To get kids actively using the admit slips, say, "Now pass your card back three people in your row [circle, table, etc.]. When you receive someone else's card, read it, then turn it over and write a response, rejoinder, or question of the back. Make it thoughtful and interesting for us all to consider." Then invite volunteers (or call on individuals) to first read the front side, and then their own written response. Invite all class members to comment or question. The original author can reveal herself if she wishes and defend her initial comments—or discuss how her unforeseen partner has elaborated or changed her thinking. And you can keep tying these reactions back to the text you assigned in the first place.

4 Don't let the cards become a grading burden or you'll just tire of assigning them. Don't worry about spelling and grammar—these aren't senior theses, but just quick notes to you and the class. Instead, glance over them for a quick view of how students are doing and whether you can move on or need to further explain a concept. If you absolutely need to give credit, use quick check marks on the cards and in your gradebook.

VARIATION: If there is a controversial issue at the heart of the text kids are responding to, collect the cards first. Flip through them quickly, standing right in front of the class, and scan for a couple of provocative/unique/incendiary cards. You know you can do this in one minute or less. Read one bomb-throwing card out loud (without identifying the author) to spark class discussion about various views of the reading. And another . . .

TO LEARN MORE

Daniels, Harvey, Steven Zemelman, and Nancy Steineke. 2007. *Content-Area Writing: Every Teacher's Guide*. Portsmouth, NH: Heinemann, 34–44.

Short, Kathy, Jerome Harste, and Carolyn Burke. 1996. *Creating Classrooms for Authors and Inquirers* (2nd ed.). Portsmouth, NH: Heinemann, 466–471.

EXAMPLES

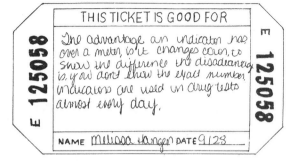

THIS TICKET IS GOOD FOR

E 125058

The advantage an indicator has over a meter, is it changes color, to show the difference the disadvantage is, you dont know the exact number, indicators are used in drug tests almost every day.

NAME Melissa Hangen DATE 9/23

Admit Slip—Indicators vs. Meters

I would have voted "Not Guilty" because the law that Congress passed was purposely against Johnson because he was favoring the south. The rule was unconstitional to the president. The republicans wanted to have one person from there group as president so they could punished the south. Most of the Congress was part of the Radical Republicans so they reallly got anything they wanted. In a big way they were criminal.

Exit Slip—Impeachment of Andrew Johnson

STRATEGY: **Word Wall**

FOCUS: **Building Academic Vocabulary**

WHEN TO USE: **Before Reading   During Reading   After Reading**

DESCRIPTION:

A word wall is a display of key vocabulary items for a unit or topic, written on individual cards or newsprint strips, and kept on—you guessed it—the classroom wall. For a math class on geometry, it might look like this:

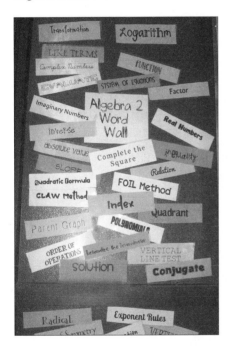

Algebra word walls provided by Sarah Hagen, used by permission.

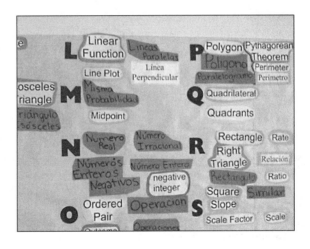

Elementary teachers have used word walls in their classrooms for years, but we rarely see them implemented in middle and high school. That's too bad, because vocabulary so often embodies *concepts*, and word walls are a way to immerse kids in the big ideas of the subject. To make word walls especially powerful, teachers actively involve students in creating them and in regularly using the information displayed to help them read, write, and talk about the subject matter. Word walls reward constant maintenance, so teachers return to them again and again, helping kids to add new terms and make connections between existing items.

Math

Why Use It?

Remember those long lists of words you studied in preparation for the SAT or ACT exam, once upon a time? How many do you remember and use now? Vocabulary is not learned effectively by memorizing lists and definitions, but by seeing words in use, in their customary contexts, and by engaging actively with them and with the ideas behind them. In return, good vocabulary study supports and deepens students' thinking about the material they are reading. So don't think that word walls are just for first-grade teachers. Reading experts remind us that if a student has difficulty with more than 5 to 10 percent of the words in a piece of reading, she will not be able to comprehend it effectively. But an actively used, effective word wall enables students to engage with language, and to refer back to their thinking about relevant words in one easily seen place, where they can put the pieces of their knowledge together and solidify it. In many subjects, the terms are essential to understanding the concepts and processes that are studied. As high school biology teacher Marnie Ware argues, "Vocabulary is at the core of my field."

So a word wall can provide crucial support for students' comprehension if they engage with key vocabulary terms before reading. And, if students have some time to read in class, stopping at some point in the middle can help to see if there are words tripping them up that need to be added to the word wall. Alternatively, reviewing vocabulary after reading can add still more to the wall, or result in rearrangements as students reflect on what they've learned.

How Does It Work?

1 Introduce the idea of a word wall and put up the first few items yourself. Choose these from the most crucial vocabulary in an upcoming unit. Seek a balance of Tier 3 technical terms and those powerful Tier 2 words that cross disciplines and mark an educated person. A useful, effective word wall should include definitions as well as information about where and when items are used. Model how you can write this information on the back of cards or strips, so that kids can walk to the front of the room, flip them over, and remind themselves of the definitions—and actively engage with the word. The word cards can be color-coded to reflect various aspects of the subject.

2 As the unit unfolds, use the word wall to highlight key concepts. Introduce terms, explain and discuss their meaning, illustrate them through whole-class and small-group activities, have students use them in a variety of ways, and regularly pause to have kids build the word wall step by step, themselves. They can fill out the cards or strips, providing definitions on the back and then leading discussions in which their classmates try to figure out as much as possible about given words. They can be asked to group, sequence, and rearrange the words according to various categories or ways of viewing the topic under study. In fields like science and math, this merges with the process of exploring and explaining the content of the course itself—so it need not become an add-on activity within a crowded curriculum.

3 Maintain the collection as it grows. Word walls should accumulate gradually, as students engage in a unit of study. Introduce just a few words at a time, so kids can internalize them and spend enough time on them to make them a permanent part of their knowledge. Then, various terms can be returned to and discussed repeatedly, so the word wall is put to regular use, rather than being posted and forgotten.

VARIATION: When Marnie Ware, biology teacher at Prosser High School in Chicago, introduces a new concept like "homologous structures"—which is also a vocabulary term, of course—she starts with an activity. In one instance, she first brought out an actual set of bones of a human arm that the school happened to possess. Then, pairs of students received sets of cut-out drawings to be pieced together—each set composed of the bones of either a cat's leg, a horse's leg, or a whale fin. Students raced to tape their bone drawings together in the proper order to complete the whole leg (or fin). They could see that while the bones were of different sizes and shapes, they corresponded to the same parts of a limb for each animal—thus illustrating the concept, "homologous structures."

Next, Marnie turned students' attention to the word wall. Along with a number of related terms on orange squares were three new ones:

* homologous structure
* analogous structure
* vestigial structure

And across from all the terms were squares with definitions written on them, arranged in random order. Now the job for the students was to identify or guess which definitions went with the three new terms. *Homologous* was the easiest, since they'd just completed the activity and pronounced the word together. The next two were from material the students had not yet studied, so now they were guessing, though with some hints deriving from the day's activity. The kids struggled with this, but didn't grow discouraged. Marnie discussed their guesses as they were offered, helped them with the various meanings, and then promised to return to the terms the next day. They were now primed for the new lesson and more vocabulary learning, and more words and definitions would be added to the word wall on the following days.

Predictable Problem

In many middle and high schools, teachers don't necessarily have their own classroom where they can leave materials, artifacts, or wall charts on display. So how can you keep a word wall if you move from room to room over the course of the day? A few itinerant teachers we know have a cart loaded with books and materials that they haul around the building—not an ideal way to work, but it does build stamina and provide exercise. We cannot let limited physical space confine our teaching strategies. A traveling word wall can become one more item to balance on the cart, constructed of large posterboard pieces taped together and folded up for easier travel. The digital solution is of course easier—keep your word wall on a flash drive or on your school's server, so you can project and work with it "live," no matter what classroom you wind up in.

TO LEARN MORE

Allen, Janet. 2007. *Inside Words: Tools for Teaching Academic Vocabulary, Grades 4–12*. York, ME: Stenhouse.

Blachowicz, Camille, and Peter Fisher. 2009. *Teaching Vocabulary in All Classrooms* (4th ed.). Upper Saddle River, NJ: Pearson.

Cronsberry, Jennifer. 2004. *Word Walls: A Support for Literacy in Secondary School*. Toronto: Curriculum Services Canada.

Harmon, Janis M., et al. 2009. "Interactive Word Walls: More Than Just Reading the Writing on the Walls." *Journal of Adolescent and Adult Literacy* 52(5).

STRATEGY: **Word Meaning Graphic Organizer**

FOCUS: **Building Academic Vocabulary**

WHEN TO USE: Before Reading   **During Reading   After Reading**

DESCRIPTION:

There are dozens of graphic organizers for vocabulary study, but this one clearly shows how to embed vocabulary learning into the wider process of reading. This particular organizer is designed to help students think in more depth about a single important vocabulary word. It asks students to view the word in a variety of ways, to notice when and how it's being used, and why it's important to know. Students complete the organizer in small groups, returning to their groups later on to add more information as they read and learn. Groups can compare versions of the same word. Or you can have various groups each tackle different words, and when the organizers are completed, post all of them. Groups can report orally or organize a gallery walk for classmates to circulate and review all of the organizers. With the right selection of vocabulary items, this can become an active process for reviewing an entire unit of study.

Why Use It?

Words gain their meaning in connection with other words, and through the ideas, concepts, and information that comprise a field of study. Thus, good vocabulary study supports and deepens students' thinking about the material they are reading. An effective vocabulary graphic organizer allows students to gather their contextualized experiences of a word in one place, where they can put the pieces of their knowledge together, actively process it, and solidify it.

How Does It Work?

1 Demonstrate how you create an organizer yourself. Have kids read a short chunk of text that includes the word and then invite them to help you fill in several of the boxes. To keep this from becoming simply the performance of a couple of students who already know the words, have every-one turn and talk in pairs (see the turn and talk strategy on pages 134–137) briefly before each step. Then you can call on several pairs to compare possibilities for filling in a particular box.

2 Put students in small groups to try it out. The more complex graphic organizers work best as whole-class or small-group activities, rather than individually. As Janet Allen explains, "If you truly don't know a word, it is virtually impossible to complete the form. If you do know the word well enough to complete the form, you don't need to complete it. Students learn extended meanings of the target word here by virtue of their *joint* knowledge" (Allen, 1999, 57).

3 As students read, they meet periodically but briefly in their groups to discuss which aspects of the word they've learned about, and then decide together how to fill in the boxes on the sheet. Explain that they shouldn't expect to fill in every box right away; the idea is to discover more about the word as they go along. The group meetings could take place for a couple of minutes at the start of each class period over several days as you work through the reading involved in a particular unit. Thus, these meetings can serve as a good, socially oriented activity for refocusing students on your subject at the beginning of each period.

4 The groups can have a number of organizer sheets going for the key words in a study unit, and add various entries as they encounter information that expands their understanding of each word. Alternatively, assign various groups to focus on particular words, to be shared with the rest of the class at some point during the unit.

5 Put the organizers to work in the process of students' learning. Otherwise they can easily become just another set of worksheets to be completed and forgotten. We've mentioned a gallery walk as one structure for students to share and review the vocabulary terms. Another can be for groups to exchange and place sticky-note comments (respectful, please!) on each other's completed organizers. Or students can pair up to discuss and compare organizers from their groups. This kind of activity is especially useful as an effective review process at the end of a unit.

TO LEARN MORE

Allen, Janet. 1999. *Words, Words, Words*. York, ME: Stenhouse, 57.

Blachowicz, Camille, and Peter Fisher. 1996. *Teaching Vocabulary in All Classrooms*. Upper Saddle River, NJ: Prentice-Hall.

Target Word

Exothermic

Topic where word is found:

Whether an overall reaction is exothermic or endothermic depends on the quantity of energy added (endothermic) compared to the amount of energy given off (exothermic) in the bond-making steps.

Parts of the word we recognize:

Thermic—like thermal underwear.
So it's about being warm?

Examples:

Gasoline burning in a car engine
Explosions

So the word means:

If heat is released overall when the steps of a chemical reacton are all added up

Why it's important:

If you are trying to combine two chemicals, you need to know whether to heat them or provide cooling because it's going to give off heat.

Where is the word used?

Our chemistry book—chapters on energy. Web article on making your own hotpack for muscle injuries. Chemistry sites on the web.

How it connects with other words:

Types of chemical reactions—maybe combination reactions are often exothermic ones.

Word Meaning Graphic Organizer

STRATEGY: **Vocabulary Tree**

FOCUS: **Building Academic Vocabulary**

WHEN TO USE: **Before Reading   During Reading   After Reading**

DESCRIPTION:

This graphic, shaped like a free-form—if not very aesthetically pleasing—tree, focuses on linking groups of related words or ideas, and allows for plenty of flexibility in the number and placement of branches (and roots, if the student so desires) to illustrate the relationships among the various key words in a unit, book, or study project. The trunk carries the core word or concept, and the branches show connected elements, along with examples. The graphic is something to be added to as students read and learn more about the words' usages, connections, and roles in carrying the meaning of the topic being studied.

Why Use It?

Each of our vocabulary graphics focuses on a different aspect of words and their relationships. The previous one takes a single word and asks students to go deeper with it. This one helps students think about relationships among a set of words from their reading. So often, the list of vocabulary terms at the end of a textbook chapter simply arranges them in alphabetical order, which has very little connection with the concepts being studied, or how they are related. This not only takes away from the overall conceptual understanding of the topic, but also makes learning more difficult because it becomes an exercise in memorizing a large number of discrete items instead of building a single integrated picture. When students create their own vocabulary tree, they are led to think about how the concepts behind the words are related to each other, and they can develop a much stronger, fuller understanding of the material they are studying. Further, the graphic enables students to go beyond simply a sentence that defines a word to understand the role of the word in conveying ideas and information about the topic they are studying.

How Does It Work?

1 Students should begin with four or five of the important words in the reading they are doing. You can provide these, especially if this is the first time the students are using this organizer. Alternatively, you can supply a longer list from which the students choose a smaller number. Or if they're really getting comfortable with vocabulary work, you can ask them to identify important words by themselves as they read. Four or five words are plenty to start with—the aim is to explore them in depth and pick up additional vocabulary along the way. And learners can really internalize only a small number of new words at one time.

2 Now put kids to work trying out the trees. Have each student draw a rough version of a tree with a trunk and branches, and begin arranging the words to represent how he or she thinks they are related. More important or general words go along the trunk and subcategories get placed on branches that show their connection to the more important words. Words can be rearranged and more added as students read and learn more about the topic.

An alternative, particularly if there is a lot of new vocabulary to deal with, is for students to place each key word on a separate sheet of paper with a tree on it and the word near the bottom of the trunk. Then as students read, they are to add related words, information, and/or examples on the branches, one item to each branch. The branches may have branches of their own, of course. A third option is to have the whole class or small groups work together on vocabulary trees that are drawn on newsprint, hung on the walls, and elaborated as a study project proceeds.

3 Students should be asked to return to the vocabulary trees periodically in the course of a unit, to continue adding to them or altering them to reflect their improved understanding of the topic. Pairs can compare their trees and discuss why they've made various decisions on how to show word relationships. And as students read more widely beyond the textbook, they can return to the tree diagrams to add notes on the ways they see the words used in other materials they encounter.

TO LEARN MORE

Kirby, Dan, and Carol Kuykendall. 1991. *Mind Matters: Teaching for Thinking*. Portsmouth, NH: Heinemann.

EXAMPLE

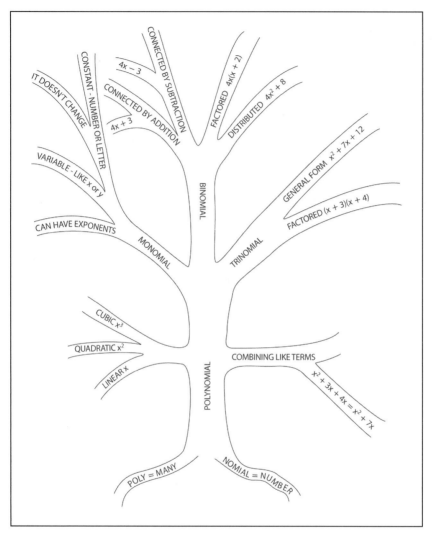

Vocabulary Tree

STRATEGY: **List-Group-Label**

FOCUS: **Building Academic Vocabulary**

WHEN TO USE: Before Reading   **During Reading   After Reading**

DESCRIPTION:

The name tells the story. The class develops—or the teacher may provide—a list of twenty to twenty-five key vocabulary words from the assigned reading. In small groups, students arrange the words in clusters based on something the words have in common. In many cases, particularly if you use the activity in the midst of a unit rather than at the end, the students are unlikely to know the exact meanings of many of the words, but they should be encouraged to share their knowledge and their guesses in their groups. A cluster must contain at least three words in order to count, but words can be used more than once. The students then decide on labels for each cluster.

Why Use It?

Effective vocabulary learning requires that students work with words, think about them, and see them in a context. Like the vocabulary tree, this is about finding relationships among words rather than defining them in isolation. The thinking that is involved is somewhat different, however, because the students are creating groupings and categories for the words, rather than linear relationships. Working together, students pool their knowledge and learn from one another. Even though a student may not yet know everything he needs to about a particular word, the clusterings help the process of making sense of it, connect it with other words he knows more fully, and suggest where he might look to find out more about it.

How Does It Work?

1 At a midpoint in their reading, or after students have completed a reading selection, organize them into small groups for this vocabulary work. Balance membership in the groups, so each includes students of varying achievement levels. That way, the students can help one another, and no one group is left completely at sea. Provide a group of vocabulary items for kids to work with.

A list for a set of U.S. history readings on African American soldiers in the Civil War might look like this, including some of the military terms and Latinate words favored by mid-nineteenth-century writers and leaders:

chattel	retroactive	contrabands	auspices
edifice	frock coats	philanthropic	quartermaster
escalating	serfdom	avocation	commissary
permeated	fatigue duty	remuneration	mustered out
reprisal	sagacity	amenability	parapet

If many of these terms are unfamiliar to the students, provide time for the groups to look them up or determine them from context—after all, if the group knows nothing about the words, the activity can't really go forward.

2 Now, working in small groups, students can pool their background knowledge and powers of inference to place the words in clusters, however they think the words might fit together. When all the words are arranged, the students decide on a label for each cluster.

3 After the work is finished, have students look back through the reading to see if their increased understanding of the words helps them comprehend the text better—and vice versa. To make this go efficiently, you can identify short passages beforehand that contain various of the vocabulary terms and assign each group one passage to read and discuss. Then have the groups report and explain one or more connections that they see between the words in a particular cluster and the passage that they've just reread.

VARIATION: Have the groups record their lists on newsprint, so they can be hung around the room for ongoing reference. Then kids can watch for the words as they read further. They can also add more words to the lists as they continue to read and learn about the topic.

TO LEARN MORE

Blachowicz, Camille, and Peter Fisher. 2009. *Teaching Vocabulary in All Classrooms*. New York: Prentice-Hall.

"List-Group-Label." 2013. "All About Adolescent Literacy." www.adlit.org/strategies/19780/.

STRATEGY: **Clustering and Mapping**

FOCUS: **Visualizing Meaning**

WHEN TO USE: **Before Reading**   During Reading   **After Reading**

DESCRIPTION:

The idea of graphically displaying key concepts has many variants: trees, of course, but Venn diagrams, timelines, concept maps, and semantic maps are also all in the family. You're probably familiar with most or all of these, and information about them, not to mention the templates and lesson plans that abound. Here, we'd like to draw attention to a couple of valuable graphic organizers that are used less often.

Gabriele Rico (1983) first popularized clustering as an aid to students' writing, describing it as "a nonlinear brainstorming process akin to free association." *Clustering* is a kind of brainstorming that links ideas in a two-dimensional map, with lines to show connections based on students' mental associations as they think about a topic, adding an important visual aspect to the process. *Mind mapping* is similar except that it is a more structured visual arrangement of ideas after students have completed their reading.

The teacher may provide a template or have students create their own, individually or in small groups. Both clustering and mapping can be used either for individual students' work or recorded on a whiteboard or document camera for a whole class.

Why Use It?

Like brainstorming, clustering helps students discover things they already know—or think they know—about the topic they will be studying. In her book *Writing the Natural Way*, Gabriele Rico describes how clustering not only helps access ideas, but reduces the anxiety people feel as they wrack their brains about a topic. As a person thinks and perhaps gets stuck, "This relaxed receptivity to ideas usually generates another spurt of associations." In other words, it is meant to open students up to connections and possibilities they might not have realized when they started. This is why the activity requires, like brainstorming, that all ideas be accepted, and that the students toss them in as quickly as possible, without censoring or questioning the connections they make.

Mind-mapping looks very similar, and similarly helps students to organize their thinking about a topic. However, it usually serves this purpose after a piece of reading or study is completed, enabling readers to put the pieces together, so to speak, and see how they are related. Because clustering and maps are two-dimensional, they enable students to more easily see the multiple connections that are harder to illustrate in the one-dimensional linearity of the printed word.

This strategy especially asks students to identify larger concepts in their reading, and then to group lesser elements under them. So mapping presents a great opportunity to teach a minilesson or two on this important thinking strategy. Cognitive researchers tell us that our minds, particularly in short-term memory, can deal with only limited numbers of items at once. But batching together a jumble of items in some logical way makes them one larger mental unit—your friend's phone number is easier to remember than a separate string of ten numbers if it reminds you of a famous historical date. Understandably, as we work through a unit of study we often break it down into smaller pieces so that students are not overwhelmed and can grasp one aspect at a time. The downside of this is that they might never add up the pieces into something larger that connects with big ideas and issues in their lives. So we need to make sure that the bigger picture doesn't get lost as we teach. This activity invites students to synthesize many aspects of an idea, rather than simply march dutifully and mindlessly through a series of tasks.

How Does It Work?

1 As with many of our strategies, it's advisable to model the activity, have the class practice and compare results, and observe as students use the activity in order to help them and inform yourself about how they are doing. Use short samples of text to show students how you do this, as a competent adult reader, and to give them plenty of practice at it.

2 For conducting a clustering or mapping activity with a whole class, write a key "nucleus" word—e.g., *infinity*, *erosion*, *manifest destiny*—on the whiteboard or project it on a screen.

3 Students may work separately at first, writing the nucleus word and circling it in the center of a piece of paper, and thinking of words and ideas that connect with this word. They write these related terms around it, drawing circles around the words and connecting these with lines to the nucleus word. They then share their ideas one at a time as the teacher constructs a class diagram for all to see. As more connections occur, these get added to the diagram, with lines to show which terms they connect to. Students should do this quickly and avoid rejecting anything. If students are to create their own kind of map, be sure they understand that there are a wide variety of ways to represent their thoughts.

4 As with brainstorming, you can refer back to the clustering after students have read the relevant material, to help them notice which ideas emerged as important in the reading, what was surprising or different from what they expected, and what they learned. Mapping that takes place only after the reading leads to the same kinds of reflection.

VARIATION: There are already a couple of cool iPad apps that students can use to arrange words in variable and creative relationships with each other, very parallel to the mind-mapping and clustering they might do on paper. Popplet and Big Mind are popular right now, and there will probably be eighteen more by the time you read this.

EXAMPLES

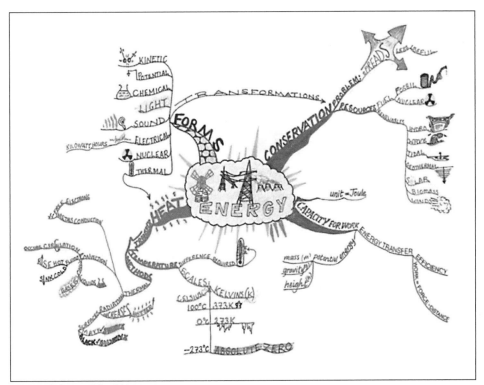

Energy Science Mind Map

From *Teach Yourself Revision Guides GCSE Science* by Eileen Ramsden, Tony Buzan, Jim Breithaupt, and David Applin. Copyright © 1997. Reproduced by permission of Hddder and Stoughton Limited.

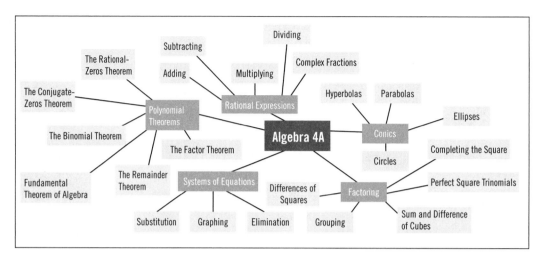

Source: http://deverett.wikispaces.com/ Reproduced with permission.

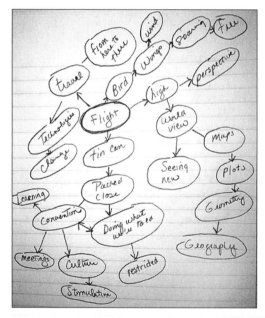

Source: www.writingthroughlife.com/a-weeks-worth-of-journaling-prompts-creative-clustering
Reproduced with permission.

TO LEARN MORE

Billmeyer, Rachel, and Mary Lee Barton. 2002. *Teaching Reading in the Content Areas*. Denver: McREL.

Rico, Gabriele. 1983. *Writing the Natural Way*. Los Angeles: Tarcher.

Think Buzan, Inc. 2012. "Beginner's Guide to Using Mind Mapping in the Schools." http://blog.thinkbuzan.com/education/beginner's-guide-to-the-use-of-mind-maps-in-elementary-schools.

STRATEGY: **Written Conversation**

FOCUS: **Sharing Ideas, Discussing, Debating**

WHEN TO USE: Before Reading   **During Reading   After Reading**

DESCRIPTION:

Kids love to write notes to each other in school—but those notes rarely have anything to do with what we're trying to teach. Written conversation harnesses the universal urge to share, but brings it into the curriculum. After reading (or discussing a topic, or watching a video, or doing a science experiment), students in pairs or small groups write short notes and responses to each other about the experience. Also called dialogue journals—or write-arounds when the groups involve three or more students—you can think of written conversation as legalized note-passing in your content area that gets students thinking by putting their thoughts into words and responding to one another. We can easily structure this so that students are taking and defending positions, based on evidence in the text they have read.

Why Use It?

We often use "class discussion" as a key after-reading activity. But when you think about it, what is a class discussion? It is usually one person talking and twenty-nine others sitting, pretending to listen, and hoping that their turn never comes. This ain't exactly what the standards documents call "engaged learning." In fact, while whole-class discussion may be ubiquitous in our schools, it is a pretty passive form of instruction, since most kids at any given moment are not actively engaging the material. If the point of talk is to help students get more deeply into the subject matter and the meaning of what they've read, then everybody in the room ought to be doing it. Smokey and his wife Elaine just published a whole book on this activity, which they call "the best-kept teaching secret" (Daniels and Daniels, 2013).

The solution, then, is quite simple: with written conversation, you can have a "discussion" where everyone is actively talking at once—though silently, in writing. Sure, you may have a few kids drift off the topic or say they can't think of anything—but you'll also have a solid majority of the class actually thinking and exchanging ideas about your subject.

How Does It Work?

1 After the reading (or other shared experience) is completed, have students identify partners or a small group for their written conversation. Four is the max. Each student needs a full-size blank sheet of paper and a pen at the ready, as well as the material being studied.

2 Explain the activity first, if this new to them, so the students understand that they will be writing simultaneous notes to one another about the reading selection, swapping them every two or three minutes at your command, and continuing the process for as long as your time constraints allow—and of course keeping quiet along the way. They are to write for the whole time allotted for each note, putting down reactions, questions, connections, ideas, wonderings—anything related to the passage, or responding to what their partner or other group members have said, just as they would in out-loud conversation. Spelling and grammar do not count—after all, these are only notes, not polished papers. Just to be clear, *all students are writing all the time*—no one is watching someone else write and waiting for a turn.

3 You can leave the topic open ("whatever struck you about this reading") or give an appropriate open-ended prompt: "What do you understand or not understand in this selection?" "What are the most important ideas here?" "Do you agree or disagree with the author, and why?" You can also use very narrow and precise topics: "Talk about Holden Caulfield's attitudes toward sex as they are revealed in Chapter 9 of *Catcher in the Rye.*"

4 Both students in each pair—or all in a larger group—write an initial note (e.g., "Dear Bobby, When I read this chapter, I was amazed that General Eisenhower actually said . . ."). Meanwhile, watch the time, and after a minute or two ask students to pass their notes to their partners or to the next person in their group. Explain to everyone: "Read what your partner said, then take a minute to answer, just as if you were talking out loud. You can write responses, feelings, make connections of your own, or ask your partner questions—anything you would do if you were talking face-to-face. Just keep the conversation going."

With each succeeding pass, you need to allow a little more time since students have to read what the increasing number of classmates on the page have contributed.

For dialogue journals in pairs, it's a good idea to have the notes go back and forth three or four times so that an extended conversation gets going. For groups of three to five, students can keep passing their notes around the circles and writing until each group member gets his or her original note back.

5 After the exchange is complete, the payoff begins when you say: "OK, now continue the conversation out loud with your partner(s) for a couple of minutes." If you worry about kids making that switch, first have them read back through all the notes on their sheet and then circle the "one most interesting sentence" that anyone wrote. Now have them use these as discussion starters for the face-to-face conversation. You should notice a rising buzz in the room, showing that kids have plenty to talk about. Circulate and sit in on groups as they talk, to get a flavor of their thinking.

6 Now a short whole-class discussion can be much more engaged and productive, because everyone will have rehearsed their thinking about the topic. Ask a few pairs to share one highlight or thread of their written conversations as a way of starting discussion. Biology teacher Lisa MacArtney collects the papers and reads aloud some of the marked sentences—which allows for anonymity for students who wish it. Lisa reports that the students especially enjoy this step, and once it's a regular practice, it serves as a strong motivation to write thoughtful comments. Lisa, by the way, uses written conversation with the real-world articles that she employs as high-interest starter reading for just about every unit in her course.

Predictable Problems

The first time you try this, a few kids may shift into oral conversation when papers are passed (adults also do this—it's a normal human response when you are bonding with a partner or a group). Be ready to remind them to "keep it in writing" during the transitions. Then, even with the best instructions, some kids will write two words and put their pens down, wasting two good minutes of writing time with each pass. You have to keep stressing that "we write for the whole time."

Because this activity has a lot of positive social pressure to work fast, we've taken to projecting four or five "safety net topics" just for the kids who need a jumpstart—or a restart. We tell them to use these only if they're really stuck. Usually the comments from classmates will give them plenty to respond to. Finally, when you call kids back to order at the end, when they are talking out loud with their partners, you may find it very hard to regain their attention. This happy little "management problem" shows you that kids are connecting to each other and the material.

EXAMPLE

> Melly, Did Mr. Gridley say that microwaves gave off ionizing radiation? I thought that kind was dangerous, and I don't understand why they'd let us have something in our homes that's dangerous. Did I just hear him wrong?
>
> — Rose
>
> Yea, microwaves do give off ionizing radiation which is dangerous. But microwaves give off such small amounts so they're not dangerous. Mr. Gridley said that we can only have under 5,000 mREMs a year. Microwaves give off such small amounts that we won't come close to ~~having~~ reaching 5,000 mREMs.
>
> Melly
>
> That still kinda creeps me out though. I don't want to grow a third ear just cause I wanted to make some oatmeal in my microwave. Jeez
>
> — Rose

Written Conversation About Ionizing Radiation

TO LEARN MORE

Daniels, Harvey, and Elaine Daniels. 2013. *The Best-Kept Teaching Secret: How Written Conversations Engage Students, Activate Learning, and Grow Fluent Writers.* Thousand Oaks, CA: Corwin.

FOCUS: **Recalling and Summarizing**

WHEN TO USE: Before Reading   **During Reading   After Reading**

DESCRIPTION:

The teacher selects a piece of content-area material that rewards rereading. Usually, this means that the text has multiple, easily missed layers of meaning; is prone to superficial readings; or taps into common misconceptions that lead readers astray. Then, the teacher plans and leads students through two (or three) successive readings of that text, taking responsibility to make each rereading feel like an adventure, a second helping of something delicious. In other words, the teacher entices kids to dig deeper, not through coercing them, but by evoking their curiosity.

Why Use It?

Every teacher has heard—and many have been intimidated by—the Common Core's insistent call for kids to do multiple readings of very hard text. When we first saw the standards ourselves, back in 2010, we immediately envisioned having to flog high school kids through Emerson's impenetrable "Society and Solitude" (a CCSS "exemplar text")—over and over and over and over. But you know what? Whether we think particular selections should be included in the curriculum or not, some text is just too damn hard to be comprehended in a single pass by any normal human being.

Many kids feel that being asked to read something a second time is a punishment because they didn't "get it" or are just "bad readers." This bespeaks their lack of understanding of the cognitive process of good readers, not a straight line but a back-and-forth process filled with rereading. Remember our thought experiments back in Chapter 2 (batsmen and bowlers, Columbus, RNA interaction), which showed how recursive reading is, how skillful readers are *rereading all the time*, though often unconsciously? Rereadings, second readings, and multiple readings are cognitive moves that good comprehenders routinely make.

And here's another reason that second readings are necessary. Both kids in school and many grown-ups in our society often do crappy first reads. Yeah, we said it. Readers zoom through an article once and are perfectly delighted to offer commentaries about it with little or no understanding at all. The habit of closer, careful rereading is vital for all of us.

The trouble with the CCSS vision of rereading (and the countless mechanical online lesson plans it has spawned) is that teachers merely *command* kids to "read it again." So the student's only purpose is to be obedient. How many teenagers are galvanized by that? So, our version of second readings stresses giving kids a motivating, meaningful, dare we say a "fun" reason to reread. That's why we call this strategy "second helpings"—because that's something people ask for when they are having a good time.

How Does It Work?

1 Have students read the text one time through to get the gist, the basics, the plot. If you have them annotate, steer them toward getting the factual information clear in their heads. After this first reading, stop to have several kids offer comments and reactions. Try to evoke questions, uncertainties, and misconceptions.

2 "Now we are going to read it again, but this time we are going to look at it in a different way." This is the core of second helpings, creating a reason for rereading that motivates kids. Each prompt will be very individual to you and to the subject matter at hand, so we cannot give you a generic list of these prompts. But here are some examples that communicate their flavor.

> **Literature:** "Some people who have read this short story think that the main character is a terrible mother, and others think she is doing the very best she can. Now let's read it again with that controversy in mind: be on the lookout and mark specific evidence in the text that shows how good or bad a mother she is."

> **Math:** "Now that you have read about the Fibonacci series, let's go back and reread with the question in mind: How does this connect to the Golden Ratio? Look for evidence of the relationship and make some notes in the margin to help you remember it."

> **Science:** "Now that you have read about the phenomenon, reread the passage, looking for information that can help you draw the process—and use it to make a diagram."

> **Social Studies:** "Now that we have studied this portion of the Constitution, reread it with this issue in mind: Many judges have held that there is an implied *right to privacy* in the Bill of Rights. Mark any such evidence you think they might have used to come to such a conclusion, and be ready to share it."

SCIENCE   **VARIATION:** When Smokey was recently guest teaching some eighth-grade science in California, the topic on the curricular agenda was *orbital mechanics*. The timing was good for this topic since the comet ISON was at that time approaching the sun. To deepen kids' understanding, Smokey wanted them to read the NASA article "Ten Thousandth Near-Earth Object Unearthed in Space." But the piece was quite challenging, and a single reading was not going to be enough for kids to really understand the science. Here's how the kids worked through second and third helpings of this fact-filled text.

1. I handed out the article to kids and asked them to "read for the main ideas."

2. Next, we had some initial whole class discussion—what were the big ideas they learned about near-Earth objects? Mostly this discussion centered on the different types of objects, not so much on how they moved.

3. Next, I asked students to reread to locate and mark information that helped them *visualize* the solar system. "What kinds of objects are out there, how big are they, and how do they move? Then make a drawing—a diagram, cartoon, mind map, close-up, or cross-section—any kind of graphic representation that helps us understand near-Earth objects better. "

4. After about five minutes of quiet work time, I had groups of four pull together and share their drawings. The task was to connect their drawings to specific passages in the article, explaining to classmates exactly what they were trying to represent in drawing.

5. Then I asked that each group nominate one to be shared with the whole class. Predictably, many kids showed a picture of an asteroid hitting the earth, and then enthused about NEO-themed movies like *Deep Impact* or *Armageddon*.

6. Picking up on that curiosity, I called for a *third* helping. "Now read through the article one more time looking for any information that could help you develop a technology to deflect a large asteroid or comet headed for Earth. Work with a partner to develop your strategy—you can go online to see what others have proposed (there are many options). It's up to you to determine, based on this article and our other studies, which strategy is most plausible. Be ready to share your chosen Earth defense strategy with us tomorrow."

7. The next day's discussion—celebrating our third time through the article—was a festival of science and invention. Kids had discovered and were advocating a wide variety of Earth-protecting theories. Many had learned that simply sending up a nuclear missile would probably be too little, too late. Given the physics of the solar system, more effective action had to be taken far in advance, when a slight change in trajectory could avert disaster.

TO LEARN MORE

Jago, Carol. 2012. "Closer Reading for Deeper Comprehension: Uncommon Sense about the Common Core." AdLit in Perspective. www.ohiorc.org/adlit/inperspective/issue/2012-10 /Article/feature.aspx.

STRATEGY: **Where Do You Stand?**

FOCUS: **Taking and Supporting a Position**

WHEN TO USE: Before Reading   During Reading   **After Reading**

DESCRIPTION:

This up-and-thinking activity one has more names and variations than you can count. Maybe you've heard of Four Corners, the Human Continuum, Living Likert Scale, Barometer, or the Human Bar Graph. All these kindred structures invite students to vote with their feet, representing their thinking by where they stand and who they talk to when they get there. We move kids through a series of conversations with other students in which they must defend their interpretation of a complex text and listen respectfully to other points of view. These activities are extensively used (and documented) by an organization we much admire, Facing History and Ourselves.

Why Use It?

The CCSS strongly emphasize learning how to develop an argument, using evidence from a text, and defending that position in vigorous debates and discussions. But did we really need to be reminded about this kind of high-order thinking? Whatever field we teach, our most challenging issues are not usually about factual recall, but about differing interpretations of those facts, alternative hypotheses, clashing paradigms, opposing viewpoints, or value trade-offs. This structure makes it possible for students to join in those debates in a way that's physical, sociable, and energizing.

How Does It Work?

1   As we have said, there are many versions of this activity—so we'll give you one example and then talk about some alternatives. It all begins when you are teaching a complex or controversial topic in your subject field. Smokey has often used "Where Do You Stand?" to help kids explore the United States' decision to drop atomic bombs on Japan. After reading varying accounts of Truman's decision—including Eisenhower and MacArthur's adamant opposition, America's refusal of an earlier Japanese surrender offer, and implications in Secretary of War Henry Stinson's memoirs that he coached Truman to extend the war until the bomb was ready—you pose a question. "Based on all you have read about this issue, where do you stand? In a couple of minutes, we are going to stand in a line, based on your interpretation of all the materials you have studied." Then stand up and indicate specific locations for a lineup, beginning at one end of the room:

* "If you are **absolutely sure** that the U.S. did the right thing by using nuclear weapons on Japan, you will stand here."
* "If you are **fairly sure** that the U.S. was right, stand here."
* "If you are **fairly sure** that the U.S. was wrong to drop the bombs on Hiroshima and Nagasaki, stand here."
* "If you are **absolutely sure** that the U.S. was wrong, stand here at the far end of the line."

2 Next, tell kids: "Now I am going to give you a few minutes to review your notes and annotations, consider all your learning, and decide where you belong on that line. You will need to explain to the people standing around you what specific evidence supports your viewpoint." Have kids jot a few phrases on a note card to bring along.

3 After that think time, have students grab their notes, stand up, and assume their places. "Now, turn to one person beside you and take turns explaining your position. Where you are standing right now, you are going to mostly agree with nearby people, right? But your partner may well have different reasoning or evidence, so listen carefully. Explain your interpretations, and support your claims. Take about one minute each." This stage—working with someone who *agrees with you*—helps kids to clarify their position and potentially strengthen their argument.

4 With everyone still in position, call for quiet and ask several pairs to share their thinking. Ask them to explain how their argument was validated, challenged, or improved during the partner conversation.

5 Now "fold the line" at the middle. The kids at the two extreme ends walk toward each other so that the line is now two people wide, and every student is now facing someone with a *different* position. (You may have to do a bit of swapping around in the middle to make sure kids get a new partner.) Invite the students to argue their positions, taking one minute each. If you like, you can make rules allowing for two stages of discussion, with opening arguments and rebuttals.

6 Once again, call students to attention to process the conversations. First, ask if any students have changed their position on the issue as a result of their debate with a classmate. If anyone has, have him explain how his opinion changed, what evidence convinced him. Invite that person to actually move to his new spot on the continuum before you continue—when this happens, it's dramatic. Next, invite several pairs to recount how their mini-debate unfolded, what they noticed about each others' evidence, and how they might make even stronger arguments in a subsequent debate.

VARIATION: Hopefully this example helps you envision the many iterations of this versatile up-and-thinking activity. Depending on the subject matter, you can have kids stand in the four corners of the room to represent their thinking, or physically arrange themselves into a bar graph or pie chart. Whatever shape you use, the key is to plan the interactions in advance: How can you arrange and shift kids so they talk with several others during the meeting? Plan for sharing and debriefing between each setup.

Predictable Problem

All these standing structures require very active teacher management. You should be in the crowd, moving people around, coaching and supervising. Kids who are unused to these mingling activities will tend to cluster in too-large groups and stare at each other. Just walk up and physically split these clumps into pairs: "You two are partners now, continue the discussion." If you get an unbalanced line, with everyone at one end and no one to debate with, you haven't picked a sufficiently debatable topic. Life lesson. But the lineup still works and it can still be folded; the conversations will just be among people with the same viewpoint.

TO LEARN MORE

Facing History and Ourselves. 2013. "Teaching Strategies: Four Corners." www.facinghistory.org/resources/strategies/four-corners.

Facing History and Ourselves. 2013. "Teaching Strategies: Barometer—Taking a Stand on Controversial Issues." www.facinghistory.org/resources/strategies/barometer.

STRATEGY: **RAFT Essay**

FOCUS: **Recalling and Summarizing**

WHEN TO USE: Before Reading   During Reading   **After Reading**

DESCRIPTION:

RAFT stands for Role/Audience/Format/Topic. This is a more extended writing activity for digging into topics in content-area classes. When students are ready to create larger written pieces, this strategy helps make them much more interesting than just a straight essay or summary. While a RAFT assignment may specify the topic to be explored, students have real choices for each of four aspects of the writing. In other words, each student designs her own personal "assignment" by choosing from lists for the four aspects:

* the **role** the writer takes—the person who is portrayed as speaking in the piece
* the **audience**—the person or group to whom the writer is speaking
* the **format** of the writing—letter, news article, poem, brochure, email, etc.
* the more specific **topic** within the material

The chart on page 172 shows some possible choices for a chemistry writing assignment on a collection of articles about radioactivity. One student might choose to take the **role** of Marie Curie as the discoverer of radioactivity, and decide to send to her university department chairman (her **audience**) a letter (the **format**) arguing about why it's important to let her further study this just-discovered force of nature (her **topic**). Another student might choose to write as Albert Einstein, sending a letter to President Truman about how the United States could build a new, very powerful weapon—an atomic bomb. (And then she could look at the real letter Einstein *did* write.) Thus the writing can involve students in addressing a topic from the point of view of a historical figure, a fictional character—or in some applications, even an animal or an object.

Why Use It?

While this activity takes more time than most in our collection, it also enables students to dig deeper into the content. Radioactivity might receive just a few pages of explanation within an eight-hundred-page textbook. But by reading further and then writing an entertaining piece that captures the attention of fellow students, the author engages in a memorable activity that helps permanently cement concepts and information in her mind. Reformulating ideas in writing and in a different voice helps students internalize them. We also know that students respond especially positively when creative choice is built into their assignments. But the choices must be serious and meaningful, so that they really steer the vocabulary, style, and focus of the writing. While you may not have the time to use a RAFT project for every unit in your course, conducting it for several key concepts or focal points in a course can help ensure that students really understand material that is essential in your subject. And as we'll see from middle school teacher Laurie Hendrickson's practice, the project can expand to encompass as much material in your course as you'd like to include.

How Does It Work?

1 First, you need a list of choices for each aspect of the writing, within your topic—something like the chart on page 172. You can develop the lists yourself, or better yet, brainstorm lists with the class. If the kids are ready for it, ask them to create the options on their own.

2 To introduce RAFT writing, lead a minilesson in which the class together creates the opening of a written piece while you hold the marker or type in the text. This means that once you focus students on a chunk of content they've been studying, they brainstorm the four lists, and then collaboratively draft the first few paragraphs of the writing.

3 Once students are ready to work on a fresh topic, provide class time for the activity, so you can confer with individuals and keep track of their progress. In-class work time not only helps to actually get the writing done, it also enables the teacher to observe on the spot, to ensure that students are moving successfully through the steps in the process—making their RAFT choices, marshaling the information they need, getting their drafts written, and so forth. This essentially means using the classroom workshop structure described in Chapter 8. We say "writing," here, but increasingly the *format* for projects like these will involve Web tools—PowerPoint presentations, videos, blogs, websites, podcasts, or Web-based videos.

4 Sharing the outcome is important. Real writing (and any other type of communication) is not just about getting a grade, but also informing, influencing, or entertaining someone else. Including this dimension converts the work from an assigned exercise into an authentic exchange of ideas—so it becomes much more meaningful to the students. If there's time, students can read to or perform for the whole class, but it's also fine to use smaller groups, so more presentations get heard in a limited time span. Obviously Web tools greatly increase the efficiency of this sharing, enabling multiple exchanges to take place simultaneously, as well as at various additional times outside the class period.

VARIATION: Laurie Hendrickson, language arts teacher at Roosevelt Middle School in River Forest, Illinois, has expanded the RAFT strategy in a very effective way, using the acronym CRAFTS. The added **C** stands for "Context" and the **S** is for "Structure of Text," added steps to help students decide how to organize their writing. She altered the **T** to stand for "Theme," and asks students to make more of a claim, rather than just address a broad topic. Laurie has built the approach into a biography project in which students choose two important figures to learn about and compare. They study biographical materials for each one. Laurie and her partners have compiled extensive lists of biographical and informational books about people in a wide variety of areas—civil rights, the Civil War, the Holocaust, the Roosevelts, the Kennedy family, the Founding Fathers, labor history, women's rights, famous scientists, famous baseball players, famous jazz musicians, famous artists, and more.

The students write context pieces first, using the voices of their chosen personalities or telling narrative stories about them. Then their CRAFTS projects take a variety of forms—green screen movies, Prezi keynotes, websites, mock journals. These must include more than one perspective, though the voices can portray various people talking about their subjects, rather than only the famous figures themselves. These projects are challenging—students must read and digest at least a hundred pages of nonfiction material. But Laurie observes, "When you give kids choices, not just about the topic but for many aspects of a project, it's amazing what they create." Laurie credits Elfrieda Hiebert's "Seven Actions That Teachers Can Take Right Now: Text Complexity," from the Text Project at the University of California Santa Cruz, for guiding the development of this project.

TO LEARN MORE

Daniels, Harvey, Steven Zemelman, and Nancy Steineke. 2007. *Content-Area Writing: Every Teacher's Guide.* Portsmouth, NH: Heinemann, 156–166.

Hiebert, Elfrieda, 2012. "Seven Actions That Teachers Can Take Right Now: Text Complexity." http://textproject.org/professional-development/text-matters/7-actions-that-teachers-can-take-right-now-text-complexity.

Northern Nevada Writing Project. 2012. "Writing Across the Curriculum: RAFT Prompts." WritingFix. www.writingfix.com/wac/RAFT.htm.

Simon, Cathy Allen. 2013. "Using the Raft Writing Strategy." IRA/NCTE ReadWriteThink. www.readwritethink.org/professional-development/strategy-guides/using-raft-writing-strategy-30625.html.

Strayer, B., and T. Strayer. 2007. *Strategies for Differentiating in the Content Areas.* New York: Scholastic.

EXAMPLE

Directions: Choose one option from each column to create your own writing assignment. Some choices can be mix-and-match. Others pretty much go together.

Raft Chart for Radioactivity Unit			
Role	**Audience**	**Format**	**Topic**
Antoine Henri Becquerel	Pierre and Marie Curie	Personal letter	The mysteriously ruined film in his desk drawer, and what it might be caused by
Marie Curie	Director of Paris Industrial Physics School	Written request	Explaining why it's important to use a lab in the school for experiments on radioactivity
Albert Einstein	President Truman	Formal letter	How a new, more powerful bomb could be built
Mother of a U.S. soldier in 1945	Newspaper readers	Op-ed piece	Why an A-bomb should/should not have been used on Japan
Nuclear medicine doctor	Medical patients	Brochure	How lung and heart problems can be diagnosed using radio-active chemicals
Home repair company owner	Home owners—potential customers	Advertisement mailed to homes	Why home owners should use the company to have their basements radon-proofed
Head of Atomic Energy Commission	Members of environmental organization	Speech at organization conference	Why it's a good idea to build new nuclear-powered electric generators
Head of environmental protection organization	U.S. senators	Testimony for Senate hearing	Why it's not a good idea to build new nuclear-powered electric generators

STRATEGY: **Password**

FOCUS: **Building Academic Vocabulary**

WHEN TO USE: Before Reading   During Reading   **After Reading**

DESCRIPTION:

This is a speedy and energizing whole-class vocabulary review, played as a competition among several teams. It is a school adaptation of the old TV game show *Password* that we learned from Jackie White, an awesome literacy coach in the Milwaukee Public Schools.

Why Use It?

We've stressed the importance of kids acquiring Tier 2 vocabulary—those versatile academic words that reach across many disciplines. But occasionally kids must also memorize subject-specific technical vocabulary (Tier 3 words) that they may never again use in their lives: *mitochondria, phloem, kleptocracy, iambic, plesiosaurus.* When students do need to remember terms like these *for a while,* here's a way to review and short-term memorize.

How Does It Work?

1 After the class has worked on a set of new vocabulary items (ten to twenty words works well), have students get into groups of five. Using chart paper and markers, each group simply makes a list of five of the words, terms, or names studied that day. These are written big enough to be seen across the classroom. Now one student from another group volunteers (or is dragooned) to play, and stands in front of the class.

2 The first group hangs its list of five terms behind the volunteer, who is not allowed to look back at it. A timer is set to sixty seconds. When the clock starts, the whole class shouts out clues to the volunteer ("It's a way of shaping land"; "Something farmers do to prevent erosion"), who has to correctly identify the term. At one minute the turn ends. The timekeeper notes the number of words correctly identified and the time elapsed.

3 The next group posts its list, another player is selected, and the game continues until all groups have had a turn. The student who correctly names five vocab words in the least amount of time wins for his or her team. Applause all around.

4 You can do this with technology, of course. Have teams submit (text, email) their five words to the teacher, who can project them on a screen behind each player. There are even blank password game templates in PowerPoint, loose on the Internet, if you trust their sources. We suggest: run but don't save.

TO LEARN MORE

Holbrook, Sara, and Michael Salinger. 2010. *High Definition: Unforgettable Vocabulary-Building Strategies Across Genres and Subjects.* Portsmouth, NH: Heinemann.

How to Use
A Textbook

We talked earlier about what makes textbooks hard. Now let's talk about what can make them easier, more accessible, and more useful for young readers. In Chapter 5, we described twenty-six specific, into-through-and-beyond strategies that can help students better understand what they read, including textbooks. In this chapter, we are going to add six more structures and strategies that work especially well with textbooks. But before we get to those activities, we need to look at the number one question we always face in determining the role of textbooks in our teaching: How much is enough?

Don't Assign the Whole Textbook

Too often, we just divide the number of pages in our textbook by the number of days in the school year (e.g., 1,200/180) and then assign those six or seven pages every day to "get it done." But in our hearts, we know that this kind of "coverage" doesn't really work. Sure, we can make students read daily sections of the textbook as a matter of compliance and obedience. And then we can claim that we "covered" all 1,262 pages of Western civilization. But how many of those names, dates, places, and big concepts will the kids remember one week after the final exam? By the Fourth of July, most of those ideas will probably be, sadly, history.

When we use a textbook this traditional and mechanical way, we aren't doing it out of cussedness. Maybe we believe that kids *need* to read the whole book to understand the main ideas in our subject. Or maybe our department or district requires that we assign the entire text. Perhaps our state's high-stakes test covers a vast inventory of details that matches the index of our textbook to a T. Or maybe the textbook has a sticker right on the cover saying "Correlated to the Common Core." Each of these seems like a good reason to assign the whole book, page by page. But still, as professionals, we have to interrogate our decisions bravely and honestly. Inertia affects teachers, not just objects in space. We too have unexamined, comfortable habits, and the textbook may be one of them. After all, the simplicity of a one-book curriculum, especially one we have practiced for many years, has its own siren-like attractions.

American schools have embraced the coverage model of curriculum, as embodied in our supersized textbooks, for most of the last century. This commitment has not, to put it kindly, served us well. If all the worrisome test scores and ranting pundits mean anything, it's that textbook-based teaching doesn't work. Still today, as the National Assessment of Educational Progress (NAEP) tells us, while a reasonable number of U.S. students have basic factual and operational knowledge in most subject areas, only a tiny fraction (only 1 percent in eighth-grade math, and 2 percent in twelfth-grade math, for example) are capable of doing "advanced" thinking in those fields (NAEP, 2011).

Be Selective

It's simply not enough to mention ideas, either in a textbook or in a lecture. No matter what learning theory you subscribe to (constructivism, information processing, behaviorism, cognitivism), all agree on one thing: to remember ideas, learners must *act upon on them*. Period. You can have students move their noses across any number of pages, left to right, top to bottom, but that is neither teaching nor learning.

The harder the text—meaning the more content-loaded, the more "inconsiderate"—the more help young readers need. They need you, the teacher, to break the work into steps and stages, and to give them tools and activities and attitudes that help. But all this helping takes *time, time, time*. And, as far as we know, schools aren't handing teachers any more of that commodity to use. So you have to prioritize; you have to decide to teach a few things well and fully—and let some other stuff slide. Like the U.S. history teachers at Deerfield High School, you could try to identify the twelve or fourteen absolutely key, overarching themes in every course you teach. You might agree in principle that kids would do better to understand a dozen key ideas deeply, than to hear a thousand ideas mentioned in passing. But what are the right themes and concepts for *your* subject, *your* course?

In their work on *Understanding by Design*, Wiggins and McTighe (2005) remind us that the content of any subject field has different levels of importance. There are some anchor ideas we want students to understand in a deep and enduring way, others that are important to know about, and finally, some aspects where a passing familiarity is sufficient. In other words, as we look at our textbook, we need to be asking: What are the really big ideas here; where are the places to slow down, dig in, and "uncover" ideas, not just cover them? What are the ideas or procedures that we want kids to really remember and deeply understand, long after the course is over? Wiggins and McTighe (2005, 10–11) say we can find these core ideas by using four filters:

1. Does the idea, topic, or process represent a big idea with enduring value beyond the classroom?
2. Does the big idea, topic, or process reside at the heart of the discipline?
3. To what extent does the idea, topic, or process require uncoverage?
4. To what extent does the idea, topic, or process have the potential for engaging students?

What a healthy exercise to filter our textbooks through these questions! We recently heard some mathematics teachers vigorously arguing whether the long division of polynomials constitutes an "enduring" idea or not. And down the hall, the English teachers were debating whether one Shakespeare sonnet was too many—or not enough. These are vital conversations to have, among colleagues and within ourselves, not just to determine what sections of the textbook to use, but to be sure we are planning the most powerful and memorable learning experiences for all our students.

Focus on Academic Vocabulary

From the Common Core Standards to our state departments of education to school reformers of all stripes, *academic vocabulary* is the watchword of the day. But what does this infectious phrase really mean? Researcher Isabel Beck (Beck et al., 2013) is credited with developing a powerful three-tier model for understanding vocabulary acquisition, which we have already referred to several times.

Tier 1 contains everyday words that your students already know. Or, as the eminent reading researcher P. David Pearson puts it, these are "familiar labels for familiar concepts" (Pearson et al., 2011).

Tier 3 contains narrow, often technical words (*bituminous, shoal, medulla, cryptographic, ex parte*) that are normally used only within a specific content area or domain. Some Tier 3 words can also be very important to building knowledge and conceptual understanding within the various academic subjects. But while these Tier 3 words may be taught in school, and can help build understanding of broader concepts, they are rarely encountered in the daily life of most educated people, and are likely to be looked up when needed.

Tier 2 words, in the long run, are the most important ones. These are words that cut across multiple disciplines and serve us in all kinds of thinking, throughout life. Examples: *slope, abstract, property, rotate, level, transform, curve, analogy, combustion, base, verify, evidence, force, record, prediction, infer, habitat, dialogue, adaptation, reciprocal, equation, replicate, theme, inherit, mystery, gothic, negotiate, habitat, regression, cellular, structure,* and *parallel.* Words like these embody rich, deep concepts that help students build a structure for understanding big ideas in many domains.

In traditional schooling—and especially with textbooks—we have spent a lot of time having students memorize lists of obscure, low-utility Tier 3 words. Instead, we should have been providing robust instruction in the powerful, conceptual, and discipline-crossing Tier 2 words. As the *Revised Publishers' Criteria for the Common Core State Standards in English Language Arts and Literacy* (Coleman and Pimentel, 2012, 11) put it:

> Sometimes curricula ignore these {Tier 2} words and pay attention only to the technical words that are unique to a discipline. Materials aligned with the Common Core State Standards should help students acquire knowledge of general academic vocabulary because these are the words that will help them access a wide range of complex texts.

This is a big change in our thinking about subject-area vocabulary.

But there are so many Tier 2 (and crucial Tier 3) words in history, science, math, and literature! How do we choose? Isabel Beck offers three criteria for selection:

importance and utility: words that are characteristic of mature language users and appear frequently across a variety of domains

instructional potential: words that students can use to make connections to other words and concepts

conceptual understanding: words for which students understand the general concept but which provide precision and specificity in describing the concept

And once we have chosen the key words to focus on, what does "robust" vocabulary instruction look like? In the past, we aimed at "multiple exposures," based on some older research suggesting that people could acquire a word by seeing it thirty or more times. More recently, attention has shifted from mere exposure to *use*. As Pearson et als. newer research (2011) suggests, vocabulary work should be multimodal and multisensory; kids should be seeing, reading, talking about, writing, doing, and experimenting with vocabulary, introduced in richly thematic networks or families of words. All the academic vocabulary building activities in back Chapter 5 (pages 143–154) offer you the chance to plug in the Tier 2 and Tier 3 words that matter to your discipline, and give kids just such engaging, multisensory experiences with words. And we provide a specifically textbook-friendly approach later in this chapter (pages 192–193).

Find Out What's *Really* on the Big Test

We may believe that the upcoming PARCC, or Smarter Balanced, or state test "requires" us to cover everything in the textbook, however thinly. Sounds plausible, given the current fervor of outsiders to supervise us, but we'd better be sure. Everybody thinks they know what's on the test, but they are often wrong. On one Illinois exam, the U.S. history test strongly stressed World War I to the present. Teachers who went too slowly, carefully covering everything from precolonial times forward, never got there. Thus, the kids who got "too much" early American history (including a full and respectful treatment of the native peoples) were "wasting their time" as far as the state assessment went. This has happened to teachers across the curriculum who make assumptions about what's on a standardized test but never check to be certain. We still hear English teachers saying that they are doing grammar drills to "get the kids ready for the SAT," even though the SAT has never had any grammar questions since its inception sixty years ago.

> *Whichever of the current high-stakes tests your kids will face, you need to study that test and its released sample items very closely.*

Whichever of the current high-stakes tests your kids will face, you need to study that test and its released sample items very closely. (You'd be crazy not to, since in many states your salary will be partly determined by how well your students can answer these questions.) In general, the newer generation of exams still has its share of old-style factual recall, multiple-choice items. But usually, the kids will be asked to recall facts or summarize information from a selection *printed in the test itself*, not remembered from any textbook. This means that even these factual items are measuring content-area reading skills as much as subject-matter recall. Kids who can quickly and strategically make sense of informational text will do well on these items.

> *... we can breathe a little more easily about skipping the occasional textbook chapter, and focus on making sure our kids can read like a scientist, mathematician, historian, or writer.*

Then, kids are likely to face "constructed response" items that present some multiple pieces of information (a chart, article, an excerpt, an image, some data, a primary source) and then ask students to work with them, connecting, comparing, analyzing, making judgments, or building arguments. Often, these items call for fairly extended written responses that are later scored by "live" reviewers. This kind of task tries to determine whether, given an authentic set of materials, students can reason and write effectively within a subject area. Again, these tasks generally provide the information—the students' job is to apply the broad concepts, principles, and procedures they have learned in their courses to understand the new material presented.

With these kinds of tests dominating the assessment horizon, we can breathe a little more easily about skipping the occasional textbook chapter, and focus on making sure our kids can read like a scientist, mathematician, historian, or writer. It's not about coverage anymore—it is about *thinking*. Students don't need more time with their noses in the textbook—they need tons and tons of practice time reading, talking, and writing about important subject-matter content.

Ways to Use Textbooks More Effectively

In a minute, we'll launch into a half-dozen strategies that can help kids get the most out of their textbooks, while sustaining engagement and keeping the classroom reasonably lively. By way of introduction, let us preview some key themes from all the activities that are coming up:

* Have empathy. Remember, not only are you a grown-up and a subject-matter expert, you have also read your textbook five or twenty times before. The material may seem easy to you, but it may really be Greek to the kids.

* Help kids get started. In the old days, the teacher's main role was to assign reading, and then check for understanding later. Now we *frontload* our teaching, giving students support before and during reading, not just handing out quiz grades afterwards. That's what all the prereading activities in Chapter 5 are for, along with a few new ones coming up here.

* Don't leave kids alone with their textbooks. We can harness the social power of collaboration, having kids work in pairs, groups, and teams at all stages of reading to discuss, debate, and sort out ideas in the book.

* Choose wisely. Make more selective assignments; instead of plowing through the whole book, make strategic choices about what is most important, assigning fewer pages and helping students study them much more carefully.

* Supplement richly. Our textbooks are no longer the sole source, the "bible" for our courses, but simply one important resource, coordinated with magazine articles, newspapers, websites, blogs, trade books, primary sources, and more.

ACTIVITY 1: **Checking Out the Textbook**

If you look in the very front of your textbook teacher's edition, you will probably find a section advising you to teach kids about the design of the textbook, to review its features and organizing principles, at the start of the course. But how many of us actually do that? Between getting to know kids' names, handing out all the materials, and filling out all the paperwork, we often end that first day of class by saying, "Read Chapter 1 for tomorrow." Mistake! A little time invested introducing the textbook now can pay big dividends down the road.

Sometimes the publisher's suggested "introducing the textbook" lesson is a combination of genuine orientation and PR flak—hardly what the kids need at the beginning of the course. Our colleague Jim Burke has developed a generic "meet your textbook" model that's both teacher and kid friendly, and it follows, with Jim's kind permission. This is a pretty extensive process; you may decide to do several, but not all, of the activities listed here, depending on the nature of the textbook and the experiences of your students. Sure, it would be ideal to do the whole activity at the beginning of the year, but if your kids are struggling with the textbook *anytime*, it is a wise decision to stop and take a couple of class periods to carefully uncover the text's structure.

Your Name: _____ Date _____ Period _____

ACCESS: Textbook Feature Analysis

Directions: Use this activity to better understand the textbook in this class. Its purpose is to teach you how the textbook works by showing you what it is made of and how these elements are organized.

Types of Text 1. Skim through the book and make a list of all the different types of documents or types of text you will have to read (include graphic texts like graphs, maps).	
Sidebars and Pull Boxes 2. Find examples of pull-out boxes or sidebars. What kind of information appears in these? Are they standardized throughout the book (e.g., "Profiles in History," "Science in the Workplace")?	
Feature: Typography 3. Find examples of different type faces and styles. Write down the examples and where they appear (e.g., large, bold type for chapter titles [e.g., twenty-four-point font], eighteen point font for subheadings throughout the chapter). How does this book use boldfaced type? What does it mean when they *use italicized words?*	
Feature: Color 4. Does the textbook use color to convey information (e.g., what does it mean when you see words in red ink on the page)?	
Feature: Symbols and Icons 5. Does the textbook use symbols or icons to convey information (e.g., if you see an icon with a question mark in it, what does that mean? Are you supposed to do something, like ask a question? Does it mean this is a potential test question? Or is it a link to a theme running throughout the book?)	

Features: Images and Graphics

6. What kind of information accompanies illustrations or images? Find examples of a map, chart, and a photograph and then look for captions or sidebars that explain or discuss the image. How is the image identified (e.g., Figure 2.6)?

Organization

7. How are chapters organized? Make a brief but accurate outline.

Navigation: Headers and Footers

8. Look at the top and bottom of the pages of the book. These are called the header and footer. What kind of information is contained in this space? What do you notice as you flip through fifty consecutive pages (e.g., does the content of the header or footer change? If so, in what way, for what purpose?)

Testing! Testing!

9. Imagine you must now prepare for a big test. What features of this book would help you to prepare for that test? (Hint: Do not limit your answer to the practice or study questions.)

Reading Speed

10. While your teacher times you, read one page of the book, taking notes as you normally would while reading it for homework. How long did that take you? Now do the math: If your teacher tells you to read the opening section for tomorrow and this section is ten pages long, how much time do you need to allot for your homework in this class?

Concerns

11. After familiarizing yourself with this textbook, you may have concerns or questions. Getting these answered up front might help you read the textbook with greater success and confidence. Take this time to list any concerns you might have (e.g., reading speed, vocabulary).

ACTIVITY 2: **Jigsawing**

Even if you are laboring under tough requirements to cover material, having every student read every page in the textbook may not be the only alternative. There are some cases where we can divide up the text, letting the kids specialize in a smaller number of topics (and pages). Instead of reading everything in the textbook (recognizing that reading doesn't necessarily guarantee remembering), they can hear oral summaries of some sections.

Our friend Donna Stupple certainly risked her colleagues' disapproval when she jigsawed *A Tale of Two Cities* in her English classes. While some colleagues tut-tutted this insult to a sacred text, Donna figured the language was just too hard for her kids to plow through. But she did want them to hear a sample of Dickens' voice and to pick up some cultural background from the era. So instead of having every kid read the whole novel, Donna created five "leapfrogging" jigsaw groups. For the first assignment, Group A read Chapter 1, Group B read Chapter 2, and so on. Then, in the next round, Group A would read Chapter 6, Group B Chapter 7, and so on. This way, each kid read every fifth chapter, all the way through the book.

In class, it worked like this: The kids would first meet in their "expert groups"—the students who had read the same chapter met to review the content and make sure they had a common understanding of the main characters, key events, and big ideas in the text. Then kids re-formed into heterogeneous "base groups" composed of one expert on each chapter, 1 through 5. Then, in chronological order, the expert for each chapter would recount the key elements of the chapter to the rest of the kids, who hadn't read it. After this round of highlights from each chapter, the group transitioned into general discussion, with Donna at the helm.

> . . . *textbooks frequently* can be *easily subdivided.*

Many novels couldn't be studied this way because information in earlier chapters is crucial for understanding later ones. But textbooks frequently *can* be easily subdivided. Let's see how this might work. Chapter 8 in Holt McDougal's *The Americans* covers the reform movements between 1820 and 1850. Four distinct strands emerged during this period—religious renewal, abolitionism, the early women's rights efforts, and workplace reform—each of which receives several pages of coverage in the book. Since these movements are part of a wider trend in society (and because the page number totals are about the same), this period presents a fine opportunity to jigsaw. Instead of reading the whole chapter, each student specializes in one of the four topics by: (1) studying just that section of the chapter; (2) meeting in an expert group to review key elements of their chosen reform movement; and (3) attending a heterogeneous group to brief classmates, and to hear from them about the three other reform movements. When students set off to do their

English

History

Textbook Jigsaw Sheet

Step 1   Reading

To prepare for your Expert Group and Base Group meetings, please respond to the following items, either while you are reading or after you have read.

Passages: Please mark any words, lines, or sections of the text that "stick out" for you. These passages might be important, puzzling, curious, provocative, or surprising—whatever strikes you. You may use sticky notes or our standard coding system if you wish.

Big Ideas: Jot down two or three of the main points, big ideas, or key terms in this section.

*

*

*

Reactions/Connections: What were your feelings and responses to this reading? What personal connections did you make with the text? Did it remind you of past experiences, people, or events in your life? Did it make you think of anything happening in the news, around school, or in other material you have read?

*

*

*

Step 2   Expert Group Meeting

In just a few minutes, each of you will explain your section of the chapter to classmates who have not read it. So now, meeting with other experts on this section, you need to review the key points, confirm your understanding, answer any questions you may have about the reading, and make sure you're all "on the same page."

Step 3   Base Group Meeting

When the group meets, the discussion will have two stages. First, each person should take about one minute (no more!) to give the group the big points, the highlights, of their chapter section. Next, everyone joins in general conversation about the readings as a set. Try to find connections, similarities, and differences, or themes in the different readings. We'll have a whole-class discussion when we get back together.

MATH textbooks are different

We have been talking here as though textbooks in all subject fields are basically alike, which clearly they are not—and in mathematics, the differences are greatest. Can we take a moment to empathize with our math colleagues? All of us who teach school must cope with grown-ups who say "Oh, I hated X (your subject) in school." But math? It seems like everyone's got it in for math. As Arthur Hyde, author of *Comprehending Math* (2006), points out, mathematics is the only school subject in which virtually every American citizen can tell you exactly when they "hit the wall" and gave up—whether it was long division, right triangles, or quadratic equations. Singer Jimmy Buffet has even penned a crude little tune called "Math Sucks" that evokes a hearty sing-along every time at his margarita-soaked summer concerts.

Actually, math does not suck at all. But mathematics textbooks are typically the hardest of all to read. Think about yourself reading a novel. One hundred percent comprehension is not really required to follow a narrative. You can skip over a hard word—maybe you get it from context later, maybe you don't; either way, it probably doesn't materially affect your understanding of the book. Shucks, you could probably doze off for a minute here and there, and still come away with a good enough understanding of the characters and events. But try that in a math textbook! If you misread *one character*, the whole meaning of the reading can be

chosen reading, it is important, as always, to use some good prereading activities (chosen from Chapter 5) to activate their prior knowledge and send them into the text thinking. Or you can use the sheet provided here, which gives support for students both during reading and at each of the meetings.

We know that jigsawing can be controversial—or simply out of the question—for teachers who are required to be on the same page with colleagues throughout the year. Or for teachers who worry, sincerely, whether hearing an oral summary from other students is as good as reading an expert's version in print. However, as we weigh the "risks" of jigsawing, it is important not to overestimate the impact of standard, read-the-chapter work. We changed. Math textbooks have the highest content load per sentence of all the secondary textbooks (Barton and Heidema, 2002), are full of abstract ideas, and use symbolic signs and signals that are specialized and different from other kinds of text. Further, the explanations of concepts are typically short, compared to the amount of the book given over to problems and applications.

There are two main approaches used in current math textbooks. In one style, the authors present a concept and then provide problems that allow students to practice the idea that was introduced. In the other procedure, the authors lead students through a more step-by-step process, where they set up experiences so students can "discover" concepts for themselves. There is plenty of controversy in the math world about which approach is best; the more inductive approach seems to have a potential advantage in student engagement. But both types of texts are still filled with abstract ideas, symbolic language, and very high concept density. When you compare this genre of text to a novel or a historical report, you might even question whether *reading* is the right term for what goes on when students use some math textbooks. Still, math teachers tell us (and the National Council of Teachers of Mathematics standards confirm) that into-through-and-beyond reading strategies (like the ones here and in Chapter 5) are one key to helping students think mathematically.

need to always wonder: Is covering material the same as understanding it? Are kids actually working, thinking, engaged with the text we assign—or are they just imitating a sentient life form, while remaining functionally unconscious? With jigsawing activities, when kids sit down to find the links between movements like abolitionism and workers' rights, they are coming pretty close to "doing history," not just dutifully accepting what the textbook says. And in other subjects it's the same; when you have to read, write, talk, and listen, it's much harder to "fake it" than it is to slide through a textbook assignment without understanding. Plus as we all know, accountability to peers can often be more motivating than the risk of teacher disapproval.

ACTIVITY 3: **Guide-o-Rama Study Guides**

Some teachers these days are "flipping" their classrooms by preparing their own video mini-lecture for each textbook section, and then saving classroom time for hands-on work and conferences (Brame, 2013). We'll talk about that movement in more detail shortly. But meanwhile, here's a lower-tech way of supporting students through dense textbook readings. Guide-o-Rama involves creating not a video but a handout that shows students the way through a chapter. This strategy does more than activate prior knowledge and set purposes for reading—it actually leads kids through the thicket of text, terms, charts, diagrams, and pictures step by step, *while they are reading*. Now, we are not talking about those old-time reading worksheets, which basically forced kids to outline the chapter (thus implying what items might pop up on the test later on). With this kind of reading guide, we can have a conversation with kids while they read, be a little bug in their ear, coaching, modeling, and mentoring them right at the moment of need.

> *This strategy does more than activate prior knowledge and set purposes for reading—it actually leads kids through the thicket of text, terms, charts, diagrams, and pictures step by step,* **while they are reading.**

That's why we like the Guide-o-Rama, a funny name for a special kind of handout that combines a genial reading road map with a think-aloud written down. Sounds weird, we know, but there's a sample on the next page. This one was designed to accompany the opening chapter of an astronomy text.

Astronomy

Get the drift? The Guide-o-Rama lets you informally coach, support, and chat with kids as you steer them along. It also invites you, as the most experienced reader in the room, to open up your head and show students how you "thought your way through" the same text they are reading. On the practical side, now that we are using textbooks more selectively and strategically, the Guide-o-Rama is a handy place to embed written directions about where to dig deep, what to skim, and when to skip ahead.

Of course, creating a really useful guide takes significant preparation time on the teacher's part. But the tool really helps kids—and once created, it can be reused, as long as you stick with the same book. You definitely do not have to make a guide for every chapter; after all, we are looking for kids to develop their own textbook attack strategies from all these good structures we are modeling. But you may find, once you have created your first Guide-o-Rama, that this is a pretty fun way to infuse even dull textbook chapters with a bit of your own spin, personality, and humor.

Star Search Guide-o-Rama—Chapter 1

Page #	Tip
111–113	Read this introductory section slowly and carefully. It sets up the big ideas you'll need later.
112	When I was a kid I always wondered where all those goofy constellation names came from. And why so many of them don't actually look like the crab or the spider or whatever they are named for. I mean, Big Dipper, I can see it, but Ursa Major (Big Bear)?

Have you ever tried to spot Betelgeuse before? Do you think you could find it now, using the Orion's Belt key? |
| 113 | The diagram on the lower left is really helpful.

The sidebar on tilt in Earth's axis is a good reminder of how the seasons work, if you don't remember. |
| 114 | So, will any of us live to see any perceptible change in the heavens during our lifetimes? How do you know? |
| 115–119 | Since this is October and we will be studying the fall sky, you can skim the pages covering Northern Hemisphere winter, spring, and summer. |

Page #	Tip
120	The "Looking West" diagram sure confused me, how about you? I just relied on the whole-sky map instead. Anyone who can explain Fig. 5 to the class gets extra credit.

There are thirty-nine fall constellations listed, too many to find them all. I started with the most familiar ones, and found about ten before I moved on. |
| 121 | When we go out stargazing Thursday night, we will be following the instructions in the box on the right, to orient ourselves to the star map. Read the steps now and see if you "get it." |
| 122–129 | You can skip the whole Southern Hemisphere section, but do this one experiment as you flip through: What big or general differences do you see in the "look" of the southern sky year-round from the northern sky? (Hint: check the Milky Way.) |
| 132–135 | Lots of tough vocab here. The three to understand are *celestial sphere, celestial time,* and *celestial latitude.*

Don't sweat the "planisphere" stuff for now. We'll get to that next week. |

ACTIVITY 4: **Vocabulary Word Sorts**

One thing that makes textbooks so tough for kids is all the new vocabulary and the high rate at which it is typically introduced. Without some advance guidance, students have no idea where, mentally, to hang all those new words. That's why it is so important for teachers to conduct effective prereading activities focused on vocabulary, so kids enter the text thinking, on the lookout for words, actively making meaning right from the start. In Chapter 5 we shared four vocabulary strategies that also work well with textbooks. Here's another that's a special favorite.

In her eighth-grade class at Baker Demonstration School, Kathleen McKenna is preparing for a unit on soil conservation. But before she assigns the chapter in the textbook, she wants to introduce her students to some of the key words they will be encountering. So Kathleen has brought to class several sets of words, each one hand-printed on a little 1 × 3 inch piece of paper. Among the terms included:

carbon dioxide	topsoil
subsoil	contour plowing
abrasion	decay
conservation plowing	mechanical weathering
decomposers	acid rain
sod	ice wedging
erosion	chemical weathering
mites	conservation
earthworms	

Kathleen has carefully included some terms that kids already know (*earthworms*, *sod*); some familiar words that are used in an unfamiliar way (*ice wedging*); and others that are brand new (*contour plowing*). She gets kids into groups of four or five and hands each a set of word strips to work on. Her instructions are simple: "Using the best thinking you can, put these words into categories that you can agree on as a group. What goes with what? If you have no idea what a word means, then guess. Choose someone to be the official 'spotter' in your group and report on what you did. OK? In about five minutes, spotters be ready to explain how your group sorted the words."

The students take a few minutes to scan the whole set, confirming some meanings and guessing at others. Then individual kids start suggesting groupings ("Let's put the plowing ones together"), trying out different hypotheses ("I think these are different kinds

Science

of erosion"), and dealing with anomalies ("Do earthworms erode the soil or help it?"). There's still plenty of buzz in the room when Kathleen calls kids back together and asks the spotters to briefly share their group's categorization scheme. As reports are collected, there's lots of overlap in the categories, and some good questions are posed along the way ("Isn't soil erosion a natural process too? Is it something we humans should always be trying to prevent?").

By now it's only ten minutes into the class, with plenty of energy present and lots of ideas left to be shared. But Kathleen just says: "Well, I guess you guys are ready to read the chapter now." While the kids don't quite storm the pile of textbooks, they don't waste any time either. Within one minute, the classroom is hushed, as kids read about soil erosion and conservation. Some kids silently nod or smile as now-familiar terms pop up and categories, some predicted and some surprising, emerge.

The magic of this activity is in its process. Word sorts are pretty fun; they are social and collaborative, and if you set them up right, they go very quickly. In Chapter 5, the similar List-Group-Label strategy is structured for learning vocabulary during or after reading. But the goal in this case is not for kids to correctly classify all the vocabulary or even know what all the words mean before they read the selection. In fact, a wrong guess is just about as useful as a right one, because it still prepares the kid to meet the word in the textbook (Kornell, Hays, and Bjork, 2009). There, he can confirm or disconfirm his prediction; either way, that's an active process and a big help in remembering. So word sorts, even when kids don't know the definitions, set a purpose for reading: they get students watching for key vocabulary and prime them to stop and think when those words appear in the text.

ACTIVITY 5: **Textbook Circles**

In Chapter 9, we introduce a small-group reading activity called book clubs. This structure is simply a school adaptation of the adult reading groups you sometimes see meeting in bookstores, libraries, or maybe your own living room. Basically, this is just people picking books they want to read and talking about them with their friends. In school, we mainly use this structure when students are reading trade books connected to a teaching field—like historical novels set during the Civil War or biographies of famous scientists (genres specifically recommended by the new Next Generation Science Standards). But some teachers have also successfully applied the book club structure to textbooks. There are a few challenges. Most textbooks don't provide the narrative structure or emotional engagement that novels or trade nonfiction books typically do. Still, even if textbooks are a little dry and overpacked, the social power of working and talking together can enhance students' understanding of them. There's robust research showing that if kids just talk to each other about what they are reading, their comprehension improves significantly (Allington, 2013).

In Peru, New York, Jodie Bonville uses textbook circles with her middle school social studies class. Here's how she describes it:

Social Studies

Our social studies curriculum deals with the history of the eastern hemisphere (the development of civilizations of Mesopotamia, Egypt, China, India, Greece, Rome). The textbook we use is a multivolume set, and we used the book *The Ancient World* for our "textbook circles." Before we started reading the text, I had students fill out a KWL chart on what they **Knew** about the Romans and **Wanted** to know about these people. The kids showed a high interest in the aspects of everyday life in Rome, which was good because this volume had lots of information on "The Daily Life of the Romans."

I formed the textbook clubs myself, balancing student strengths and weaknesses in reading. As always in my classroom, I wanted to keep a balanced, mixed-ability model. It wasn't too hard to get our Roman textbook circles going, because earlier in the year I had taught students the basic procedures for book clubs with literature. Back then, I trained students with short pieces of text and introduced them to various tools for note-taking and annotating text (see page 121). All these tools were explained, practiced, and reinforced. So peer-led small-group discussions were already a part of our classroom culture.

When adapting book clubs to the social studies textbook, I needed to redesign some of the roles that students use while they are reading—and that they bring to the group to feed the discussion (see pages 121–124). I used some of the regular roles, like Connector, Illustrator, and Researcher. I also made up some new ones, including the "Amazing Re-enactor," whose job was to dramatize aspects of Roman daily life, based on what they read in the text. (I supplied them with a chest of props, like sheets for togas, etc.) I also gathered some other materials for different group members and their roles, including reference books about Rome and websites about ancient civilizations bookmarked on the computer.

The textbook circles met on a simple schedule. Groups first met for one class period to read a selection from the textbook and make notes with their assigned task in mind. Mostly kids read silently and jotted notes, but some groups read certain passages out loud to each other, and talked about them as they went. The next class period, the students had another forty minutes to work on the tasks associated with their roles. Because we teach social studies every other day due to block scheduling, the students also had an extra day outside of class to continue working on their roles, so they would come to class really prepared and ready to share the following day.

During the book club meetings, my own job was to facilitate and guide. I circulated around the room, listening as students discussed each section of the text. At first I just wanted to make sure that students were all engaged in the discussion, but after a while I could also sit in a group and take notes on the various interactions between students. After each textbook circle session, we gathered as a whole class to debrief, to discuss positives and negatives of their interactions and discussions, so that the next meetings could be even more productive.

As far as assessment was concerned, I created an informal Textbook Circles Self-Assessment sheet for kids to rate themselves as group members and as emerging experts on the content. I also kept the anecdotal notes from my visits to the individual groups. And, oh yes, I did give a unit test over the textbook, and the kids did very well on it. The students reported that they really enjoyed using literature circles in social studies. They felt that being able to discuss the textbook in a group helped them to remember information better. And they really enjoyed the different roles, because these helped bring the text to life for them—something I just love to do in my classroom.

For more information about book clubs, including many of the classroom tools and forms that Jodie used as well as further assessment ideas especially adaptable to textbook circles, see Chapter 9.

ACTIVITY 6: SQ3R—Remembering Facts from Long Texts

Back in 1941, a guy called Francis Robinson (1970) came up with a comprehensive model to help students remember big chunks of nonfiction text, such as textbook chapters. He called it SQ3R, standing for Survey, Question, Read, Recite, and Review. Today, if you look at any study skills website, homework center, or college help desk, you'll find some version of SQ3R. It is still the number one, most famous, most widely used comprehensive model for textbook study. It is old as the hills—but maybe it is old for a reason, like because it works. It ain't exactly what you'd call "a really fun activity," but when kids simply must retain large quantities of content-packed text, SQ3R can help.

The underlying assumption of SQ3R is this: if you really want to remember big textbook chapters, you cannot simply read straight through them like a novel—you need to attack the text in a whole different way. You need to slow down, break the work into stages, and take multiple, conscious steps to retain information. Here's how it lays out.

Survey

* Preview the structure, organization, or plan of the chapter.
* Think about the title.
* Read the introduction and/or summary.
* Read the headings and subheadings (boldface, color text, etc.).
* Look at any pictures, charts, or graphs.

Why do this? By predicting what will be included in the chapter, you will remember more details.

(Do the next three steps for each subsection of the chapter.)

Question

* For the section of the chapter at hand, pose some questions you would like to have answered.
* There may already be some questions in the book, at the beginning or end of the chapter.
* You can formulate other questions by changing subheads into questions (for example, the subhead "Causes of the Civil War" could be turned into the question: "What were the causes of the Civil War?").

Why do this? Having questions in mind results in (1) a spontaneous attempt to answer with information already at hand; (2) curiosity until the question is answered; (3) a criterion against which the details can be inspected to determine relevance and importance; and (4) a focal point for crystallizing a series of ideas (the answer).

Read

* Read to answer the questions you have developed.
* Mark or highlight the answers as you find them.
* Adjust your speed—if content does not relate to a question, move on.

Why do this? Reading the text in light of your own questions makes you a more active reader and helps you understand, evaluate, and determine the relative importance of material.

Recite

* After reading the section, stop and take a minute to paraphrase or summarize the information.
* Jot down the question you were pursuing.
* Answer the question in your own words; use only key words needed to recall the whole idea.
* Test your comprehension of the section by asking: What were the main points here?

Why do this? It's important to solidify your understanding before moving on—there's lots more content coming!

Follow the above plan for each section of the chapter.

Review

* Review your notes within twenty-four hours of making them, and again within a week.
* First, read your written question(s).
* Try to recite your answer(s). If you can't, look at your notes. Five to ten minutes should suffice for a chapter.

Why do this? You can significantly increase retention if you use both immediate and later review.

You might notice that many steps of this procedure encourage kids to use the exact same cognitive strategies that research says proficient readers rely on (and which we discussed in Chapter 2). In SQ3R, students are explicitly posing *questions* about the text, quite intentionally *inferring* and *making predictions*, consciously *monitoring their comprehension*, and repeatedly *summarizing* what has been read.

Obviously, getting students fluent with the SQ3R program will require some training and experience. Smart teachers provide lessons early in the year when they first demonstrate, and then kids practice each of these steps, with immediate guidance and feedback from the teacher. You can also make it sociable, putting kids into small groups to compare the predictions they made after surveying, the questions they are developing for a subsection, and so forth.

SQ3R has proven quite popular with teachers and effective for kids in terms of content retention, but as we warned, this is not the kind of experience that turns kids on to a content area or galvanizes a lifelong interest. It can be a grind, chapter after chapter, and becomes laborious and mechanical if overdone. So while we certainly think this strategy should be in the repertoire of every teacher with a textbook to teach, it is not the whole package. Combining SQ3R with other approaches in this chapter, and in the rest of the book, will provide a deeper, more balanced, and more engaging experience.

Substituting for the Textbook

Jeff James teaches Introduction to Physical Science to freshmen at Andrew High School in suburban Chicago. "Honestly, I hate textbooks," he says. "They're full of mistakes. They're boring to the kids, and they're too simplistic. They don't go deep enough, and they include a lot of stuff that 95 percent of my students will never need to know, even if they go into a science career. I mean, quantum physics for ninth graders?" Jeff is also concerned because the textbook adopted by his department doesn't even match well with the Illinois state assessment, which

Physical Science changes every year as let's-get-tough legislators pile mandates on the schools.

So now Jeff teaches without a textbook—almost. The first time he tried it, he forgot to tell the parents in advance. "A political mistake," Jeff admits, ruefully recounting the barrage of questions he fielded at that fall's go-to-school night. "The parents think the textbook is the subject, I realized. So what I do now is tell them in advance how I teach, and when they hear the rationale, they have no problem with it. They remember they didn't like the textbook when they were in school either. But now I do issue the textbooks to the kids. I say, 'Use this as a reference, use the glossary if you need it.'" But Jeff makes no regular reading assignments in the textbook. Doesn't he use the textbook for anything else? "Well, I'm a really awful artist, so I do project some of the drawings and diagrams in the book."

So what do the kids read instead? For the backbone, Jeff writes his own text, far shorter than the textbook, focusing on a much smaller number of topics. And he delivers this text to kids in the form of a PowerPoint presentation, both projected and in paper printout form. Why is this better than a textbook? "Well, for one thing," Jeff laughs, "the author is there to answer questions and talk to the students."

What does the minitext include? What does it leave out? Jeff says there are two criteria for including a topic in his homemade baseline text, one of which he's proud of and one not. "First, as the science expert in the room, I've got to ask, what are the ideas that are fundamental to science, things kids have got to understand so they can continue their study of science in the future, and be able to consider a career in the field?" For Jeff, the gotta-haves include things like Newton's laws of motion, the kinetic theory of matter, and the origin and history of the universe. The second criterion that Jeff's not so proud of? "What's on the state exam."

The rest of students' reading includes a wide variety of articles on physical science, chemistry, and earth science (all of which are covered in the state's physical science exam, taken after the fifth semester of high school). Jeff makes extensive use of the *Chicago Tribune* and the neighborhood's own daily newspaper for real-life examples. Years ago, when Chicago Cubs home-run king Sammy Sosa was suspended from baseball for using a cork-filled bat, the class read about it avidly. Using their knowledge of physics, they determined that "corking" a bat is a bad idea, scientifically—increasing bat speed but decreasing the force that helps you hit home runs. Jeff also directs students to a number of Web resources for science information and stories; his favorite is the NASA website. But he is adamant about teachers checking Internet sites before sending kids their way: "You've got to screen the Web stuff first—it's even less reliable than the textbook."

Finally, Jeff's students read science magazines (*Science News, Discover, Nature, Scientific American*) and trade nonfiction books. Last year, some favorite books for students were *Big Bang: A Short History of the Universe* and $E = mc^2$: *A Biography of the World's Most Famous Equation* (see pages 65–67). Kids also read selections from more challenging science trade books, with coaching and conversation from Jeff, including *Genome: Autobiography of a Species in 23 Chapters* and Stephen Hawking's *A Brief History of Time*.

So how well does this textbook-free physical science course work? Pretty well, judging by the kids' grades and test scores, which Jeff reports are higher than under the old textbook-based model. "I call this No Secrets Education. I tell the kids what we are going to study, we study it, and that's what I assess. And they do great. Plus, I know I'm sending a few young scientists into the world, which makes me really happy."

Get a Better Textbook!

One day, a group of math teachers from California came to visit one of our schools in Chicago. An hour after the initial orientation had concluded, while everyone was supposed to be sitting in classrooms, Smokey was surprised to see one of the visitors trotting down the hall with something clasped to her chest. "This is amazing!" she shouted, pointing at the textbook she was clutching. "It's fabulous! Where did you get this? Can I buy this copy from you? I've gotta show this to my colleagues back home!" The woman literally would not let go of the textbook, which she was holding like a drowning person with a life ring. In the end, we did get the book away from her, but only after sitting down at the computer and ordering an examination copy sent to her home.

The textbook happened to be *Interactive Mathematics Program* (Fendel and Resek, 2013), published by It's About Time in Mt. Kisco, New York. The math teachers at our school had decided a few years earlier that IMP's hands-on, real-life-applied, NCTM-standards-based program was the best fit for our kids and our school. But the moral of this story is not that all

Math

TEXTBOOKS in the FLIPPED classroom

A hot and sometimes controversial trend in secondary education these days— which even caught the wandering eye of the *New York Times* (Fitzpatrick, 2012)—is the "flipped" or inverted classroom. In this model of technology-enabled learning, the classic teacher lectures are not given in class—but instead are watched by kids as homework. Typically, flipping teachers prepare a compressed video version of their normal lecture on a topic, usually between eight and twelve minutes long. (Doesn't this sound like a video version of Jeff James, whom we just visited— creating a shorter, custom-tailored textbook of your own?) Then students are supposed to watch the video minilecture at home, with some sort of accountability tool in hand, often a note-taking sheet or journal. When kids arrive at school the next day already familiar with the topic, the teacher can then spend class time clarifying key points and answering questions, offering more hands-on-activities, having one-to-one conferences with kids, and supporting students in doing experiments, inquiry projects, book clubs, or other small-group work.

From what we have seen, heard, and researched, there seem to be a million variations of flipping. Some iterations seem highly progressive, and teachers really take advantage of the newfound class time to make learning more experiential you math teachers should go out and adopt IMP or any other competing math series. We're just pointing out that it's possible to be using the wrong textbook and not even know it.

It's important to be vigilant, to be on the lookout for new materials that might suit our students better. It is so easy to take the path of least resistance and keep readopting the same text over and over, without carefully scanning what else is available. Sure, doing systematic review of the alternative textbooks in any subject area can be a time-consuming process. Once you request the examination copies, the sales rep is always on your case and you never find a series that pleases everybody in the department. But even if you don't end up changing textbooks, the conversations with colleagues that emerge while you are evaluating materials will be some of the best staff development you'll ever get, guaranteed.

and interactive. In other models, the kids now have teachers talking at them both day and night. The flipping pioneers (there are many creation stories, and we don't want to slight anyone) are inarguably top-rank, incredibly hard-working teachers. Just think of the extra work they tackled to create all these new materials, learn video editing, restructure classes, train their kids, inform parents, develop new assessments, and on and on.

At the same time, we are always on the lookout for "innovations" that can boomerang. So when we see thousands of these flipped lectures for sale on the Web, we wonder where this all leads. Those pioneer flippers created original, custom-tailored lessons for their own kids. But now the Gates Foundation is vigorously backing the collection and distribution of generic online lectures for everyone, everywhere. Bill Gates himself gloats that within five years they will have all the great lectures in the world collected. Obviously, this move reinforces the idea that *lectures are teaching*. But worse, what happens when school districts start choosing and buying the lectures to replace teachers? Maybe so long to the creativity, autonomy, and professional ownership that the flipping pioneers have embodied so well.

If you have come this far in the book, you already know that we are rather fond of teaching kids to *read* informational text, just as the Common Core calls for, and that we don't think lectures, live or canned, are the main way that teenagers achieve deep conceptual understanding of content.

Building a Community of Learners

Forgive us for starting a chapter by quoting research, but here's a report that really hits home. A recent study by the Chicago Consortium on School Research at the University of Chicago reviewed research showing the importance of "noncognitive" factors (that is, attitudes, social skills, and behaviors) in students' achievement (Farrington et al., 2012). One particular category, academic mind-sets, relates directly to the kind of atmosphere teachers establish in the classroom. These mind-sets include the following:

* I belong in this academic community.
* I can succeed at this.
* My ability and competence grow with my effort.
* This work has value to me.

These reflect not only how students relate to others and the teacher, but also the extent to which classmates and the teacher are supportive, especially when the work grows challenging. In one study, for example, a randomly selected group of students saw a video and read a pamphlet about older peers who described how they overcame initial difficulties and grew more successful over time. Even a year later, after this very minimal intervention, their GPAs were higher than those of a control group that didn't see the video or pamphlet.

And while we're at it, here's another recent study on the importance of classroom climate and personal relationships in raising student achievement. Joseph Durlak and his colleagues at Loyola University (2011) conducted a giant meta-analysis of 273 studies of social skills training programs in schools around the United States. Their findings? In schools where teachers explicitly taught the social skills of small-group interaction (active listening, turn-taking, agreeably disagreeing), the students gained an average of 11 percent on both their course grades and on the high-stakes standardized tests given in their state. Are you kidding? We know plenty of schools that would *kill* for an 11 percent score gain—and this came not from test prep or cramming, but from teaching kids how to act friendly and supportive toward each other.

So now, the focus on such non-tested phenomena as student attitudes and social relationships is growing intense. Paul Tough's book *How Children Succeed* (2012) explores these in depth. A classroom management program called Positive Behavior Interventions and Supports (PBIS) has been adopted by a growing number of large school districts. Even a conservative commentator, former Gates Foundation executive Tom Vander Ark has jumped on the social-emotional learning bandwagon. We certainly hope this is not just another fad or mandate to be piled onto teachers, however.

So while we've argued in this book that it's crucial for us to expand *what* kids read and show them *how* to read it, good teachers know that the work of teaching runs far deeper. We need to make the classroom a community, a place where students feel safe to take the risks involved in learning, where they see it connected with their lives, and where they help and learn from one another instead of working only as isolated individuals. And we do this not just to make students feel good, but to enable them to learn meaningfully in our subjects, through reading as well as the many other avenues we use in our teaching.

Teachers have many ways to build community, but we know students respond strongly when they sense that the teacher knows something about them as individuals. Humor helps break a lot of the ice. Surveys of students show that giving them choices, even in small things, helps students feel respected and viewed as people who are maturing and worthy of trust. While some might think this means a loose or disorganized classroom, it's really quite the opposite. A class where students work well together and respect one another needs to be an orderly group. But in our competitive, individualistic society, students need to develop specific habits of supporting and encouraging one another. Students who know each other well and have been taught to listen supportively to one another are more likely to take risks and stretch beyond their comfort level as they learn. The importance of climate and community are reflected deeply in the first core proposition of the National Board for Professional Teaching Standards (2002):

> Accomplished teachers understand how students develop and learn. They . . . are aware of the influence of context and culture on behavior. They develop students' cognitive capacity and their respect for learning. Equally important, they foster students' self-esteem, motivation, character, civic responsibility and their respect for individual, cultural, religious and racial differences.

It may seem like the simplest truism to say all learning happens in a context that colors everything taking place. But that must be factored into every teaching activity we plan: whatever strategies we try won't work if kids are turned off to school, or are just passively waiting for the teacher to give them the answers. School needs to be a place where kids feel some ownership and control (see Glasser, 1986, *Control Theory in the Classroom*), where they have the confidence to recognize and work on their confusions, where they take responsibility and learn how to help one another and why it's important to do so, and where they inquire into the big questions that matter for them. Otherwise, even when we teach strategies to help students deepen their understanding, they will only learn them mechanically, not recognizing when or why such strategies are needed.

Another insight into the context of reading is found in Jeff Wilhelm's research, in *You Gotta BE the Book* (1997). In his interviews of resistant eighth graders, Jeff found that to them, reading was simply "finding the answers to the questions at the end of the chapter," or sounding out the words on the page, whether these made any sense or not. Kids' struggles as readers, in other words, reflected not just a lack of skills, but an unproductive conception of their role as readers and learners in the classroom. Wilhelm and Michael Smith's work, *Reading Don't Fix No Chevys* (2002), reveals that boys particularly are more engaged when reading and learning provide perceived benefits within the experience itself, rather than serving only a vague future goal like getting into college or joining the job world.

> *We need to make the classroom a community, a place where students feel safe to take the risks involved in learning . . .*

So unless the classroom is a place where kids see learning as useful and meaningful—connected to their individual interests, or shared with their friends, or focused on large issues they care about—teaching content reading "skills" or comprehension strategies or anything else simply doesn't stick. In this chapter, we'll share some of the ways that effective teachers actively shape classrooms so that the message is consistent and repeated and enacted: this school is a place where we all help each other learn, where the learning is for students, not just to keep the teacher off your backs, and where the experience of learning is engaging in itself, and not just a set of skills you'll need "later."

There are five main ways that teachers build community as they go about teaching their subjects and using reading to do so. We'll describe each one in more detail in this chapter. Teachers:

1. Make the classroom a place where students trust the teacher and believe it's safe to take risks.
2. Organize learning so that students work together and help one another.

3. Provide students with choices and opportunities to take responsibility in the classroom.

4. Connect learning with students' lives and the larger issues around them.

5. Read aloud from engaging and powerful writing in their fields so kids can fall in love with ideas.

Taking Action in All Subjects

The Common Core Standards focus pretty much on learning outcomes rather than classroom processes—but not entirely. The speaking and listening standards explicitly call on students to learn to work collaboratively, share ideas, and build on one another's thoughts. The standards documents of all our professional organizations across subject areas, too, urge many community-building strategies, not as feel-good frills but as powerful ways to teach content so that students really do learn. Of course, in lab science courses the role of group work has long been recognized and made an essential ingredient of students' learning process. And in any classroom where collaborative work in pairs or small groups is employed, and where the task involves discussing and thinking through ideas rather than just filling in blanks, a supportive community connection is needed to make it work. The following box outlines strategies we can use to build this community, based on the basic categories introduced above.

STRATEGIES for building community in the classroom

Make the classroom a place where students trust the teacher and believe it's safe to take risks, a place where it's OK to ask questions when they don't understand something, and they can expect to receive the support they need to handle challenges.

* Model and share your own passion for your subject, your thinking processes when reading about it, and your own challenges as a student and a reader.

* Value students' questions, both those that express confusion about the material being studied and those about larger implications or related topics.
* Hold brief in-class conferences with individuals to discuss their questions and set individual learning goals, to help make vulnerabilities less public, and to learn what support each student needs.

Organize learning so that students work together and help one another.
* Provide explicit training in collaborative interaction.
* Orchestrate small-group activities in which students help one another to understand course material.
* Provide class time for book clubs, using books from your classroom library.

Provide students with choices and opportunities to take responsibility in the classroom.
* Hold class meetings to co-create norms for the community. Then follow up with periodic meetings to address needs or issues as they come up.
* Develop as many jobs and responsibilities for students as you can possibly think of, and rotate these periodically.
* Schedule in-class reading time with choices of articles and books about your subject.
* Use "jigsaw" activities in which small groups of students give presentations to help the rest of the class learn about various aspects of a topic.

Connect learning with students' lives and the larger issues around them.
* Conduct surveys of students' interests and past experiences that are related to the course subject.
* Conduct inquiry projects within the course subject area, or connecting several subjects.

Read aloud from engaging and powerful writing in your field. Reading aloud evokes the sense of a group gathered around the fire to hear the stories that hold them together as a community.

Of course, no classroom is likely to employ all of these strategies all the time. However, it's clear that they need to be present often enough to ensure that students truly believe their teachers care intensely about them and their learning.

Following are more specifics for these strategies to promote community in the classroom. There are few surprises here; all are approaches that good teachers have employed for years, and that education experts and teacher-authors have described in books on pedagogy and reading. These most definitely are not fluffy "team-building" exercises, but well-structured and thoughtful approaches for teaching important subject matter. Several of the key strategies will be described in greater detail later in this book—see Chapter 8 for more on classroom workshop, and Chapter 9 for more on book clubs.

Make the classroom a place where students trust the teacher and believe it's safe to take risks.

> ✶ **Model and share your own passion for your subject, your thinking processes when reading about it, and your own challenges as a student and a reader.**

Prosser High School biology teacher Marnie Ware spends a considerable amount of class time with her students, many of whom are English language learners, on issues around

Biology

healthy diet, which she views and explains to the young people as a social justice issue. And she turns this into inquiry projects that are integrated into the curriculum. Students view excerpts from the film _The China Study_, which documents an extensive inquiry into the effect of nutrition on illness (Campbell and Campbell, 2006; and see www.thechinastudy.com). Her more advanced students analyze data from the study to determine their own conclusions about it. Others interview family members to generate their own data, which is then compiled and analyzed by the class, working together. Marnie explains that she understands adolescents don't have total control over their diets, since they are still dependent on their families. Nevertheless, many are influenced by this work. One recent student decided to major in biochemistry in college as a result.

At the same time, it's important to help students understand that along with our passion, we adults also experience confusion and uncertainty, especially with new ideas or new skills. Foreign language teacher Theresa Hernandez encourages her students in French to risk the inevitable mistakes they'll make as they try to speak the language, by describing the many

Foreign Language

faux pas she uttered while living in France. One story she tells them: Complaining to a French friend that her eye hurt, she kept repeating "mon oeil!" The friend thought she was saying "moneil," which is slang for "I'm just kidding." She grew increasingly frustrated at the ensuing lack of help, while the friend couldn't understand why she seemed upset when she insisted she was only kidding. Not knowing the slang, Theresa could make no sense of the growing conflict. Theresa adds that for practicing a foreign language, pairing kids with friends helps reduce their timidity about speaking.

Teachers can find comfortable ways to take risks themselves, thus signaling to students that they value and support this behavior. Cris Tovani, in *I Read It but I Don't Get It* (2003), tells kids about her own difficulties with reading when she was in high school, and the techniques she resorted to for faking book reports. Other teachers enjoy including occasional mistakes in their calculations or information as they work out a problem on the chalkboard. The glee kids display as they point these out helps to confirm that it's safe to risk errors by nailing the teacher in the same situation.

> ✻ **Value students' questions, both those that express confusion about the material being studied and those about larger implications or related topics.**

This requires more than just a quick "Any questions?" at the end of a lecture. Actively initiate the process by having groups confer briefly and jot down their questions, followed by reports of one or more questions from each group. Then be open about the fact that you don't always have the answers, and there's nothing wrong with that—though of course if you come back the next day with some new information on the topic, it's especially good. Even better, *show* kids how you find answers by doing a search-aloud, projecting your computer as you seek information on the Web, and vocalizing your decisions as you choose keywords, vet websites, and click through information. Following a digression and loosening up on your timetable shows that you value students' curiosity. If we complain about students' lack of engagement in our subject matter, we must be ready to respond positively when they do show interest. And of course national standards such as those for science and social studies urge us to strongly emphasize the value of questioning.

Math teacher Marianna Jennings, at Prosser High School, reiterates regularly to students that she especially appreciates "wrong answers," because they bring up issues that students need to understand. As we visited one afternoon, a student asked about one problem for which her solution didn't match the answer key at the back of the textbook. Which was correct? Rather than simply answer, Marianna replied, "Well, sometimes the textbook is wrong. Let's all do the problem and see what we think." Later she tells Steve, "I try not to be the

Math

know-it-all who just delivers information." She also follows what she calls "the five-second rule," having everyone pause before raising hands or calling out an answer, so that the more hesitant kids get a chance to respond. It's invigorating to observe a math class in which these strategies result in a room filled with highly engaged kids.

✶ Hold brief in-class conferences with individuals.

It's important to discuss with students their questions, to set individual learning goals, and to help make vulnerabilities less public, while you learn what support each student needs.

Science   In Northbrook Illinois Junior High School, science teacher Pam Mendelson circulates among her students as they write summaries that help them understand their reading. She talks briefly with individuals or pairs—she likes to call this "catch and release"—to see how they are doing. "You really learn a lot about the kids, their struggles with comprehension as well as their abilities. Sometimes students who are having difficulty say amazing things in a conference that they would never have volunteered in class discussion. I ask them to share, which can really boost their confidence. And I get to be able to anticipate what they'll need. For example, I'll learn that a particular student has trouble with oral directions. So I'll get to him and check on whether he needs help with what to do next or not."

Pam recalls one student who had been failing, and in a conference she found his understanding was way ahead of the other kids. But she could tell that he didn't know how to study for tests. "I can see what an amazing thinker you are, so let me help you learn how to study," she told him. She did this in some afterschool sessions, and afterward, she reports, he became a completely different, and successful, student. This change all grew out of a brief in-class teacher-student conference. One-on-one conferences, Pam has learned, are far more than simply occasions for monitoring or helping with a specific task. They enable a teacher to learn things about individual students that he or she would never otherwise discover.

History   History teacher Seth Patner, teaching at the Renaissance Charter High School in New York City, found that his most valuable conferences were the informal ones that take place in the halls as he spots students who need support. "The one-to-one relationships are a huge part of the work," he observes, offering the example of a girl who was doing nothing in class until they began talking about her family's origins in Aruba. "Why would you care?" she at first pouted. No surprise that, after he asked lots of questions and they looked at a map together, her attitude changed completely. "You've got to know what's going on in their heads," he explains.

**Organize learning so that students work together and help one another.**

> ✴ **Provide explicit training in collaborative interaction.**

Turning students loose to work together in pairs or groups without helping them learn how to do it is a recipe for chaos. But we've learned a tremendous amount from our colleague Nancy Steineke (see _Reading and Writing Together_, 2002) about how to build students' collaborative skills as well as supportive relationships. She systematically teaches and maintains friendliness and support among students, using interview activities, discussion about what good listening very specifically _looks_ like and _sounds_ like, and what she calls "home court." Students brainstorm the factors they believe lead sports teams to win more games on their home turf than games played away. This helps students to understand the value of helping and cheering one another along— and to recognize the destructive power of put-downs. Nancy teaches various collaboration skills (like listening, asking good questions, taking turns speaking, encouraging others to speak) using T-charts to list what each one looks like (in one column) and sounds like (in the other). And she doesn't just teach the skills once. Students need to review, provide mutual support (with structures like "skills coaches" in each discussion group), and reflect on how they are doing by writing down specific skills and behaviors their group did well with. The teacher can listen in on discussions, jot down effective statements and behaviors that she witnesses, and describe them to the class later. Along with Harvey, Nancy has written two more recent books that include step-by-step lessons for teaching these critical social skills (Daniels and Steineke, 2011, 2013).

One way that Prosser High School math teacher Marianna Jennings builds friendship and collaboration with her students is to orchestrate math problem get-acquainted icebreakers. Each student receives a sheet containing a number of math problems equal to one less than the number of students in the class. Students then circulate around the room finding others to pair up and solve a problem with them. As each problem is solved, the student collects the signature of his or her latest partner and gets the answer briefly checked by the teacher. The goal is for all students to get comfortable working with everyone in the class.

Math

> ✴ **Orchestrate small-group activities in which students help one
> another to understand course material.**

More and more, middle school and high school teachers are rearranging their rooms so that students sit and work in small groups and teams, rather than in rows. Students are encouraged to confer as they work on assigned problems, and to discuss ideas in their groups before responding to a teacher's question. That's just how it looks frequently in Marianna Jennings' algebra class. Marianna's kids work in groups of four, using the following roles: discussion leader, task conductor, secretary, and time keeper. Prosser High School history teacher Bryan McKay prefers placing students in pairs because he finds that the work tends to get shared more equally, whereas in larger groups it's easier for one or two students to sit by while just a few do the tasks. One of Bryan's favorite group activities is a set of his-

tory "trials" in which pairs of student lawyers each research an issue, take one side, and then present their case to a panel of three judges—who must also do the research so that they can evaluate the arguments. (Note the relevance of such a project for helping students learn argumentation strategies prized by the Common Core.) A typical history trial will address a question like, "To what extent did John Brown's Harpers Ferry raid cause the U.S. Civil War?" The students use the website Edmodo to communicate and plan with each other on their teams outside of class. This sort of project takes a number of days to carry out, with time for library research plus three class periods to get through all the trials. But the payoff in student engagement and learning is huge, and the students enjoy working together. Bryan finds it easy to monitor as the teams work and to help kids problem-solve if they have difficulty collaborating.

> * **Provide class time for book clubs, using books from your**
> **classroom library.**

This is another strategy so important that it has its own chapter later on. Book clubs are explored more thoroughly still in Harvey's *Literature Circles: Voice and Choice in Book Clubs and Reading Groups* (2002). This structure takes the next step beyond simply allowing students to read independently, and features student-led discussions in small groups that share an interest in a particular topic or piece of writing. While the popular term "*book* clubs" may seem to imply that it's meant only for reading long novels in English classes, this structure works equally well for short articles in any subject area.

When a group tackles a whole book, the students decide on the number of pages to be read by their next meeting. Especially when students are first getting accustomed to this work, everyone in the group may have specific note-taking roles to accomplish while doing the reading. These tasks might include jotting down potentially lively discussion questions or marking critical passages the group can to return to. Then, kids can use these notes to feed discussion when they sit down face to face. However, teachers who frequently employ book clubs usually do away with such narrow tasks once the students become accustomed to this work, since the jobs can make students' participation a bit mechanical, compared to simply having engaged discussions on issues in the reading. Many teachers use self-evaluation forms to help group members to monitor and improve their participation in the group. (We'll have more to say about book clubs in Chapter 9.)

Provide students with choices and opportunities to take responsibility in the classroom.

> ✱ **Hold class meetings to co-create norms for the class. Then follow up with periodic meetings to address needs or issues as they come up.**

When science teacher Pam Mendelson works with her students to establish the class norms at the start of each year, she also asks them to write about the best and worst qualities and actions of teachers they've had in the past. Each student then writes out one rule he or she would like *her* to adhere to, along with a consequence if she violates it. These are all listed for the class to discuss and then choose one for her to follow. At times she'll explain how a particular rule may be unrealistic (a typical example: requiring that she like all students equally—she's only human, she says, and can try to treat them all fairly, but can't avoid natural feelings she may have). Thus, more than just outlining the rules, the process involves an extended discussion of the values that matter to her students.

> ✱ **Develop as many jobs and responsibilities for students as you can possibly think of, and rotate these periodically.**

Micheline Cosentino, teaching sixth-grade science at Northbrook Junior High, asks students to each think of one question about the topic under study that he or she would like answered. When we visited, the focus was on "weather wonders." The students must then find information on their particular questions, and the kids take turns, one each day, to briefly report on an answer that was discovered. These mini-inquiries also set the stage for deeper curricular investigations later.

Science

On a larger scale, we just recently came upon a report about Childersburg High School in rural Alabama, where it was decided to have students take on the work of reimagining the culture of the entire school. A leadership team visited other schools with effective programs, created lists of priorities, shared them with faculty, created a school creed, and worked to get all students behind it. Now they lead guided tours for community members, businesspeople, and interested visitors from other schools. As Jennifer Barnett, the teacher who has written about this, describes it, "Students at our school demonstrate their ownership of their learning community each and every day. I pinch myself often, just to make certain that I'm not dreaming" (Barnett, 2013). We don't see why this couldn't be happening in every school across the country.

> ✳ **Schedule in-class reading time with choices of articles and books about your subject.**

We'll explore this strategy in depth in Chapters 8 and 9 with independent reading workshop and book clubs. To give students wide options for reading, you'll need to build up a classroom library and collection of interesting articles on your subject, as we discussed in Chapter 4. Teachers who use reading workshop regularly often begin with a minilesson on some aspect of their subject, or on the process of reading thoughtfully, before the reading time begins. They conduct conferences with individuals during the reading session, as described above.

English English teacher Molly Rankin's freshmen at Prosser High School enjoy reading workshop two or three days every week. The students read books of their own choice, after Molly reads aloud for ten minutes from a young adult novel that reflects the kids' interests. The students take notes, both on what's taking place and their own reflections on it, and use these as aids for discussion in pairs or with the whole class. After a short strategy lesson, the kids do their own reading and continue at home for at least fifteen pages, or twenty minutes, per night. The students write responses that she calls "reading rants and raves." They email their thoughts to outside adults whom Molly has lined up (by drafting her friends and even her mom), and these gracious volunteers each respond to five students, providing the kids with regular adult pen pals. We see this as a remarkable way to help students feel like they belong to a club of engaged readers.

Other teachers have students share their responses by writing "dialogue journals" with a partner, creating posters, or presenting their thoughts to classmates. It's important to emphasize students' respect for one another and commitment to listen, learn from, and question one another as this sharing proceeds. *Enact* this with explicit requirements for audience participation—oral performances should be aimed at informing and helping the whole group, not just obtaining a grade for the presenter. The class as audience should take notes on presentations and respond to each presenter with questions and reflections.

> ✳ **Use "jigsaw" activities in which small groups of students give presentations to help the rest of the class learn about various aspects of a topic.**

This is a powerful and lively way for students to share with one another what they've learned from the reading they are doing. There are many ways to divide up the work and share it, so that students are teaching each other. When Pam Mendelson worked on the concept of "introduced species" with her junior high science students, she first acquainted them with some invasive plants in the area, such as purple loosestrife and buckthorn (Steve can attest to the annoying proliferation of the latter in his yard). After the class brainstormed questions about this problem, the students divided into two groups, with each group reading a separate article on their problem plant, looking for answers to their questions. Finally, pairs from the two groups exchanged information on answers they found in their reading.

Science

When exploring the topic of inheritance, Pam introduced four types not covered by the standard Mendelian pattern (we'll leave it to you, readers, to look these up and refresh your memory of biology courses):

* incomplete dominance
* codominance
* multiple alleles
* polygenic

Since these can be confusing, she had students in pairs read relevant sections of the textbook, after which each pair wrote a brief summary about two of the patterns. Pairs then came together in groups of four to share and discuss what they'd learned. A friend whose children had attended Pam's school confided to Steve that parents clamor to get their kids into Pam's class.

Connect learning with students' lives and the larger issues around them.

> * **Conduct surveys of students' interests and past experiences that are related to the course subject.**

Some educators who speak and write about the Common Core Standards assert that connecting students' reading to their own lives is not an approach we should encourage. The research on the importance of noncognitive factors in students' learning very clearly says otherwise. A student mind-set that connects a kid's life to the school community leads to higher grades (Farrington et al., 2012). And in fact, the standards themselves never reject such connections, for they can readily serve as one source of the evidence that can be used to build an argument or analyze a passage.

Donald Graves, one of the fathers of modern literacy research, often said that if you don't know ten specific things about a student, you don't know him or her well enough. He kept a journal page for each kid to record what he discovered about students' lives and interests. So as you learn about your students, bring in articles, magazines, books, and other materials that appeal to their interests. Janet Allen, in *It's Never Too Late: Leading Adolescents to Lifelong Literacy* (1995), explains how she uses surveys repeatedly during the year to learn about students' attitudes toward her subject, their prior experience with it, the subjects and issues they are interested in, their attitudes toward school in general, their life experiences, their preferences as to various classroom activities—all to learn what particular strategies might make the difference for students who are struggling.

Science At the start of the year, science teacher Pam Mendelson asks students to write in their journals about what they're excited to learn in the coming year as well as what they're worried about and what helps them learn. She provides a list of metacognitive thinking strategies and asks which work best for them and which they think they'd like to learn to use. She asks about their afterschool activities, what book they are reading, and—especially revealing—what book they'd recommend to her.

History At Prosser High School, history teacher Bryan McKay honors students' real-life concerns by scheduling a period for discussion on relevant topics every two or three weeks. The discussions are organized in a variety of ways—sometimes conducted as a whole-class activity, other times by groups that take pro or con stances to discuss separately and then debate with one another. Topics include issues such as cloning, artificial intelligence, euthanasia, and free speech. Obviously, Brian leaves the debating to the students and does not insert his own opinions into the mix.

> ✱ **Conduct inquiry projects within the course subject area, or connectingseveral subjects.**

Such projects (described in more depth in Chapter 10) generally start with a large question or controversial issue—for example, energy consumption and renewable sources of energy, or types of social discrimination and how to reduce their occurrence. Individuals or teams of students choose to focus on particular aspects of the problem, based on their interests. Skills and information related to the subject area of the course are then introduced at times when students need these for their inquiry. A couple of years ago, Harvey and our friend Stephanie Harvey wrote a book about managing such curricular inquiry projects called *Comprehension and Collaboration* (2009).

Josh Stumpenhorst, who teaches seventh-grade English and history at Lincoln Junior High in Naperville, Illinois, has his students working on "passion projects" of their own choice every Friday. At the start of the year, after being inspired by Morris Lurie's story "My Greatest Ambition" (about a young teenager with frustrated aspirations to become a comic-strip creator), students write briefly about their own passions and aims in life. Based on this, they embark on long-term projects to learn about and in many cases create products reflecting these desires. Some typical projects:

History

English

* claymation videos
* programming of video games by a group of eager boys
* Web research and writing about sea turtles
* a catalogue of fishing in the various lakes and streams in Illinois
* a survey to identify factors influencing students' test performance
* creation of a video cooking show focused on various kinds of cookies (with samples brought to class, of course)

These involve a variety of research, with help provided by the school media specialist/librarian. Some, like the sea turtles, will look like normal webquests. Others, like computer programming or videos, will involve study of the skills and techniques for creating specific products. Josh uses small-group and individual conferences to help students who are uncertain about the direction their project should take—but he finds that most who at first lack direction usually latch onto another student whose inquiry grabs their attention.

Some teachers may be surprised to hear that Josh does not grade or evaluate the projects in any way. The only requirement is that students share their work with the class twice each semester. Nevertheless, the kids pour their energies into the work, and this builds a great sense of commitment and belonging in the classroom. We visited on "Innovation Day," when all kids in the sixth grade presented their projects. When we talked with the students about the lack of grades, they used the word *passion* again and again. "You can't really put a grade on that," one student observed.

Read aloud from engaging and powerful writing in your field.
We've already talked about how reading aloud isn't just for little kids anymore. We all love a good story, and hearing it together opens up a lot of opportunities to reflect and relate as a group. As English teacher Molly Rankin finds, it engages students with literature. And as history teacher Ken Kramer describes (see Chapter 4, page 73), it helps students

comprehend more challenging texts. And as we outlined on pages 98–99, reading aloud is not just a delightful coming-together experience; it is also encouraged by the Common Core for all texts and topics.

Putting It All Together

When we review all of the steps and strategies that we've described in this chapter for promoting a strong learning community in the classroom, they clearly reflect what group dynamics experts tell us make for well-developed groups. According to Richard and Patricia Schmuck, in *Group Processes in the Classroom* (2000), a class becomes an effective learning group when it features:

* high positive expectations on the part of both students and teacher
* leadership that is shared and diffused throughout the class
* a strong sense of friendship and cohesiveness within the classroom
* norms that are clear but flexibly adapted to the activities in which the class is involved
* communication that flows easily in all directions, among students and between students and teacher
* conflict resolution that allows differences to be addressed constructively

If these features are present in effective human groups of all sorts, we can be sure that they are essentials in any effort to improve students' reading and learning in our subjects.

Independent Reading Workshop in Content Areas

Sometimes, when we hit a lull in the maelstrom that is teaching, when the storm of paperwork and standards and standardized testing calms for a moment, we slip back into our idealistic mode and reflect on the big goals that brought us into this work. For many of us, the overused but still important term "lifelong learner" figures prominently in our hopes for students. Sure, we want them all to pass the state exam and be "college and career ready." But we hope for more. We want our students to leave us with an enduring curiosity about our field, plus the motivation and the tools to continue learning.

So looking out at the adult community around our school, how do we recognize our "success stories," the alumni who are living the kind of thoughtful life we wished for them? Well, one thing they have in common is: they read—newspapers, magazines, and books—and they scan the Web with skill and purpose. They read not only what's required by their jobs, but also for recreation, for information, for citizenship. For these lifelong learners, being informed, having a book going, or exploring a new field are normal parts of life. And sometimes, these lifelong learners don't just read by themselves. They join book clubs or reading groups. They gather in living rooms, in the back rooms of bookstores, community centers, or church basements, and talk about books. They read and discuss old-time classics and hot best sellers, novels and biographies, books about people and history and science, about investing and dieting, politics and economics. And when they finish talking over each book, they pick another and set a date for the next meeting.

Individual and Small-Group Independent Reading

We've just described the two main kinds of independent reading that real, lifelong readers engage in: *individual* and *small-group* independent reading. When the reading is done individually in school, we call it "reading workshop." When it takes place in groups that read books or articles together, the label is either "book clubs" or "literature circles," though the material can just as easily be interesting articles as whole books. The common feature is *choice*: adult readers select their own material, whether from their easy chairs at home or as members of a discussion group. Typically, the chosen materials are interesting and accessible, written at a level people can fluenty digest. There are no assignments, study questions, quizzes, grades, or tracking. Reading flows from intrinsic motivation (curiosity, wonder, pleasure, etc.) and is not driven by external rewards or punishments. We use the term *workshop* because it's something like the traditional artisan's shop where a master craftsman guides apprentices who are all working on individual projects.

*Kids should be acting like lifelong learners while they are **still in school.***

So if we want this future to become reality, to grow the community of lifelong learners in our schools, part of every school day must be devoted to independent reading. This means students picking material and talking about it with their friends. Kids should be acting like lifelong learners while they are *still in school*. It doesn't make a lot of sense to wait until they graduate and hope they will develop good habits someday, maybe.

In this chapter and the next, we show how some time can be set aside for independent reading *in every school subject*—and we'll offer specific classroom structures to organize it. Yes, English teachers may be in a somewhat better position to employ this kind of activity. Indeed, language arts teachers in your school, if they follow the guidelines of the National Council of Teachers of English or the National Board for Professional Teaching Standards, already sponsor independent reading in their classrooms, perhaps dividing time between teacher-directed activities and student-driven workshop or literature circle time. But independent reading within content fields is for everyone. Remember our dream? Passing the state exam is not enough—we're trying to raise informed citizens and enthusiasts here!

The classroom structure that can help you move students is this direction is known as reading workshop. See the following box to see what it looks like.

READING workshop schedule in a typical content-area class

5 minutes	*Short* minilesson—can be on how to use workshop effectively, on a reading strategy, or on some aspect of content being studied
5 minutes	Reading choices introduced by teacher—either a wide range or a selection centered on a curricular topic
15–30 minutes	Reading and journal-writing time, with teacher circulating for brief one-on-one conferences with students to provide help, answer questions, or observe how students are doing
5 minutes	Reports on interesting ideas students have learned, discussion of issues brought up in articles, or self-reflection on doing this kind of reading, which isn't like the textbook

Of course you won't be able to do this every day—you have your subject to teach. But as you'll see in the following classroom examples, subject-area teachers find natural places in the schedule to fit in reading workshop time.

Meghan Dillon is an art specialist who uses reading workshop in her teaching at many different grade levels in the Kettering, Ohio, schools, outside Dayton. With the GM plant long gone, this town has become much more of a low-income community than in the past. So, you might ask, reading in art? But while Meghan loves to work in the studio with her students, she also asserts, "We're readers. Every lesson ties into a book"—especially picture books used as mentor texts. "I'm a picture book fiend," she tells us, and since she's an artist, we can understand why. Whenever students finish a project early, they are expected to read. But this can happen only if you have plenty of books and articles for students to choose from. Meghan maintains a subscription to *Scholastic Art* (check it out at http://art.scholastic.com) along with an endlessly growing collection of art-focused reading materials. Meghan has collected books

Art

on art and art history for years, ever since graduate school. She maintains a list on the Web, on Shelfari. She cadges PTO funds for more books whenever she can. She borrows from the school library and the public library. "I flood them with books over the course of the year," she says of her classes. It's this large collection that enables her to give students lots of choices of valuable texts to read. And to whet their appetites, she reads relevant excerpts aloud whenever there's an extra scrap of time.

> *. . . subject-area teachers find natural places in the schedule to fit in reading workshop time.*

Meghan weaves student-choice reading into her more direct teaching as well. To expose students to a wide variety of artists, Meghan uses *Getting to Know the World's Greatest Artists*, a forty-four-book series. Each book is just thirty-two pages long, but is filled with high-quality photos of each artist's work. Meghan starts by having the kids mull over the various books in the set for about fifteen minutes, looking for an artist they might be especially interested in. Then each student chooses one—they battle over the most famous, of course, but the previewing helps to reduce this, and it's OK for several students to choose the same person. After the kids read their books and complete an organizer to record key information, Meghan takes them through a series of slides, one for each artist. With each slide a student pops up to provide a brief summary of information about that artist, so the whole class takes over the teaching role for the period. When Meghan's students first arrive at the start of the year, they are skeptical to find reading a part of art class, but they quickly grow accustomed to it. Meghan knows that not all her students will become great artists, but she aims to make them all advocates for art, and reading supports this goal.

Further, Meghan periodically sets up centers to enable students to engage in a variety of activities during a class period. ("Centers aren't just for first graders, you know.") Of five centers in the room, three are for doing quick art activities, one is for student-choice reading, and one involves technical reading of directions that students must follow to create a small piece of art—how to do a water-color resist, or one of the paper-folding arts. With modeling and practice, the kids become expert at moving through most of the centers within a one-hour period.

Math If student choice of nontextbook reading seems like a surprise in art, how about math? At Westbrook High School in Westbrook, Maine, math teacher Tina Soucy schedules student-choice reading time about once every ten days in her Financial Literacy course. The reading is part of the once-per-quarter inquiry projects that the students complete. They browse articles on the Internet (with help from lists and websites that Tina provides) to find topics they wish to research, and then to find additional articles to expand their knowledge of chosen topics. Their reports must include at least four references, though Tina urges that wider reading is likely to produce a stronger report.

The topics tend to range widely, but always focus on financial aspects of the issues that engage the kids. Some typical topics are the economics of genetically modified foods, food safety, the marketing of pharmaceuticals, government deficits, and the recent "fiscal cliffs." Students often gravitate to controversial issues, though Tina is careful not to communicate her own positions on them, instead simply helping students to find as much accurate information as possible. Fortunately, the Internet is readily available since the state of Maine provides laptops for all middle and high school students. Tina welcomes many modes of reporting, including PowerPoint presentations and more traditional oral reports.

The Financial Literacy course does have a textbook on financial algebra that Tina uses, plus two additional resource texts. However, these tend to be very dry, so she supplements them with contemporary news articles that bring the topics to life. This use of wider reading is now migrating gradually to other math courses in the school. Fortunately, the Common Core math standards support the application of mathematical concepts to real-world applications. But it's not surprising that Financial Literacy is very popular with the Westbrook students, even though it's a course that involves plenty of work.

> *Classroom workshop is not a piece of content or a unit, or another maddening mandate that overloads your curriculum . . .*

Classroom workshop is not a piece of content or a unit, or another maddening mandate that overloads your curriculum—it's simply a powerful classroom management structure that allows students to work on individually chosen topics *for learning in your subject* and to receive individualized attention from the teacher. It's a strategy that secondary English teachers and elementary teachers have employed for reading and writing for many years, guided by experts like Donald Graves, Lucy Calkins, and Nancie Atwell. A workshop approach is also a regular feature of science, shop, art, music, drama, and just about any other lab or performance class. But we shouldn't allow only a limited group of our teaching force to monopolize such a valuable instructional tool, particularly when it's so handy.

Along with providing a structure for students' real-world reading in your curriculum, there are some further powerful advantages to using reading workshop:

Eight Benefits of Independent Reading Workshop

1. Workshop signals that reading and studying a subject is important enough to give students class time for it.

2. Workshop offers students a wide variety of real-world reading in any subject.

3. It can be run in short chunks of time, and does not have to involve extensive assessment.

4. Workshop allows the teacher to directly teach learning strategies or course content through short minilessons, with students immediately applying what is taught while it's fresh in their minds.

5. It enables the teacher to easily observe students' understanding or difficulty with a concept through one-on-one conferences that take place during reading time. This can alert the teacher to reteach difficult material, correct misconceptions, or add information that she discovers the students need.

6. Through a workshop structure, the teacher can provide students with individualized support. As more schools introduce differentiated instruction, classroom workshop is one of the most effective tools for addressing students' greatly varying needs.

7. Workshop promotes student buy-in because it introduces individual choice into the instructional mix. In research studies, students strongly state that choice is a major motivator for their reading—but they also testify that school rarely provides this opportunity (Worth and McCool, 1996).

8. Workshop enables the teacher to employ interactive student involvement as a significant element of instruction—through immediate application after a minilesson, through dialogue with the teacher during conferences, and through sharing time at the end of the workshop session. Again, research tells us how important this is. The Consortium on Chicago School Research (Smith et al., 2001) found that through grade 8, students' scores on standardized reading tests were 5.2 percent higher than average in classrooms with high levels of interactive instruction, and 4.5 percent below average in settings where interactive instruction is neglected.

MAKING reading workshop work

* The classroom has a good assortment of readings, from library resources to copied articles to bookmarked websites. Most teachers who use workshop have to gradually build up their collection over time (see pages 78–84).
* The teacher provides an opening "minilesson" on content or a reading strategy. The teacher gives brief descriptions of the various reading selections so students can choose meaningfully.
* Individual students decide which selection they will read.
* Reading time is provided in class.
* While reading, students take notes or jot responses, applying the concept or reading strategy just taught.
* During reading time, the teacher confers with individual students to answer questions, provide help to those who are confused, and gain information on students' level of understanding.
* The teacher records observations briefly to develop a record of students' progress and/or needs.
* At the end of the reading period, several students report on what they've learned, or how the reading strategy worked.
* Other students are encouraged to respond or ask questions, so that the reporting becomes a learning activity for everyone.
* Assessment is brief and simple—give points for participation, completed notes, presentations.

Conduct Minilessons

Minilessons are important not just for teaching or reteaching content, but also for showing students how to use workshop time effectively and for initiating activities that help kids focus on and process the ideas they are reading about. So these lessons are key for both content and effective classroom management. Minilessons should, indeed, be mini. The idea is to briefly refresh or focus kids on one important idea or strategy that will be relevant to the reading they're about to do—and then let them get reading, so they can apply it. Minilessons can be divided into three main categories: (1) the rules and procedures of workshop itself, which you will conduct primarily at the start of the year, when you first introduce the structure; (2) reading and thinking strategies (many of which we've provided in Chapter 5); and (3) lessons on course content.

Here's a generic minilesson structure that makes sense at any grade level, in any subject. It's built around the Gradual Release of Responsibility structure that we describe on pages 89, 92 in Chapter 5, as well as the approach described by Lucy Calkins (2013) in her numerous workshop resources.

* First, the teacher establishes a connection with material that the students have recently been working on, or a concept or process they've struggled with: "I noticed yesterday when you were working on those problems in class . . . "
* Then the teacher explains and models her thinking or application of the process or concept.
* Third, students as a whole group help the teacher with a second quick application of what's being taught.
* Next, students try it out once again on a fresh example, this time individually or in pairs.
* Finally, the teacher links the lesson to today's reading—"So as you're reading these articles, be sure to think about . . . and explain in your journal some spot in your reading that connects with it"—and sends students off to use it on their own.

And now for a few typical minilessons for helping workshop to run smoothly:

Minilesson on how to choose reading matter wisely. Model the process yourself, showing kids how to read a few sentences to see if the piece focuses on what they need or want to learn, and whether it is too hard or too easy (a quick application of the think-aloud strategy described in Chapter 5). Use several examples, one very technical and difficult, one that you gauge as too easy and unchallenging for your students, and one that is just right. Perhaps also include one that turns out not to be relevant to the topic you are interested in. This will help students learn to skim the reading to get a quick sense of what it's about and whether it's likely to be relevant, or of interest to them.

Minilesson on what to do if the student needs help but the teacher is busy. Young people need to understand that you can't help everyone at once, so they need to have useful alternative activities while they wait for you. Brainstorm with the students to identify some options—quietly ask a fellow student for help; write in your journal about what is giving you trouble; look up confusing words in the dictionary; find another article on the same topic and see if it explains the concept more clearly or answers your question; and so on. But we hope you don't use our list. Instead, have the class propose such items and record them on a large piece of newsprint to be posted on the wall so you can refer to them instantly when students gets antsy.

Minilesson on how to ask for help in a conference with the teacher. Students having difficulty often express only a global sense of being stuck or lost. Model for them how to pinpoint where the confusion lies, so the conference can zero in on their real needs. This will probably involve solving a problem or answering a quiz question using a think-aloud, in which you talk through each step of your thinking. Build in a couple of spots to portray yourself as confused and describe the confusion in detail—"Wait a minute. I'm not sure if I should add here, or subtract. What was that rule again?" In addition, explain to students the kinds of questions you'll be asking them in conferences, and again model the sort of responses that are helpful.

Other valuable minilessons on helping students use reading workshop effectively:

* what kids can do when finished with their reading (record thoughts in a reading log, list vocabulary words learned or unrecognized in the reading, complete a project on the reading, choose a new book or article—whatever you and the students have agreed to be the most productive next steps)
* what needs to go into each student's reading folder
* how to work quietly with other students, if student-to-student conferences are a part of the process
* lessons on any of the other aspects of workshop, which we are now about to describe

Keep Students on Task During Reading Time

Effective and creative classroom management is key to making workshop go well. A valuable strategy used by teachers experienced with this structure is a practice called "status of the class," initially popularized by Nancie Atwell's groundbreaking book *In the Middle* (1998). After completing a minilesson and reviewing students' reading choices, the teacher asks each student to briefly—in a simple phrase—state what he or she has chosen to read during the workshop period. Some teachers jot these choices on a list with the students' names preprinted, while others have the students themselves record their reading in a log in their reading folder. This process establishes a quick contract with students about the work they are about to do, and also lets the teacher know if particular students need help or are unsure of how to proceed. These will be the first ones she gets to for conferences during workshop time.

Conduct One-on-One Conferences During Reading Time

When helping individual students during workshop, ask questions to assess their progress and needs. Ask them to summarize one main idea from the material they've been reading, explain one important concept, or indicate a question they have. If you've just taught a new concept or a learning strategy, you can ask about it—"Can you tell me about the last comment that you wrote in your journal?" Give some responsibility to the student by asking what help he or she wants from you. Then respond briefly and teach just one thing, to keep the conference short and focused, so the student can learn but not feel overwhelmed.

Your aim in the conferences is twofold—well, maybe three. First, to provide help where it's needed; second, to see for yourself quickly and promptly whether the kids are getting it and learning what they need to; and third, to keep them on task by maintaining your presence around the room. That's why it's much better for you to go to the students, rather than having them come up to your desk. And also why it's important to keep the conferences short. If you see that a student needs a great deal of help, this isn't the setting to provide it. Nor will you get to every student in a single workshop period; indeed, you shouldn't even try. Think in multiperiod stretches. Just keep track so you don't completely miss some kids over the course of several sessions. We're also looking for efficiency here, so if you notice most of the class experiencing the same problem, it's a time-waster to repeat the explanation with each individual. Instead, call a brief halt to the reading and do an on-the-spot minilesson. Or use some debriefing time at the end of the workshop session. Minilessons can come before or after reading time. The idea is to give kids exactly what each one needs, when they need it.

Record Observations of Students' Reading and Understanding

Meeting with students during reading workshop enables you not only to assess students, but also to inform yourself about their learning needs and their achievements. But you'll need some tools to help you keep track of all the data in simple and manageable ways. Many teachers have students keep folders containing not only ongoing work, but also handy forms that summarize their progress—sheets that list books and articles they've read, learning goals they've set for themselves, skills and concepts they've mastered, and reflections on their learning. A good resource for this record keeping is *Classroom-Based Assessment* by Bonnie Campbell Hill, Cynthia Ruptic, and Lisa Norwick (1998). It includes a great collection of forms on a CD-ROM disk so you can alter them to suit your own needs. One inspired and easily recreated tool is a sheet with squares the size of small sticky notes, plus space above each square to enter a student's name. After you talk with a student, simply jot on a sticky note a few words about what took place or what you observed and slap it in the student's square. As these notes accumulate, transfer them to separate sheets for each student and, presto, you've got a continuous anecdotal record of each student's progress without any extra time or effort expended. When we first learned about this we slapped our foreheads—why didn't we think of that!?

Make Student Sharing and Presentations Really Work

The goal of student sharing at the end of workshop is not merely to monitor whether kids did the reading, but to make the classroom a more active learning community. As research reminds us, creating a community of learners is one of the keys to better reading and higher student achievement. In our highly individualized and competitive culture, however, we're often working against the grain when we attempt to promote community in the classroom. Students who are new to workshop structures may be accustomed to just sitting absently as their friends deliver their reports. To reverse this, teachers need to make explicit that class members are to respond, ask questions, and connect what they've heard to their own reading. Thoughtful teachers address this in a variety of ways.

One model we really admire comes from first-grade teacher (yes, you heard that right) Kristin Ziemke at Burley School in Chicago. When her students or teams are presenting to the rest of the class, every kid who's listening has a clipboard with two columns of Post-it notes preattached. As they enjoy the presentation, they use the Post-its to jot down several "new learnings" on the left side of their clipboards and some "questions for the presenters" on the right. When a report is done, audience members get up and place their signed Post-its on one of two charts labeled (you guessed it) new learning and questions. Kristin then orchestrates a debriefing during which the presenters notice and celebrate what they have successfully taught people—and then answer questions from the ample posted list. Badda bing, audience accountability.

Use Web Tools for Sharing and Publishing When Possible

The Internet is home to a constantly growing number of valuable tools that students can use to share responses to their reading, hold extended discussions, and create and share presentations on what they've learned from what they've read. Of course, your school needs to have the resources for ready student access to networked computers, and this varies widely. Maine, as we have noted, provides laptops for every middle and high school student in the state. Schools in communities with strained budgets aren't as fortunate right now. But as costs for equipment come down, hardware becomes easier to use, and technology becomes more universally used, we hope that most schools will be able to provide machines for all students.

Here are the tools that tech-savvy teacher Mindi Rench of Northbrook Junior High School (near Chicago) currently likes and sees various online colleagues use. We know there will be new ones by the time you are reading this book, but the list will give you a good idea of what's possible:

> ✳ **Edmodo.** This website is designed especially for school classrooms and enables a teacher to communicate with all the students in a class, and vice versa. Teachers can post assignments, have students upload written pieces and presentations to share with the teacher and one another, communicate with parents, and much more. The following screenshot shows an Edmodo page from Sara Ahmed's eighth-grade social studies

Oct 5, 2011 | Reply | Public | Tag

Me to Language Arts -201-, Language Arts -203-

Homework: 10.5.11
Reading: 30 mins
SS: Truman Doctrine/Iron Curtain Speech Article FILES ATTACHED
Question sheet and hypothesis #1 Who was responsible for the Cold War?
Science: Bibliography, hypothesis
Math: None
XC MEET TOMORROW AND NO PRACTICE ON FRIDAY.

truman_on_greece.docx ⌕Preview

coldwardocs.docx ⌕Preview

Edmodo Screenshot

From the top, here's what you're looking at in the screenshot above:

Date

Ms Ahmed's Avatar

Me to Language Arts (note from Ms. Ahmed to two classes, 201 and 203)

Homework: date

Reading: expected amount of reading time

Social studies: titles of the two attached articles

Question sheet and hypothesis: #1 (line two of the social studies homework; refers to a handout kids have containing the big question: Who was responsible for the Cold War?)

Science: homework assignment

Math: homework assignment (none tonight)

XC: note to members of the cross-country team (Ms Ahmed is the coach)

Thumbnails of two attached articles

class in Chicago. As you can see, Sara is using it to assign homework, distribute two handouts, and give a discussion topic for this evening's online posting—and even letting the cross-country team members know about their practice schedule.

* **Google Drive.** At this widely used site, students can store written work, collaborate on documents they've posted there, and add comments for one another. Along with written documents, students can include PowerPoint presentations, videos, music, pictures, spreadsheets—just about anything that can be stored electronically. One advantage is that large files can be easily shared, which can be problematic on email.

* **Kidblog.org.** Blogs are excellent for enabling students to reflect informally on their work as they do it. Whether a student is struggling with a math problem, celebrating that she's finally solved it, seeking help from a friend, or sharing thoughts on her own real-world reading about your subject, a blog is an easy place to just get the thoughts down. Obviously, there need to be rules for what can be discussed, and monitoring to maintain decorum, mutual support, and respect among the students.

* **Padlet.** Here we have the electronic equivalent of sticky notes, admit slips, and exit slips (see Chapter 5, pages 118–120, 140–142). Each student can create his or her own word/idea wall for responding to reading, brainstorming, or otherwise processing ideas. A teacher can create a class wall as well, where all the students can add their comments.

* **Glogster.** A cross between a blog and a poster, this app allows kids to combine text, images, and video clips onto an animated, distinctively designed poster that allows viewers to explore many dimensions of the glogger's thinking.

* **Today's Meet.** This site enables a teacher to set up student discussions. Some people use the site for "backchannel" exchanges that students carry on during a presentation or class activity, though this can be difficult to keep focused on the curriculum. Specifically permitting discussion times, on the other hand, can allow for silent student interchange among one group while others are reading or working on other tasks.

* **Animoto.** A number of sites enable students to combine presentation of content with music or other sound effects. Animoto has been around for

several years (a lifetime in this industry) allowing kids to upload photos, video clips, text, and music. Then the Animoto "engine" combines them into a slick video podcast. This is a great ways of sharing the results of research reports. One cool feature: every time you upload the same materials, Animoto makes a fresh program. So kids can remix several times, tinker with ingredients, and then choose a favorite.

What About Assessment?

If you do a good job with workshop and provide lots of fascinating stuff for young people to read, you won't, in the long run, need to grade their reading. Since our goal here is to create habits of intrinsically motivated literacy, a nonevaluated reading period is what we'd all probably prefer. However, we know this is the real world, and kids are so accustomed to receiving some sort of grade for everything they do that it can be hard to wean them from that expectation. Still, the more we can reduce the role of grading, the more workshop will serve its long-range goal—and the less burdensome it will be for you, the teacher.

So our suggestion: have students keep reading journals in which they both record ideas they've read about and respond with their own thoughts. The double-entry journal described on page 128 is a very serviceable model for this task. It's not difficult to quickly review the journals later and give simple checks or points for completed entries. Just don't discourage yourself by taking home armloads of journals from all your classes at once. Spread out the paper load by rotating collection dates. You'll get a clearer picture of the progress and understanding in each class that way, as well. And *don't* mark or grade those learning logs for grammar, spelling, or neatness. The journals are informal notes, tools of thinking, not formal papers for a public audience. Enough said.

Always the Big Question: Time

There is still one big question about workshop that teachers most frequently ask: How do I possibly find time to fit independent reading workshop into my schedule? After all, very few of us have big chunks of time lying fallow in our teaching days, waiting for some activity to come along. So first, if time is tight, focus the readings on content you know you must teach, but as much as possible, look for short real-world articles and essays that cover the topic rather than just the textbook.

Start with short SSR (sustained silent reading) time periods for reading and expand them if it's working well and achieving your learning goals for kids. Many teachers struggle at first with how to fit workshop into their time schedule, but increase its use as they find they can spend less time on lecture, covering the same material more effectively with this interactive strategy. "Coverage" is, in some ways, an imaginary issue. If you skim over everything lightly and the students don't get it, they'll still do badly on the final exam. Conversely, if they've really grasped some central concepts of your course through their own choice of lively readings, they're more likely to become engaged and learn more from even the pedestrian stuff.

So when first getting started, hold reading workshop at least once a week to make sure students are familiar and comfortable with the process. Then later, you can vary the frequency according to need and the amount of time available. If you simply can't squeeze it in at least once a week, run workshop frequently for a period of four or five weeks and then let it rest, so you achieve some sense of continuity and focus on real reading for periods of time during the year. In addition, teachers often use the basic workshop time pattern even when having students read from whole-class assigned textbook material; it helps get them accustomed to the structure and take advantage of the many benefits that workshop provides.

> *So when first getting started, hold reading workshop at least once a week to make sure students are familiar and comfortable with the process.*

A final challenge: teachers may wonder, "Sure, I can make this work with a topic students will find exciting, like body chemistry, but what about something more technical, something like, say, 'moles' in chemistry?" OK, we realize that because the workshop hasn't been employed as much as it could be in most subjects, collections of good, interesting, short articles aren't precollected for us. It will take time for good teachers to build up their article sets and begin sharing them more widely. Still, let's take up this challenge, as an example of how we might proceed.

Chemistry

For those who have forgotten their high school chemistry, let's pause for a little minilesson. (And no complaining, English teachers—we expect our students to learn this stuff!) A mole is a standard number for counting atoms (or any other objects), specifically 6.022×10^{23}—a pretty huge number. It's a handy number for chemists because the amount of any element, in grams, that is equal to the element's atomic mass has exactly that number of atoms. If that sounds confusing, an example can help: twelve grams of carbon twelve contain exactly one mole or 6.022×10^{23} of atoms. This standard number allows chemists to determine the relative amounts, by weight, of each chemical that they need for a chemical reaction, and the amount of the chemical (or chemicals) that will be produced. For example, to produce methane gas, CH_4,

TIPS for helping
workshop run smoothly

* **Start with short time periods for reading** and expand them if it's working well.

* **Make minilessons work** by connecting clearly with recent work, by modeling, and by using gradual release of responsibility.

* **Provide short minilessons to help students use workshop effectively**—for example, on how to choose reading matter wisely or how to participate in a teacher-student conference.

* **Keep students productive during reading time** by conducting a "status of the class" check-in before students begin to read, and by conferencing with individuals.

* **Make one-on-one conferences effective** by asking questions that probe students' thinking and use of reading strategies.

* **Use student folders** to keep the kids' responses and record keeping organized.

* **Document students' reading and understanding** by using forms that allow for quick entry and scanning of information by both you and the student.

* **Make student sharing and presentations interactive** by having the rest of the class ask questions and give comments.

by combining carbon (C) and hydrogen gas (H_2) you don't just take one gram of carbon and four grams of hydrogen and mix them together—the hydrogen is much lighter for the same number of atoms. Instead, you'd combine one *mole* of carbon to each two moles of hydrogen gas (two, not four, because each molecule of the gas has two hydrogen atoms, and you need four hydrogen atoms to each carbon atom to make methane).

OK, stay with us one last step. To get one mole of carbon, you'd weigh out twelve grams of it—because twelve is carbon's atomic mass. And for two moles of hydrogen gas, you'd need 4.03 grams—1.00794 is hydrogen's atomic mass (a few of the hydrogen atoms have an extra neutron in their nucleus, making them heavier), times two atoms of hydrogen in each molecule, times two again. In learning about chemical reactions, students are typically asked to calculate just how much of each chemical will go into and come out of a reaction. And real chemists use this kind of calculation when they design chemical manufacturing processes so that all the source material gets used up efficiently.

Now how about some readings to connect this technical concept to the real world? Steve spent some time on the Web and easily located plenty of mole material. Of course he had to vet all websites for accuracy, and some sources were more reliable than others. But consider:

* A clear explanation of the mole as a unit of measuring numbers of atoms or molecules, why it's helpful, and how it's used in chemistry: www.wyzant .com/Help/Science/Chemistry/Moles/.

* Another excellent explanation of moles is the short YouTube lecture from the Khan Academy, at www.youtube.com/watch?v=AsqEkF7hcII.

* The number of atoms that equal a mole is 6.02×10^{23}. But how did chemists figure out that huge number? The following article explains several methods. It's tougher reading, but enthusiastic science students might want to tackle it: www.scientificamerican.com/article.cfm?id=how-was-avogadros-number.

* The number that is a mole is also called Avogadro's number. Actually, Avogadro didn't figure out the number, so who was this guy—a rather ugly but rich eighteenth- and nineteenth-century Italian lawyer and political activist who dabbled in chemistry. And what exactly did he discover that's connected with moles? A short biography can be found at http://www .famousscientists.org/amedeo-avogadro/.

* Since mole measurements are used to figure out amounts of substances to mix together for chemical reactions, chemical engineers must know about them. So what exactly do chemical engineers do in their jobs? Students can read about it here: http://chemistry.about.com/od /chemicalengineerin1/a/chemicalengineer.htm.

* And as motivation for young people to study this stuff, what do chemical engineers get paid? Actually, quite a bit: http://chemistry.about.com/od/ educationemployment/a/chemical-engineer-salary.htm.

* Not only do chemical engineers earn a lot of money, they also have a sense of humor. Read about the annual celebration of Mole Day at www.moleday.org.

✱ They even enjoy reading comic books—and of course connecting them with chemistry and the atomic number and atomic mass that are part of mole calculations. Check out the website "A Periodic Table of Comic Books" at www.uky.edu/Projects/Chemcomics.

Obviously, we could keep going with this list. We've varied the kinds of readings to cover a range of issues: a specific technical application of the concept of moles and molecular weight, the use of such information in possible student futures (of which many students have little knowledge), and a bit of sheer fun that a group of chemistry students have had with one part of the topic. Nowadays, such searches are unbelievably easy compared to life before the Internet. There's no reason for us to hesitate using it to engage kids with our subjects by providing choices among real-world articles, giving them time to read them, and freeing you, the teacher, to help individual students.

Content-Area Book Clubs

All across the country, every month, hundreds of thousands of thinking Americans gather in voluntary adult reading groups. There are countless variants—literary book clubs, beach-book clubs, bible study groups, self-help book clubs, professional journal study groups, Civil War history clubs, and online book chats. The number of such groups has exploded in the last two decades, doubtless owing to TV's Oprah Winfrey, who showcased book clubs and sparked their formation in living rooms, community centers, bookstores, church basements, and, in Chicago, we know, a few bars. So why not in middle and high schools?

In Chapter 4 we emphatically claimed that teenagers should be reading some of the same nonfiction books that thoughtful, curious members of the adult community choose. We can use book clubs to make that happen. Let's visit Nancy Steineke and Mike Dwyer's American Studies class at Andrew High School and see what school-based, content-area book clubs look like.

American Studies

This elective junior-year course puts two teachers and fifty-six kids together for two periods a day to study integrated American literature and U.S. history. Right now, the kids are dividing into their "1929–1969" book clubs. Groups of three or four students are pulling desks together, each preparing to discuss their chosen historical novel set either during the Depression, World War II, or the Cold War era. Among the choices were multicopy sets of books that Nancy and Mike have assembled over the years:

The Eye of the Needle, Ken Follett
Summer of My German Soldier, Bette Greene
Snow Falling on Cedars, David Guterson
The Great Escape, Paul Brickhill

The Journey Home, Yoshiko Uchida
Wings of Honor, Tom Willard
Fail-Safe, Eugene Burdick and Harvey Wheeler

The book clubs began two weeks ago, when Nancy and Mike book-talked all six titles and invited each student to submit their first, second, and third choices. Nancy and Mike then sat together and formed the small groups, giving kids their first choice wherever possible.

Now, as groups pull their chairs together, students take out their books, which are fletched with sticky notes, along with their learning logs. Today, the first order of business is a five-minute warm-up conversation, much like the personal chit-chat that adults typically do before undertaking a small-group task. Each day, Nancy offers a generic topic ("the best movie you've seen lately," e.g.), and the rule is that every kid in the group must say something. By now, the students prefer picking their own subject, and the group of girls in the back is definitely warming up with their home-grown question: "What do you look for in a boy?" Kids take turns asking follow-up questions and jot notes about their partners' responses.

Nancy and Mike call time and signal the switch to book talk. Since this is the last of several meetings, and the kids have now finished reading their books, there is much talk about endings, about big themes and resolutions. The *Fail-Safe* group is having an especially lively conversation. A couple of kids are truly disturbed by the ending, in which the U.S. government allows New York City to be destroyed by a nuclear bomb as payback for an accidental attack on Moscow. Bill and Alice are amazed that the Russian and American governments would accept such a double tragedy instead of engineering some kind of diplomatic escape. Chris, the group's resident tough guy, just shakes his head and says: "An eye for an eye, man." "But they're not soldiers, all those innocent people in New York," protests Farina. And then an extended argument develops about military versus civilian casualties in a war—and whether there is ever any such thing as a "noncombatant."

Circulating through the room, you notice that the students are using several tools to support their discussion, to remind them of ideas they want to share. Kids have marked important passages of their book with small Post-it notes, jotting a few key words or a question on each, hanging these off the edge of the book. In their journals, they have also made a drawing or illustration, some kind of graphic response to each section of the book. When the time seems right, they'll show their picture around, as another way of spurring conversation. And finally, each student maintains and draws conversational material from two lists in their journals: one of "personal connections" (what the book means to me) and another of "historical connections" (tracing the setting and events back to topics studied in the history class and textbook).

Origins of Content-Area Book Clubs

Over the past twenty years, Harvey has been working to transfer this naturally occurring literacy structure from living rooms to classrooms. Back in the '70s and '80s, the idea began as "literature circles" in English classes. Smokey's book of the same name (2002) has been used by teachers to set up similar reading discussion groups in their classrooms, usually with novels. Then, with Nancy Steineke, he wrote *Minilessons for Literature Circles* (2004), which showed how small, peer-led discussion groups didn't require whole novels. You can have a perfectly delightful small-group discussion about a poem or a short story. And it works with other genres too—historical novels, biographies of scientists, and works of social science, politics, or sociology—not to mention short nonfiction articles and "text sets" of several such selections.

More appropriately labeled "reading circles" or "book clubs" when we consider activities for the full curriculum, these structured discussion groups combine two powerful educational ideas: *collaborative learning* and *independent reading*. Simply defined, book clubs are small, peer-led discussion groups whose members have chosen to read the same article, chapter, or book. These groups can be organized in a wide variety of ways, but the consistent elements are:

* Students choose the reading materials.
* Small groups (three to five students) are formed, based upon choice of texts.
* Grouping is by text choice, not by "ability" or other tracking.
* Different groups choose and read different materials.
* Students keep notes that help guide both their reading and the discussion.
* Groups meet on a regular, predictable schedule to discuss their reading.
* Discussion questions come from the students, not teachers or textbooks.
* Personal responses, connections, and questions are the starting point of discussion.
* A spirit of playfulness and sharing pervades the room.
* The teacher does not lead any group, but acts as a facilitator, fellow reader, and observer.
* When book clubs finish a cycle, groups may share highlights of the reading with classmates through presentations, reviews, dramatizations, or other media.
* New groups form around new reading choices, and another cycle begins.
* Evaluation is by teacher observation and student self-evaluation.

In other words, if you walk into a classroom where book clubs are meeting, you'd expect to see perhaps five or six small groups of students sitting together and talking quietly about an article, chapter, or book they have chosen. Along with the reading material, students will have brought some form of notes (a journal entry, a special thinksheet, some annotations on the text itself) that they created while reading, and that now serve as a source of discussion topics. The teacher circulates through the room, visiting groups, but does *not* lead the discussions or "teach" any group.

Getting Started with Book Clubs

Let's say you've read the story about Nancy and Mike's book clubs, you've started building a classroom library in your subject area, and you have assembled some multiple-copy sets of books. Now you're ready to devote class and homework time for groups to read a trade book in your field: a biography, a historical novel, a popular trade book with good science or math content. How do you organize, monitor, and assess this work? Here's a quick rundown of the key steps.

Training

We can't plunge kids into book clubs without their knowing how they are to operate; we need to show them first. You can do that by enlisting a couple of colleagues to offer a live "fishbowl" demonstration right in your classroom—or show a videotape of an adult book club, a successful student group from another class, or your own class last semester. Or you can ask a group of students themselves (pick the most collaborative ones) to try their best at a discussion in front of the class, using a short article everyone can read first. After whatever demonstration you decide to offer, ask kids to list the specific social skills they saw in action—what did they see people doing that helped the discussion work? You can also collect negative examples (Don't interrupt! Don't hog the air! No put-downs!) and convert them into positive statements. You'll eventually come up with a list like this:

* Come prepared—do the reading, bring your notes or annotations.
* Take turns and share airtime.
* Listen actively: make eye contact, lean in, nod, confirm.
* Pull other people into the conversation.
* Ask follow-up questions.
* Piggyback on the ideas of others.
* Be respectful of others people's ideas.

* Speak up when you disagree.
* Disagree constructively.
* Stay focused on the task.
* Support your views with the article/book.
* Be responsible to the group.

If your students are already experienced in cooperative group work, this review of social skills may be all the warm-up they need. On the other hand, if collaborative learning is a brand-new way of operating, more preparation might be required before jumping into multiday, peer-led discussion of whole books.

You can practice peer-led discussion using short pieces of text (news clips, excerpts, images, or cartoons), quite small groups (pairs work fine), and short amounts of time (one to three minutes). A good way to begin is to give everyone the same minitext, have them read and make notes, and then discuss it with a single partner. Next, hold a whole-class debriefing, using your homemade list of social skills as an anchor. What worked and what didn't? Did all partners participate? How did you handle disagreements? What do you need to do differently next time? What was a question that really sparked a pair's conversation? Practice with three or four "shorties" and debriefings over a few days, until kids get a fair proportion of the social skills going (not 100 percent; they are beginners, after all). Then you can move on to bigger selections—chapters or books.

Group formation

In their pure form, book clubs are built on readers' choices of books. However, your kids may not be ready for the pure version. You may need to make some artful interventions to ensure that all groups will be functional, with a good balance of social and reading skills. We do not want you to try this activity and encounter one or two nightmare groups that career off task, undermining your enthusiasm for book clubs before it can even take root. So here's how many of our Chicago colleagues manage for "modified student choice."

Offer students five, eight, even ten different books (or articles) to choose from. The choices should encompass a range of reading levels, from thin and easy to thicker and harder, to accommodate the diverse reading levels that probably exist in your class; remember, book clubs are independent reading that should be recreational-level for comfortable, fluent reading. To help kids find the right book, give a quick (thirty-second) book talk about each title you have read yourself; for others, see if a student has read the book and can talk about it, read aloud the blurb from the back cover, or print out reviews from Amazon.com. Give students a couple of days to browse the books, suggesting that they read the first couple of pages of each book to see if the interest and readability are right. Then it's time to ballot: ask students to write down their top three choices from the alternatives. Take the ballots home and, taking your time, form wholesome (meaning, likely to function well) groups. If some kids don't get their first choice this time, because you could foresee a crashing and burning book club, you can reassure them that next time they probably will.

> *Give students a couple of days to browse the books, suggesting that they read the first couple of pages of each book to see if the interest and readability are right.*

We particularly like groups of four, because they provide for a good range of different views, while still placing significant responsibility on each member. In a group of six or seven, one or two people can always hide, hitchhiking on the efforts of others. On the other hand, groups of two or three are too small to have enough diversity, and too vulnerable to absence and other afflictions. Pragmatically, we often form groups of five, knowing that on any given school day there will probably only be four members present. Of course, we do form larger or smaller groups when the book choices point that way, but we encourage the kids to be vigilant about the potential difficulties. Six can be OK, but seven and above we usually split into two smaller groups for increased individual responsibility.

Scheduling

Book clubs need not eat up huge amounts of class time, since after initial training, the reading and note-writing is done mostly outside of class, as homework. The big scheduling questions are: How much time should we allow for students to finish a whole book, how many meetings should they have along the way, and how long should those meetings last? Many middle and high school teachers have kids divide the books into thirds and meet three times over a three-week period, for a half-hour each time. Often we use Fridays for this: read and talk about the first third of the book for this Friday, the second for next Friday, and the final third for two Fridays from now. With longer, fact-filled books like *Fast Food Nation*, you might break it into five sections, with five meetings over a three-week period. The more we use book clubs, the more we understand how important it is not to drag out a book for too long; better to hustle through it than to read just a few pages a day, thus losing the momentum of really reading. At Lake Forest High School, Maggie Forst moves things along more quickly, giving her book clubs two whole class periods a week for discussion, so they can get on a roll and finish books faster.

Note-taking choices

For student-led book clubs to work, it is vital that kids intentionally capture their responses while they are reading. Kids need to grab those thoughts right away and save them—after all, they may be reading at home, in the evening, a day or three days before the next meeting of their book club. And the last thing we want is for kids to come to their book clubs and say: "I can't think of anything to talk about." That's why we use one of several different tools to help readers capture their responses while (or just after) reading and bring them to the meeting. Three of these have already been outlined in Chapter 5:

> Post-it Response Notes (pages 118–120)
>
> Annotating Text (pages 121–124)
>
> Multicolumn Notes (pages 128–130)

The fourth tool, designed especially for book clubs, is called *role sheets*. With this device, we encourage students to focus on one particular kind of thinking that smart readers use. A role sheet not only stores ideas to bring to your group, it also helps set a purpose for reading when you sit down with the book. But use these with caution: abundant past experience has shown that these roles can swiftly morph into stultifying and mechanical make-work if used for more than a *brief initial training*. Here's one set of roles we often use for middle and high school kids who are reading nonfiction; you'll notice that many of them overlap with various thinking strategies in Chapter 2.

Connector. Your job is to find connections between the material your group is reading and the world outside. This means connecting the reading to your own life, to happenings at school or in the community, to stories in the news, to similar events at other times and places, to other people or problems that you are reminded of. You might also see connections between this material and other writings on the same topic, or by the same author.

Questioner. Your job is to write down a few questions that you had about this selection. What were you wondering about while you were reading? Did you have questions about what was being described? Why someone said or did something? Why the author used a certain style or structure? How things fit together? Just try to notice what questions pop into your mind while you read, and jot them down, either while you read or after you're finished.

Passage master. Your job is to locate key sentences or paragraphs that the group should look back on. The idea is to help people notice the most important, interesting, funny, controversial, or enjoyable sections of the text. You decide which passages or paragraphs are worth reviewing and then jot down plans for how they should be shared with the group. You can read passages aloud yourself, ask someone else to read them, or have people read them silently and then discuss why the passage stands out.

Vocabulary enricher. Your job is to be on the lookout for especially important words—new, interesting, strange, important, puzzling, or unfamiliar words—words that members of the group need to notice and understand. Mark some of these key words while you are reading, and then later jot down their definitions, either from the text or from a dictionary or other source. In the group, help members find and discuss these words.

Illustrator. Your job is to draw some kind of picture related to the reading. It can be a sketch, cartoon, diagram, model, timeline, flowchart, or stick-figure scene. You can draw a picture of something that's discussed specifically in the text, or something that the reading reminded you of, or a picture that conveys any idea or feeling you got from the reading. Any sort of drawing or graphic representation is OK—you can even label things with words if that helps. During the meeting, you'll wait until your drawing fits into the conversation, and then show your picture without comment to the others in the group. One at a time, they get to speculate on what your picture means, to connect the drawing to their own ideas about the reading. After everyone has had a say, you get the last word: you get to tell them what your picture means, where it came from, or what it represents to you.

Researcher. Your job is to dig up some background information on any topic related to this reading. This might include the geography, weather, culture, or history of the setting; information about the author, her or his life, and other works; information about the time period portrayed: pictures, objects, or materials that illustrate elements of the text; the history and derivation of words or names; music that reflects the subject matter or the time. This is not a formal research report. The idea is to find some information that helps your group understand the material better. Investigate something that really interests you—something that struck you as strange or curious while you were reading. Here are some places to look for information: the book's introduction, preface, or "about the author" section of the book; library books and magazines; online computer search; Web interviews with the author or experts who know the topic; other articles, novels, nonfiction, or text-books you've read.

These jobs can be useful because each one embodies a kind of thinking that mature readers actually use. So the roles can be a "backdoor" way of introducing or reinforcing the good reading-as-thinking strategies we outlined in Chapter 2.

There are several ways to put the jobs to work. You can simply name and explain these roles, putting them onto classroom posters, or have kids list them in the front of their journals, as a reminder. Or, if you want to be really official, you can make the role sheets into full-page handouts, color-coded by job, leaving most of the page blank for kids' notes.

When students use role sheets to capture connections or questions, we don't want to limit them to only that kind of thinking. We always want kids to talk about everything that struck them in the reading, not just their assigned role of the day, so the group conversations can be free-flowing and spontaneous. That's why we instruct kids to put their role sheets *facedown* when they start a meeting, and use them only if they completely run out of things to talk about. The roles should also rotate every meeting; we don't want one person to get typecast as a questioner or illustrator; instead, all the members of a group should try all the different kinds of thinking that good readers do.

Again, if you use the worksheet form of roles, restrict their use to a brief training period. We have consistently found that when role sheets are used for too long, the conversation around them becomes dutiful and dull. Anyway, kids will have more to draw on when they use one of the other three response-capturing tools, each of which invites a whole range of reader responses rather than limiting it to one sort of thinking.

The Teacher's Role

When student book clubs are meeting, the teacher's role is to assist, observe, and facilitate. Generally, this means circulating around the room, visiting groups for a few minutes each. Obviously, if you have groups that are struggling or off task, you'll be going there first. Tell kids beforehand that when you sit down in their group, they should keep talking, and not look to you for direction, topics, or feedback. You may eventually share an idea or question, but you'll do it as a temporary group member, not the boss. If they really need help, you can "donate" a rich question to give them a conversational spark, but then move on immediately. Kids must take responsibility for running these discussions; we cannot get tricked into spoon-feeding them topics. When groups have learned the norms and are humming along, you can take observational notes to aid in your assessment of the kids' work—or join a group for a longer time, as a real member. More on assessment in a minute.

Projects

Book clubs can often lead to valuable and energetic public performances. Our colleague Nancy Steineke (2009) has written a whole book—*Assessment Live!*—with ten ways for middle and high school kids to show what they know in nonessay forms—for example, tableaux, talk shows, found poetry, a skit with narration. Such projects can also give students a chance to use the tools of drama, art, writing, websites, PowerPoint, music, design, or other expressive outlets.

We enjoyed a social studies class where, after reading opposing materials about climate change, two teams of students each prepped their in-house lobbyist to "Brief the President." At the appointed moment, each lobbyist was separately ushered into the Oval Office, where a straight-faced classmate impersonated the chief executive and the lobbyist was allowed five minutes to make her strongest case. In the first briefing, the president sat in stony silence as a worried Sierra Club scientist begged for government intervention. A few minutes later, the president slapped the subsequent lobbyist on the back when she asserted that "global warming is a cuckoo left-wing plot." The student playing the president's aide immediately improvised mixing cocktails, and all three clinked imaginary glasses in a comic tableau of old-boyism.

Social Studies

Assessment

We find that teachers' number one question about subject-area book clubs is "What about assessment?" Yes, they can envision students meeting in small, peer-led conversations about books, but they worry about justifying the time expenditure and documenting the benefits. Of course, when we devote classroom time to *any* activity, we always want to know if it worked, if kids learned from it. But with student-centered, collaborative activities like book clubs, we are especially concerned that kids be accountable for careful reading, preparing thoughtful notes, and joining fully in a group conversation.

We also realize that overly intrusive assessments can undermine the spontaneity and trust that small-group conversations require. After all, adults who attend monthly book club meetings do not receive grades as they put on their coats to head home. In fact, most grown-up reading groups tolerate many levels of participation without penalty. It would be more natural and lifelike to have evaluation-free book clubs like the ones adults enjoy, but we are in the school zone now, where one seemingly inescapable function is to rank, rate, judge, and label kids' work. OK. Now that we are done regretting this truly regrettable reality, how can we assess book clubs without wrecking them?

First of all, you can give kids ten points for every time they arrive prepared with their reading materials and their notes, in whatever format you have assigned (bookmarks, sticky notes, annotations, role sheets). This is all-or-nothing grading, done by walking past the students, grading over their shoulders, ten or zero, no fives, no arguments. Some of our colleagues in Chicago use a rubber stamp with the day's date to acknowledge completion; others carry a clipboard with a class list and quickly check kids off as they scan. The quickest system: assume everyone gets ten points a day, and record zeros only for the unprepared.

Don't read (and certainly don't "correct") these reading notes; they are meant to spur memory and aid discussion, not to be a formal paper. If you try to grade them qualitatively, you'll get sucked into a time-eating spiral. If you are worried about kids creating fake notes, then collect one a day at random, just as a preventive. When a cycle of book club circles is completed, have students place all their notes in a folder—or a Book Club Portfolio, if you want to get more formal. This provides a written record of each student's reading and thinking all the way through a book. If students have used Post-it notes to mark their responses, they should put page numbers on each one first, then take them out of the book and stick them on a plain piece of paper in page number order—voilá, documentation!

Now assessment can get more interesting and substantive. Once your classroom book clubs are up and running, you have the opportunity to visit groups for a longer time—say eight or ten minutes—and observe how kids are discussing and what ideas they are sharing. Some of our Chicago colleagues use an observation form for each student that includes these elements.

Often these teachers say: "If I visit your group for ten minutes and you don't open your mouth once, it counts as 'not participating.'" Maybe this is a taste of Chicago-style tough love, but a small group cannot have a lively back-and-forth when some members don't join in for whole stretches of time. You may be surprised to find that in such a short visit you can easily discover who is prepared, recall one important comment from each member, determine what kinds of thinking the kids are doing, and also notice the social skills they manifest—or lack. When you have this kind of written record for each student, perhaps two or even three times during the course of a book, you are developing some pretty deep assessments of what they are learning—and creating another useful document for students' folders.

Book Club Observation Sheet

Name of student: _____

Prepared?   Yes / No

Participated?   Yes / No

One memorable comment or quote:

The kind of thinking this represents:

One noticeable social skill:

Part of any valuable evaluation plan is student self-assessment. You can design assessment forms, much like the teacher version above, with which students periodically stop to reflect on their group's process in writing, followed by a discussion of the "findings" and, later, a whole-class debriefing. At Washington Irving School, Kathy La Luz aimed a video camera at one book club each day, and that group was obligated at its subsequent meeting to review the clip, discuss strengths and weaknesses, and make plans for improvement. Back at Andrew High School, Nancy Steineke uses student observers—a single group member who steps out of the conversation for just one meeting to track their group's reading strategies or social skills, jotting notes on a simple form that is later shared with the group. Nancy talks in detail about such assessment strategies in her book *Reading and Writing Together: Collaborative Literacy in Action* (2002).

Culminating Assessments

Finally, if you must give kids an overall grade for a cycle of book clubs, we suggest you pay attention to both group and individual performance. Indeed, it is a core principle of successful collaborative learning that you maintain both *individual* and *group* accountability. Many of us can remember times in school when we were put in a group of ne'er-do-wells, and then got a "group grade" that lowered our average and made us hate those kids. Bad idea! We solve this by having both group and individual outcomes.

Back to Nancy and Mike's 1929–1969 book clubs. At the end of their book, each student writes an individual essay—but definitely not a traditional book report. As Nancy says, "Hey, I don't need any plot summaries—I've read all these books." Instead, the kids have a four-part assignment:

1. Recount in detail one conversation that you started in your book club.
2. Recount another conversation that started with someone else's question.
3. Describe one significant historical connection you made between the novel and the period we studied.
4. Write about one other element of the book that struck you as interesting or important.

Then, each group gets involved with a performance project that all members work on, like the ones we outlined earlier (page 250).

Or, here's another way of doing end-of-book assessments. If our desired outcome is for kids to engage in sustained and thoughtful peer-led discussion about books they have chosen and read carefully, then why grade some surrogate, tacked-on project every time? Let's get brave and grade the thing itself. All we need is a legitimate scoring rubric, a performance assessment tool that includes valid criteria for evaluating the work of a book club. And the best way to create such a tool is with students. After they have had some experiences with peer-led reading discussions (perhaps during the training period, when they were using short pieces), ask them: What do effective content-area book club members do? What are the specific traits or behaviors they demonstrate? How do they show that they are engaging with the subject matter? Kids will typically brainstorm a list with items like these:

* Support your argument with evidence from the book.
* Remember and share important information.
* Bring key passages to the group's attention.
* Pose thoughtful/interesting questions.
* Give partners good reasons to go back and reread some text.
* Challenge others' ideas diplomatically.
* Have fresh or unique ideas about the topic.
* Share your relevant background knowledge.
* Build on other people's ideas.
* Use an appropriate voice level and tone.
* Do the reading and come prepared.
* Involve other people in the discussion.
* Take your turn; speak up but don't interrupt.
* Don't hog the airtime.
* Respect others' opinions and beliefs.

Notice that some of these traits are more content-oriented (e.g., remember and share important information), while others are more about having a good social process (e.g., don't hog airtime). If kids don't offer a good balance, keep probing or add missing items yourself.

Next, put kids in small groups with this instruction: "Now, we don't want a scoring guide with seventeen criteria on it—that would be way too complicated and time-consuming. So decide which five or six elements are most important, and decide exactly how you want to word them. You may decide that some items on the list say the same thing in different words, so you may want to put those together in one statement." Give groups some time to create their short list of key book club skills, and then add one more job: "Now, take 100 points and allocate them to your criteria. You will decide if some behaviors are more important than others by the points you assign them." We like to have groups record their proposed rubrics digitally if technically possible, so they can later show their models to the whole class.

Finally, groups report back for a whole-class consensus-building meeting, where we make the big decision: Which will be our official criteria, and how many points will each be worth? After some usually lively debate, the class must agree and adopt a rubric. They tend to look something like this:

Come prepared (reading done and good notes)	10
Remember and share important information	20
Support your ideas with evidence from the book	30
Challenge others' ideas diplomatically	15
Ask good follow-up questions	15
Keep all notes, records, and forms	10
TOTAL	**100**

There's no "correct" rubric or point allocation to work toward; as long as your model includes some valid criteria for book discussion and everyone agrees to abide by it, you're set. Indeed, the whole rubric-creating exercise itself is a conversation about good reading and discussion habits—one of those rare moments when assessment actually does feed instruction. Now the next time a book club cycle is finished, the kids use the class-adopted rubric to score themselves on their overall performance. You can score them also and reconcile the two, or just review the students' scoring and adjust ratings up or down if needed.

If you use all these assessment ideas, here's what might wind up in a student's Book Club Portfolio:

daily check-ins, with points if needed

copies of all reading responses/notes/sheets/Post-its

teacher observation logs

peer observation form

video of a group meeting with written reflections

final assessment rubric form from student and teacher

optional ingredients (projects etc.)

Now that's what we call evidence, accountability, and, ta-da, grading. Of course, the best assessment of all, the one that really matters, is this: after doing book clubs, do young people want to read more books? More books about science, technology, history, politics, engineering, and math? We think they will.

Inquiry Units

Vanessa Brechling wanted her advanced algebra students to learn about exponential functions and their practical applications, and so she launched the kids on a study of historic population trends in various countries. She brought in population reports on Russia, China, India, South Africa, Germany, Japan, and the United States. Drawing on sources like the World Bank, the United Nations Population Program, the Organization for Economic Cooperation and Development, and the websites of individual countries, Vanessa was able to gather information that went back as far as a hundred years. The documents included data about birth rate surges and declines, steadily but not invariably rising life expectancies, and even the death rates of infants and women in childbirth. For example, one graph showed the strikingly low numbers of people born during World War II, and a previous dip among people born during the Russian famine and economic disruptions of the 1930s.

Algebra

To start the unit, Vanessa asks her students to choose which country they want to work on, with groups of three to five focusing on each one. Then, each group reads the reports on their country and creates a list of factors they think have had the most influence on that particular population. In Russia, for example, poor health care in the more remote regions appears to play a major role, as has an increased rate of abortion. In some underdeveloped countries, AIDS is a large factor, though high rates of childbirth still ensure the population there increases. The students' task is to create a mathematical model of the population trend in their chosen country.

Next, students graph the existing data and relate the graph to the factors they identified in the population reports. The graph provides the students with a visual representation of the population trends. Then Vanessa asks groups to find a mathematical equation to fit the data in the graph. The equation needs to incorporate both the general trend of population growth, which is best described by an exponential model, and any specific changes in growth patterns that may have occurred due to wars, epidemics, changes in birth control policies, and so on. Through their investigations, the students learn about using various forms of mathematical models to represent numerical changes in these patterns over time. Ultimately, the kids make predictions about future population trends for their countries.

The level of engagement in this project is high. Students take pride in choosing their countries and learning about them. They decorate their graphs with national symbols—flags, pictures of major exports, scenery, and wildlife. They have fun while performing mathematical analyses similar to those government statisticians do. They use the reports to find explanations for increases or drops in population. They get the satisfaction that comes from investigating actual phenomena and making sense of it. And they explain their charts proudly to visitors.

By the completion of this project, Vanessa's class has covered a variety of topics on her Advanced Algebra curriculum list. In Common Core terms, this lesson has helped students learn math that is reflected in the standards shown in the chart.

COMMON CORE math
standards covered by this inquiry

CCSS.Math.Content.HSF-LE.A.1 Distinguish between situations that can be modeled with linear functions and with exponential functions.

CCSS.Math.Content.HSF-LE.A.1b Recognize situations in which one quantity changes at a constant rate per unit interval relative to another.

CCSS.Math.Content.HSF-LE.A.1c Recognize situations in which a quantity grows or decays by a constant percent rate per unit interval relative to another.

CCSS.Math.Content.HSF-LE.A.2 Construct linear and exponential functions, including arithmetic and geometric sequences, given a graph, a description of a relationship, or two input-output pairs (include reading these from a table).

CCSS.Math.Content.HSF-LE.A.3 Observe using graphs and tables that a quantity increasing exponentially eventually exceeds a quantity increasing linearly, quadratically, or (more generally) as a polynomial function.

CCSS.Math.Content.HSA-SSE.A.1b. Interpret complicated expressions by viewing one or more of their parts as a single entity.

In listing the curriculum targets covered by her population project, we are "backmapping," a term we first learned from Wisconsin teacher Barbara Brodhagen (2007). Rather than start with a list of mandated standards and then design an isolated teaching activity to meet each one singly, Vanessa instead plans a longer inquiry project that has real-world significance, that is interesting to kids, *and* that involves key math concepts. Then she works backward to see which goals and standards the inquiry will address. This way, she can be sure that such an extended project is not taking time away from the items she needs to teach, but simply teaching them in a more powerful and memorable way.

CCSS.Math.Content.8.SP.A.1 Construct and interpret scatter plots for bivariate measurement data to investigate patterns of association between two quantities.

CCSS.Math.Practice.MP2 Reason abstractly and quantitatively. Mathematically proficient students make sense of quantities and their relationships in problem situations.

CCSS.Math.Practice.MP4 Model with mathematics. Mathematically proficient students can apply the mathematics they know to solve problems arising in everyday life, society, and the workplace.

CCSS.Math.Practice.MP5 Use appropriate tools strategically. Mathematically proficient students consider the available tools when solving a mathematical problem. These tools might include pencil and paper, concrete models, a ruler, a protractor, a calculator, a spreadsheet, a computer algebra system, a statistical package, or dynamic geometry software.

CCSS.Math.Practice.MP6 Attend to precision. Mathematically proficient students try to communicate precisely to others.

CCSS.Math.Practice.MP8 Look for and express regularity in repeated reasoning. Mathematically proficient students notice if calculations are repeated, and look both for general methods and for shortcuts.

Thanks for these correlations to Paul J. Karafiol, math teacher at Walter Payton High School in Chicago.

Inquiry: A New Old Idea

Engaging thematic units like Vanessa's may be fairly rare, but they are not brand-new. Dedicated and creative teachers have been creating such extended investigations for decades, maybe centuries. There is a whole family of project-based, problem-based, experiential, inquiry-oriented structures that focus on kids doing authentic and extended investigations of curricular topics. These approaches all share the goal of making kids active researchers instead of passive listeners. These instructional models also have a long and deep research base showing academic gains on a wide range of customary high-stakes measures. Linda Darling-Hammond's book *Powerful Learning: What We Know About Teaching for Understanding* (2008) is a compendium of this research.

Whatever the content and schedule, we can list some of the main characteristics of these projects, recognizing that creative teachers design many variations on the structures, adjusting activities to suit the learning needs of their classrooms.

Management Structures

Extended time: Students read, gather information, discuss, and write (or create other communicative materials) about a single topic for a substantial amount of time, usually over several class periods.

Focus on a significant issue: The topic involves a question or focus that connects with the larger world or a particular interest that students have. The topic often (but not always) crosses curricular boundaries. For example, subjects like climate change, recycling, globalization, animal extinction, child labor, space exploration, or gentrification inherently involve multiple disciplines—science, math, social studies, economics, and more.

Choice: The topic and questions around it are often generated by the students. Even with the more curriculum-driven inquiries, other elements of choice are introduced as much as possible—choices among subtopics, readings, other students to work with, kinds of research tasks (such as opinion surveys, Web searches, and phone calls to interview cooperating experts), and various ways for students to represent their learning.

Grouping: To allow for conversation and support and to tap the energy of social interaction, students often work on their inquiries in groups of three to five students. These groups are formed based on students' shared interest in a topic.

Teaming: Where possible, teachers conduct projects in interdisciplinary teams, each one helping students with a different aspect of the project.

Outcomes: Students complete reports, artifacts, presentations, activities, displays, and performances to represent their learning, share these with the rest of the class (or with a wider audience), respond to questions, and receive feedback.

Teacher Roles

Teach the research process: Provide activities and steps that help students become engaged, think critically about the topic, and work through stages to get it done (how to tell quickly if a book will be useful for your project, how to design good interview questions, how to take useful notes, how to decide whether a piece of information is important or tangential to your topic, etc.).

Build background knowledge: Build the "schema" or knowledge students need to comprehend relevant text, to understand and think about their topic more deeply and meaningfully.

Readings and resources: Share initial reading and viewing materials, and support the students in finding more (suggesting Internet websites, providing book lists).

Model research strategies: Instead of mostly presenting information, explicitly model your own research strategies. Just as we routinely do think-alouds with printed text, the inquiry teacher demonstrates through "search-alouds"—she projects the computer screen and narrates her thinking as she explores a topic online. Then she sits with kids side-by-side and coaches them as they try out these strategies with their own topics.

These principles can be brought to bear on wide range of curricular topics. In English, Jeff Wilhelm turned the classic play *Death of a Salesman* into an inquiry project by asking students to think about this question: "What are the costs and benefits of the American emphasis on sports?" Students started with a prereading questionnaire on their own attitudes about sports, and then went on to read sports-oriented short stories and poems, *Sports Illustrated*, newspaper sports sections, and athletes' endorsements in advertising, along with discussing Willy Loman and son Biff's interest in sports. They investigated particular questions related to the issue and concluded by making video documentaries and other visual displays. Three girls in the class even successfully campaigned to change the school's fall homecoming so it would recognize many activities, rather than just football. Jeff reports: "Every student completed the final project with uncharacteristic energy and passion" (Smith and Wilhelm, 2002).

In her eighth-grade social studies class in Chicago, Jacqueline Sanders meets a required consumer education standard with a unit she calls "Where does the money go?" She hooks kids by beginning: "You've been complaining that your parents say 'No' when you ask for that new Xbox. Do you wonder why? What do you think we'd need to know to understand whether your parents really can't afford those gifts, or are just putting you on?" The kids take some guesses about what rent and food costs are—a kind of KWL on family budgets. Jackie then distributes newspapers and sends the kids to the want ads to choose a job with a salary they think is adequate, and to write a resume and cover letter applying for it.

The resumes require a pause for a minilesson, a look at examples on sites like www .Hotjobs.com and www.CareerBuilder.com, and some classroom writing time. Then work on family budgeting begins, based on the pay offered in the job ad. The kids learn that after dividing their annual salary into monthly gross pay amounts, they've got to compute and subtract withholding taxes. Next it's time for apartment hunting on the Web and in the newspaper. But now there's more tough news: they'll need to post a security deposit, with some landlords asking for two months' rent up front. Some students now realize they're in much too low a pay bracket and go back to choose another job—an interesting lesson about goals for their future.

For food costs, the students return to the newspaper, with its Sunday ad pages. Motivated now to economize, the kids compare prices at Jewel, Dominick's, and other local chains. Next come utilities, with some initial discussion to clarify what these actually are. Jackie stipulates that heat and hot water are picked up by the landlord, so the kids just need to cover telephone and electricity—and cable, Internet, and cell phone service, if they can afford it. Interviews with parents confirm these costs. Using IRS instruction booklets,

English

Consumer Ed.

Social Studies

Math

students figure their final income tax returns. And at last they can determine if there's anything left over for treats and gifts. Since the seventh graders are working on a simpler version of the same project, the eighth graders also serve as "H&R Block" consultants to do the younger kids' taxes for them.

Obviously this project integrates economics, reading, writing, and math. While many good teachers have created projects similar to this one, we want to emphasize the range of reading for such a unit:

* newspaper want ads, apartment ads, and grocery ads
* sample resumes on the Internet
* booklets on wise shopping practices and guidelines for family budgeting
* news articles on the truth or illusion of price discounting in many stores
* articles on the comparative cost of living in various cities
* IRS form 1040EZ instruction booklet
* bills from home for electricity, telephone, groceries, car insurance, TV cable, cell phone, and other household expenses

By the time they are done with this lesson, Jackie says that most of her kids gain a new respect for how hard their parents work—and how expensive *everything* is!

What Is Inquiry?

In 2009, Smokey and our colleague Stephanie Harvey introduced a new version of small-group investigations called *inquiry circles*. Steph had already written a classic text about individual student inquiry called *Nonfiction Matters* (1998; a new edition is coming soon). Smokey had been updating a neglected fifty-year-old instructional model called "small-group investigations" (Joyce and Weil, 2008). They agreed that well-structured peer collaboration might be the missing link in many school research projects. After all, so many of today's most important developments, innovations, and breakthroughs are achieved by teams of people working together; think of the scientists on the Mars exploration team, the doctors conducting new drug trials, the tech wizards in Silicon Valley cooking up the Next Big Thing.

Steph and Smokey jokingly introduced these inquiry circles as "book clubs on steroids." Instead of just picking a book to read (as we discussed in Chapter 9), here small groups of three to five students pick a curricular *topic* to investigate—which opens up the whole world of resources to read, view, ponder, and analyze.

Types of inquiry projects

In their book, Steph and Smokey talk about four types of inquiry circle projects that can be done with small groups of students in any class:

Mini-inquiries: These are brief, in-class investigations of questions posed by students (e.g., why does lightning make noise?). Teachers call these "quick-finds" and use them to honor kids' curiosity as well as model how we get answers to questions of all kinds. These can last from five minutes to a couple of hours. We use these brief inquiries, especially early in the school year, to honor kids' curiosity and show them ways of getting answers to puzzling questions.

Curricular inquiries: More extended investigations of key concepts in the course (Civil War battles, probability in different casino games, marsupials, sonnets), these are the bread-and-butter version of inquiry circles. They can replace whole chunks of presentational teaching, and we use them all year long.

Book club inquiries: After reading a novel or nonfiction book, groups conduct research into lingering questions they have about the topic, issue, time period, author, or debate.

Open inquiries: Often done toward the end of the year, small teams of students choose their own "hot topics" or "burning questions" to investigate.

Steps in inquiry projects

In all types of inquiries, circles move through the same four steps of research:

* First they *immerse* themselves in the possible topics, browsing, marinating, building background knowledge, and wondering.
* Second, they *investigate*—develop research questions, search for information, collect data, develop hypotheses, ponder arguments, and question points of view.
* Third, they *coalesce* around a narrowed topic or question, intensifying research, digging deeper, synthesizing information, and building knowledge.

✽ Fourth, they *go public*, sharing what they have learned, demonstrating understanding, or taking action. This final, often neglected step is especially important because it gives students an authentic audience, purpose, and occasion for carefully presenting their findings.

Is this sounding a little abstract? Let's jump into Ben Kovacs' sixth-grade classroom at Burley School in Chicago, where the curricular topic at hand is civil rights. (For the classroom video of this lesson, see Harvey and Daniels, 2011.)

Ben's kids have already spent several class days studying the 1960s civil rights movement among African Americans in the South, and have a pretty good handle on the basic facts and the broad themes of justice, resistance, organizing, nonviolence, and negotiation. Now Ben wants them to explore the civil rights struggles of some other people, at other times in history. Inquiry circles will be the perfect tool for these explorations. Here's how the stages unfold.

Social Studies

Immerse. To open up the range of other civil rights struggles, Ben projects and thinks aloud about an article on migrant workers in California. The piece describes the difficult working and living conditions of migrant families in the 1970s. As Ben does his think-aloud, he stops to vocalize his own curiosity, reactions, and concerns and jot notes in the margin. After reading a sentence about how migrant families often live in a car, a tent, or a one-room shack, Ben stops. "Wow, I have to ask a question about this," he says. "How does a person's home affect their way of life? Turn and talk about that with your partner. What were your feelings when you heard this part of the article?" After a minute of conversation, he calls kids back to share. Ray volunteers: "If I were living there I'd feel endangered all the time. The weather gets bad. It would be hard to make friends if you were really poor and all the other kids were really rich. It would make me feel sad all the time." Ben quietly writes down the word *endangered* on the screen.

After working through the article, Ben points to the back table, where he has placed copies of seven short articles about different civil rights issues—the rights of women, homosexuals, workers, child laborers, elders, the handicapped, and illegal immigrants. Sending kids to the table a few at a time by their birthday month, Ben gives them plenty of time to peruse the choices and pick the article that most piques their interest. Meanwhile, he sits with the rest on the rug talking about their possible civil rights topics. Alexis' comments that she's interested in the rights of homosexuals: "Some people on my dad's side of the family are very religious, but

I have my own thoughts about gays and lesbians, and I want to learn more about their struggle." Alexis's assumption that all people of faith have a united point of view about homosexuality could become an important point to explore, and one that would easily be overlooked with a more traditional approach to teaching the subject matter.

Once they have made their selections, kids read and annotate their chosen article (and many read several). Ben helps them to mingle with others to find out who has similar interests, and gradually groups of three to five are tentatively formed around which civil rights struggle each student wants to investigate.

Investigate. Starting the next day, Ben and the kids have a "reading frenzy," gathering and devouring tons of stuff on the chosen civil rights topics, looking at online video clips, printing out key articles, and constantly talking with each other. They keep notes and documents in folders, but at this stage the emphasis is on hoovering up as much information as possible. Ben comes around to visit groups as they are feasting on this information. As he sits down with the group that's chosen to focus on LGBT rights, the kids are talking about how some states have passed laws approving same-sex marriage—and others haven't. Alexis comments, "As I was reading these articles, I've got a lot of questions. I believe the government was trying to deny them benefits like social security, when they're basically like regular marriages? The only difference is that it's same sex."

Anthony interjects, "Yeah, they are all citizens. It shouldn't really matter—it's not fair."

Alexis agrees. "I just feel like the government has been saying that all people have the same rights, but they don't."

At this point Ben suggests a next step. "This is such a complex situation you really have to read more about it. One thing I'm thinking is that you probably need a little comparing and contrasting between marriage and civil unions."

Tom blurts out, "I don't even know what a civil union is!"

Now, Ben helps the kids refine their search, homing in on missing information. Having offered this team a promising focus for their further investigations, he moves on to the next group.

Coalesce. Now the different civil rights groups target their key questions for deeper research. They've reshaped and refined their inquiry questions, and had a minilesson with Ben about how to turn these into searchable terms. Now they can dive into more focused research, using books, articles, websites, videos, library visits, telephone interviews of topic experts, and more. While subtopics are typically parceled out to individuals, teams meet regularly to monitor schedules, complete specific tasks, and plan for going public. A big part of Ben's job as an inquiry circle facilitator is to help kids monitor their plans, workload, and schedule by making mindful "midcourse corrections" as the project unfolds.

As kids continue their research, Ben calls everyone together for a check-in. "So, you guys have already done a lot, but there's only two weeks left." He shows them a list of tasks achieved and a calendar for the remaining class time. In keeping with the principles of collaborative learning, each student will both do an individual project (in this case, writing a "feature article" summarizing their research) and join in a group project. At Burley, students always have multiple ways to share their inquiry circle learning through podcasts, gallery walks, skits, displays, presentations, or other performances. Most of the time, the audience is the rest of the class, or the other sixth-grade class across the hall. But at this particular time, the school's annual learning fair is coming up. This means Ben's kids can show parents and community members what they have learned about civil rights at an event they call "Explore More."

Go Public. On the appointed day of "Explore More," dozens of parents and neighborhood friends (including dignitaries from the school district) pour into Ben's classroom to enjoy a series of performances about civil rights—all presented by puppets kids have made, voiced, scripted, and rehearsed. Some turn out to be giant-sized, bigger than life, while others are handheld, and a few will be seen on video. In just minutes, an audience of over seventy people has crowded into the room, including the rest of the sixth graders sitting on the floor in back.

Right at center stage is the set for a new TV program—LGBT News. Rodney and Amy manipulate two puppet newscasters (comically made to look exactly like them) at the anchor desk. The group has rigged up a screen that rear-projects headlines and graphics, just like on a real news show. "Welcome to LGBT News!" Amy's puppet declares as the show hits the air. Headlines appear on the screen and the kids run through some key events in LGBT history. "Connecticut judicially declared same-sex marriage legal in October of 2008," she reports. "Meanwhile, in California, advocates of Proposition 8 changed the state's constitution to a restricted definition of marriage, only opposite-sex couples, and eliminated same-sex couples' right to marry."

Accompanied by a frenzied graphic, Tyrone breaks in with an urgent "Bleep bleep! Breaking news!" From backstage, remote reporter Alexis intones: "Quite recently, both judicial and legislative methods sought to allow same-sex marriage in Iowa and Vermont," and gives the dates on which gay marriage became legal in those states. The kids go on to recount, breathlessly, more key events they have researched. While it's clear where the kids' personal loyalties lie, the show is balanced and doesn't editorialize. The broadcast wraps up with "Same-sex marriage has been a political issue for decades. People have positions on both sides of the issue. American citizens should be aware of these recent changes and be informed of more to come." Coming to the end of their allotted time (more puppets are waiting in the wings), anchorwoman Amy declares, "That's all we have time for, tune in next time for more LGBT news!" And finally, just to cap off the TV show theme, all the kids working backstage continue: "And we're closing in 5, 4, 3, 2, 1. We're off air!"

A VARIETY of inquiries

Structures for inquiry projects can vary widely, serving many instructional purposes. Considering the projects we've observed at a variety of schools, we can think of several types:

* inquiries on subtopics of traditional school subject matter—such as digestive diseases (as part of human anatomy) or abolitionist biographies (within U.S. history)

* inquiries focused on a large, often controversial question, such as "Is recent violent weather caused by human impact on the environment?" or "Should the USA have dropped the atomic bombs on Japan in WWII?"

* information-gathering on a subject that crosses several subject areas and/ or goes beyond traditional subjects, such as students delving into their own family or community histories

* simulation activities in which students take on particular roles, research how their characters would respond to a particular situation, and then enact the situation as a culminating role-play

* "jigsawing" projects, in which small groups of students become experts on one aspect of a subject area, meet to share their findings, and then engage with other teams to see what they have learned.

Management Tips for Inquiry Projects

Whatever inquiry variation you choose, based on your students' needs and your subject's demands, here are some important strategies we've learned for ensuring that inquiry projects don't get bogged down or backslide to traditional, mechanical, plagiarized research papers.

* Help the students identify a large, multifaceted, open-ended question, something people can disagree about, to focus and motivate their inquiry. This can be a single question for the whole class ("Why do we always have wars?" "Is space exploration worth what it costs?"), or separate questions for each small group or individual. It's most meaningful if the questions are ones students have posed, but your own can work too, if you choose well. Use interest-generating activities like questionnaires or comparison of brief, controversial cases to make the questions real and urgent for students—"If we can treat diseases with animal genes, will we still be 'human'?" "How do advertisers deceive us with numbers?"

* Create opportunities for student choice, even when you need to keep the focus on required course material. Sometimes enthusiastic teachers predesign a project so completely that students just march through the steps, rather than questioning and inquiring with real care. But even limited choices under a mandated curricular umbrella mean a lot to students, signaling that their judgment is valued and their voice heard.

* At the same time, you know your kids, and can probably anticipate some areas of probable interest. Have some materials ready in a number of likely areas so that you're not searching frantically at the last minute to find readings for ten—or thirty—different projects! Since finding good material the kids can understand is one of the most challenging of research tasks, you'll want to have books, articles, videos, and websites ready, or check on where they can be found on the Internet.

* If students are unfamiliar with the subject, arrange for them to do some reading of short pieces, or other information-gathering before they choose and begin specific projects. It helps to build prior knowledge so that students make choices they are truly invested in.

* Consider requiring kids to do some inquiry projects in groups of two to five, subdividing their main question into subtopics or aspects for which they take individual responsibility. That way, there will be fewer different

topics being researched at once, the kids can support each other, and you can more easily handle the demands for help. Of course, you'll often have the bright loner who demands to do something special on his or her own. Your own good judgment as a teacher will guide you here.

✱ Provide guidance for each step in the research process, and monitor kids' progress. If they're floundering on their own, they'll learn and succeed only if you help them. Conduct minilessons on how to take notes, develop searchable terms, ask good interview questions, organize information, create a Keynote/PowerPoint/podcast/video/blog—whatever your project requires and you see that the students need.

✱ Build in a meaningful process for sharing the knowledge that students have gained. For example, in an effective "learning fair," students not only create charts and demonstrations, but also present explanations and answer questions while visiting "judges"—parents, community members, other teachers, other kids—circulate and fill out response sheets. Science teacher Melissa Bryant-Neal also required her classes to ask questions of presenters, write entries in their journals after each presentation, and make lists of new vocabulary they're learning, so that the presentations became real learning experiences for the audience and not just recitations for the teacher.

✱ Don't start too big! A project that takes parts of three or four days can be plenty. Then if your structure works well, go ahead and expand it next time around.

✱ Team up with one or more teachers in another subject area, if at all possible. This will support integration of subjects and give each of you some welcome support. While most inquiry projects in most schools are planned and operated by individual teachers in their own classrooms, it's especially energizing when groups of kids and teachers can join in cross-subject investigations that involve several teachers and their classes. Some schools already invite this kind of collaboration with co-taught courses like American Studies. In a school that supports grade-level faculty teaming, teachers can easily work together on projects because they share the same kids and enjoy common planning time. They can divide up subtopics and each teach about one of them. Individuals can take charge of particular activities and the students cycle through all the classrooms. Teachers can reshuffle the kids according to the kind or focus of presentation they choose.

Assessment (and Grading) of Inquiry Projects

First, let's address the simpler subject of grading. For inquiry projects, we tend to use the same repertoire of grading strategies that we outlined for book club assessment on pages 250–251. That means awarding "good faith effort" points for preparation and engagement each day; collecting and reviewing work samples such as annotated articles; checking group work plans and schedules; using observation forms as we sit with individual groups; and scoring individual-accountability outcomes, like essays and reports.

When we come to the end of a multiday inquiry, we use a co-created rubric to score group projects or performances. For example, take a look at the rubric on the following page that Melissa Bryant-Neal's biology students helped her develop for scoring presentations on digestive diseases.

Biology

Hopefully, you can imagine creating a similar rubric for almost any inquiry topic your kids might investigate. We always begin by asking kids, "What would a successful performance in this domain look like? Sound like? Include? Avoid? Let's start by listing some of those criteria, and then we'll winnow them down to a manageable list of traits that we all agree are valuable. Next, we'll assign each one an appropriate weight, and then we'll affirm this as our assessment rubric for all groups on these projects. When people share their learning, we'll all fill out a form and hand them back to the presenting group. Afterward, I'll collect them all and compute the averages."

That probably covers our department and district needs, but what about state and national standards? How do we know that kids are learning what has been mandated and will be covered on the big tests? Back to the back-mapping strategy we introduced earlier in this chapter. Make yourself a three-column chart. In the left column, jot down *your own skill and content goals* for the inquiry project. Then in the center column, list items from your *district or state standards* that match those in the first column. In the right-hand column, list the *standards to be met if you are teaching a Common Core subject* like math or English, or a science class covered by the Next Generation Science Standards (2013).

Yes, We Do Have Time for Inquiry!

A chemistry teacher worried about covering all the topics for the district test, an English teacher with a prescribed list of novels to get through, a math teacher concerned about the kids' transition to advanced algebra and trig—all may wonder how to make room for these

Objectives	Low Performance 2 points	Needs Some Work 4 points	Getting There 6 points	Mastered 8 points	Earned Points
Case background detail	Fails to give background about the case, or gives very little.	Addresses patient profile somewhat, yet misses two or more necessary components.	Addresses patient profile in detail, yet misses one of the necessary components.	Addresses patient profile in detail: history, family, social, symptoms, mediations, lab data.	
Scientific accuracy	Many inaccuracies, terms not defined, group does not seem to understand main ideas.	Some inaccuracies; terms not explained. Group could respond to questions but not in detail.	Mostly accurate and research evident. Some terms a bit confusing but main ideas clear.	Well researched and accurate. Group could define and explain new terms and concepts, answer questions.	
Research questions	Many questions unanswered or incorrectly answered with little effort to tie to case.	Very little detail on questions and some inaccuracies.	Most questions answered accurately, with some detail missing.	All questions answered accurately, in detail, and group can relate them to the case.	
Teamwork	Group effort extremely unequal. One member dominated presentation and/or one person failed to participate.	Some group members seem more prepared & research-grounded than others.	Group mostly equal but at times one member dominated presentation or one left out.	All group members participated equally and helped each other research and explain case.	
Presentation style	Mainly reads from paper, rarely interests audience, lacks inspiration; little confidence in subject.	Reading often from paper, little eye contact, gets some audience attention but doesn't inspire discussion.	One of the qualities missing and lacking some confidence.	Gets audience attention, interests class in case, inspires discussion, shows confidence in subject.	
				SCORE	

ambitious projects when there's already so much to cover. And we won't tell you that in-depth inquiry projects don't take time—they do. But the reasons for doing these projects are irresistible.

First, the effect on students' approach to learning and reading is just too large and too important for them to miss out. These inquiry projects give students valuable experience in what it's like to be responsible, independent thinkers. We teachers often use the phrase *lifelong learner*, but we need to turn that platitude into a reality for kids. And these projects are often memorable, among the few learning experiences students remember long afterward. Too often, kids experience school reading as drudgery to muck through however they can. So it boils down to a trade-off. For sure, we can try to "cover" all the material, with most of our students passing a chapter test and immediately forgetting most of what was taught. Or, we can be more strategic in what we emphasize, going deeper into a smaller number of topics, exactly as the Next Generation Science Standards (2013) suggest. That way, we can make room for these valuable extended inquiries, so that more of our students will genuinely under-stand some key topics, and come to own the subjects we teach.

Project work may be even more essential for our struggling students. If they've had some time to read and inquire in depth on topics that matter to them, it's much more likely that they'll understand and engage with more of the standard textbook material we do have to cover. The choice is simple: stick to the textbook and lose most of these students permanently, or incorporate some inquiry projects that get students engaged and keep them going through the drier spells.

The national standards documents—not just the Common Core, but Next Generation Science Standards as well—desperately plead for students to be given opportunities to ask important questions, read a variety of real-world materials, think critically, and inquire more deeply into specific topics, rather than skim lightly over endless parades of facts. While test makers have not always honored these recommendations, we know that such in-depth inquiry is vital for the preparation of competent experts in our fields—as well as the fellow citizens who live on our block.

Anyway, the projects don't have to take forever. Melissa Bryant-Neal's digestive-system disease reports required a total of two double-period classes—one for her to introduce the structure and get the kids going on their research, and a second one for the groups to finish writing their reports and present them orally.

As tight as our curriculum and time schedules may seem to be, in-depth inquiry projects are some of our most powerful teaching strategies for making reading and learning matter for our students. At Addison Trail High School, in the suburbs west of Chicago, the very popular Freshman Studies program focuses much of its entire curriculum on interdisciplinary learning, combining English, history, and biology. Here are some typical student comments at the end of the year:

> "When I really thought about this year, I enjoyed most of it. I enjoyed the class and the discussions. Also, there was a connection between the students and the teachers that you don't see often."

> "Now that it is the end of the year, I am no longer afraid to go up to the front of the class to give a speech. I am much more confident."

> "When I first signed up for Freshman Studies, people warned me not to take the class because there were too many projects. I did anyway, and I am so glad that I did. I will miss this class so much."

journal

Help for Struggling Readers

Sushma Sharma's freshman physics class is working on real-world applications for relating distance, time, and speed of a moving object. The group includes many struggling readers who have not had much success in school. They have difficulty focusing at the start of the period and are easily distracted, particularly when they don't understand something. The problem they are working on describes the diving powers of the peregrine falcon, one of the fastest birds in the world. The falcon can dive at a speed of 97.2 meters per second. Sushma has posed the following question: If the falcon dives from 100 meters in the air at a rabbit down below, and the rabbit spots him starting the dive, how long does the rabbit have to scoot under a rock and avoid becoming dinner?

Physics

As we worked with several pairs of students who struggled with this problem, similar conversations were repeated:

> **Students:** We need some help!
>
> **Steve:** So what do you think is going on in this problem?
>
> **Student:** I don't know.
>
> **Steve** (*attempting to see what the student does and does not understand*):
> Well, what's the scene? What does the paragraph say is happening here?
>
> **Students:** Silence.
>
> **Steve:** OK, let's read it aloud. You start.

Students read the problem.

Steve: So now tell me what is happening in this situation?

Student: Well, there's a bird, a . . . a . . . [struggles with the pronunciation] falcon.

Steve: And what is he doing?

Student: He's, he's diving.

Again and again, challenges emerge as the students talk. First and foremost, they aren't accustomed to turning the words they read into mental pictures. They don't see what's happening in the problem until a considerable amount of discussion brings the picture into focus—exactly the problem that reading researchers say is characteristic of struggling readers.

Another issue is the sheer unfamiliarity of the content for these students. They don't have lots of opportunities to watch falcons dive for rabbits. None could recall seeing such a scene on television, though nature documentaries might perhaps include such feats. Similar challenges showed up in another word problem about shining a laser beam at a "reflecting panel" on the moon in order to determine its distance from the earth. Students didn't realize that a reflecting panel is simply a mirror. Nor were they accustomed to picturing that a beam of light "travels" like an object (or a wave, physicists would add). But again, as a result, they could not *picture* the situation.

Later, when the kids did construct a picture in their minds, they still needed to understand how to search through the paragraph for information to help solve the problem, and to have confidence that such information would indeed help, even if they weren't yet sure how. And finally, they needed to decide what equation would give them an answer, and why.

These were willing students who wanted to learn, even if they sometimes acted out when frustrated. They worked patiently when the teacher and observer helped. As a result of our observations, Sushma introduced the students to a problem-solving process that starts with picturing the situation from the reading and then locating the information needed. Several months later, though not every reading problem was resolved, the students were much more comfortable and successful with their efforts. During a similar in-class session solving problems about wave speed and frequency, the same kids worked steadily and seriously. They still struggled with the concepts and particularly with the vocabulary. But their confidence and commitment were visibly stronger.

We sympathize when teachers say to us, "I'm a physics teacher, not a reading teacher!" There's so much we need to do for our kids, and never enough time to do it all. And yet our close observation of their struggles tells us that to help students understand and learn from the tasks we assign them, we must work with their reading process. This does not mean we're doing the reading teacher's job. Rather, we're teaching one of the skills involved in learning and doing science—that is, understanding science material.

Oh, and by the way, if you were unsure about that falcon and the rabbit's fate: the basic equation is *rate = distance/time* (as in meters per second). Since we know the rate and the distance, but are seeking to determine the time, the equivalent equation is *time = distance/rate*. We plug in the numbers, *time = 100 m/97.2*. Looks like the poor rabbit has barely one second to hide. Thank goodness for Steve's long-ago study of physics and, we hope, the rabbit's quickness.

A number of great teachers have written about their insights as they've moved struggling and discouraged adolescents to become good, enthusiastic readers. And some great teacher-researchers have developed and brought together the studies that on a larger scale confirm the strategies these teachers have used. They include Kelly Gallagher (*Readicide: How Schools are Killing Reading and What You Can Do About It*), Janet Allen (*It's Never Too Late*, and *There's Room for Me Here*, the latter written with Kyle Gonzalez), Cris Tovani (*I Read It But I Don't Get It*), Jeff Wilhelm (*You Gotta BE the Book*), Wilhelm working with Michael Smith (*Reading Don't Fix No Chevys*), Richard Allington (*What Really Matters for Struggling Readers*), and Kylene Beers (*When Kids Can't Read: What Teachers Can Do*). We can draw on this fund of experience, as well as the successes of teachers we have known and observed, to learn what it takes to make a difference for the kids who need help the most.

> *... to help students understand and learn from the tasks we assign them, we must work with their reading process.*

To get close to some struggling readers and their teachers' effective strategies for helping them, we visited Downers Grove South High School in Chicago's west suburbs, where we talked with teachers and a group of students who struggle with reading. This school is working hard to ensure that all the young people are able to learn from their reading across the subject areas, with a team of six reading teachers and the collaboration of the entire faculty. In an outstanding improvement program, cohorts of teachers participate in three-year cycles of professional development on strategies to support students' reading and learning across the curriculum. Seventy-six of the faculty have participated so far. And three levels of a one-semester reading strategies course engage struggling students in a variety of the reading supports, such as text marking, multicolumn notes, and small-group discussions, that they will find their teachers using in content-area courses. While we quote and describe several teachers here, we're indebted to the entire faculty, since it's their broad and enthusiastic involvement that makes possible the success of the individual teachers from whom we learned. We realize that not every teacher gets to work in the kind of supportive professional culture that Downers Grove South has achieved. However, the strategies these teachers use will work in any classroom anywhere.

So what do we learn from the coaches, classroom teachers, and kids about the ways their teachers have helped them? Of course, all the strategies we've outlined throughout this book for students in general will help those who are struggling. Conversely, the strategies we'll describe now are also effective for all students—but they're especially crucial for kids who see themselves as nonreaders, and who have experienced a lot of failure in school. Here are the approaches that the Downers Grove South teachers and other experts tell us are paramount.

Create Supportive Relationships

All the great teachers who describe success with struggling readers focus on the essential process of developing students' trust. We've talked about this earlier in the book, but it's so essential for these students that we need to go a little further here. The psychologist-educator William Glasser (in *Choice Theory in the Classroom*, 1998) explains that people who have repeatedly failed at something usually cope by focusing their lives elsewhere to avoid still more failure. If students experiencing difficulty are going to take the risk and give math or science or a foreign language a new try, they need to know that you'll be there to help, and that they're in a safe place where they won't suffer further hurt if they don't succeed on the first attempt. In Chapter 7, we described some of the recent research showing the effect of "noncognitive" factors on students' success. These factors are actually fully cognitive in nature, but involve students' view of themselves, the possibilities for success, and the connection between their lives and the learning that they are undertaking. And as more and more research is demonstrating, these understandings make a major difference in students' learning.

When Cris Tovani shares with students her own strategies for "fake reading" from her days as a student (in *I Read It But I Don't Get It*) she's making an important move. Of course, she's showing the students she's street-smart and not easily fooled. She also explains why the students won't be doing "book reports"—they're not only easily faked but don't help students learn to read better. Perhaps most important, she's placing herself on their level—"I've been where you are. I know what it's like. But I've learned and improved, so you can too." And her admission surprises these adolescents—always a valuable tool for getting people's attention and shifting them to new ground.

KEY STRATEGIES for helping struggling readers

* **Create supportive relationships.** Show students that you care intensely about their reading, believe they can succeed, and won't accept anything less. Many struggling readers feel that adults have somehow abandoned them, or preconcluded that they are failures. Effective teachers find their own individual ways to demonstrate that this is not true.

* **Model thoughtful reading.** Use "think-alouds" (see pages 94–97), in which you demonstrate active reading strategies by reading aloud and stopping to narrate how your mind works with the material—asking questions, making inferences, and entering the world created by the book or article. Struggling readers are too rarely shown the active thinking that more experienced readers bring to the process. It is especially vital to model what you do when you get stuck, confused, or run across a word you don't know.

* **Promote self-monitoring.** Students can clarify confusion only if they stop to notice when this happens. Waiting until a teacher tells them they've got it wrong is too late. Readers can be helped to realize when they're having difficulty and shown effective ways to get back on track.

* **Use materials students can successfully read, but also give them extensive support for more challenging texts.** Students who have experienced repeated failure with reading are only further discouraged when they encounter lots of vocabulary they don't understand. For any given topic, providing materials at a variety of levels helps avoid this teaching trap.

* **Build engagement with the text.** Drawing and role-plays, arguing positions on real-life issues, helping students visualize the events and situations they are studying—all turn reading from a mechanical activity that kids avoid to one they are willing to work through.

* **Provide books and materials in various formats.** Listening to taped readings, viewing films and video clips, even reformatting texts in short chunks, with space to jot notes and write responses—all are steps that can help students enter into texts in a variety of ways.

At the start of Chapter 7 we described the research that shows the power of students' mind-sets to affect their success or failure in school. Amy Stoops, one of the Downers Grove South reading coaches, argues passionately, "Many of these kids have given up. They don't believe they can succeed in school, and are often ready to drop out. We must have ways to turn them around." There are hundreds of ways to do this, to make supportive connections with students, and the individuality of these is what makes the message powerful. One-size-fits-all doesn't, really—so each of us needs to find our own way in this work.

Downers Grove South reading coach Jennifer Hernandez described the many steps she takes:

* starting the year with a positive tone—it's crucial
* taking time with each student
* pointing out individual students' strengths
* listening—students can often verbalize much more extensively than they can write, so get them talking and point out that they can now write down what they've said
* greeting students at the door of your room and asking about their day or their weekend—this adds up over time
* sharing appropriate stories of your own struggles with challenging texts (as Cris Tovani does)
* believing in your students' potential and telling them—"You *will* get good at reading"
* being passionate not only about your subject but also about your students and their success
* using surprise (Jennifer likes to show a video of a group of students singing a wacky song about reading. Her students claim to dismiss it, but they love to watch it repeatedly.)

Downers Grove South biology teacher Lisa MacArtney uses a fascinating approach we'd not heard about before. At the start of the year, students complete a profile that helps define various types of intelligence. The profile identifies four types: students who are strong on social relationships, those who are well organized, those who are analytical, and **Biology** those with high energy. They then form a "human graph" in the hallway to see the particular strengths of their fellows. Lisa finds that when working in groups—which occurs frequently in her class—this enables students to focus on and make use of each other's abilities and understand their differences. It's easy to remind them about the various strengths, and they more frequently encourage one another and are patient with the areas in which some are less inclined. Some teachers use categories like this as well to form groups so that each has a mix of abilities.

Model Thoughtful Reading

Effective teachers help struggling kids by modeling their own mental processes as they read, rather than just exhorting students to do something they don't know how to do. Kylene Beers, in *When Kids Can't Read: What Teachers Can Do* (2003, 47), describes how teachers use think-alouds (described here on pages 94–97) to demonstrate meaningful thinking, giving instruction rather than just instructions. This is more challenging than it might sound, since so much of our thinking as we read is nearly unconscious. Beers uses the following passage to challenge students in classes she visits, asking them to figure out what's going on as they read it and then notice the mental processes they used:

> He put down $10 at the window. The woman behind the window gave $4. The person next to him gave him $3 but he gave it back to her. So when they went inside, she bought him a large bag of popcorn.*

Most of us see a girl trying to keep her date from paying for everything at the movies. Good readers make some spirited inferences to reach this conclusion, perhaps with further speculation about the two people's motives. Struggling readers often don't even see the point in deciphering the puzzle. They need to see how we do this and what we learn as a result. Of course, when we demonstrate this process for reading in math or science, we're actually showing students how to think about our subjects.

In classes across the curriculum, Downers Grove South teachers provide modeling for many reading strategies every time they begin a new lesson. Even when a strategy has been taught and used widely, it helps for students to see it applied across a variety of subjects again and again. One of the coaches' realizations has been that a particular reading process may be more complex than a teacher first imagines, since he or she is already quite familiar with the material. When reading coach Amy Stoops first observed Karen Eder model the solving of a problem in physics, Karen described four steps in the process. But particularly because Amy was not herself a science teacher, she could see that there were steps she didn't fully

Physics

* Adapted from "Where Comprehension Comes From" in *Creating Support for Effective Literacy Education* by C. Weaver, et al. Copyright ©1997 by Constance Weaver, Lorraine Gillmeister-Krause, and Grace Vento-Zogby. Portsmouth, NH: Heinemann.

understand, so the two teachers identified many more mental actions that Karen was performing. Karen's first broad step, for example, was to identify what she knew and what the problem was asking. Within that step, however, were many smaller ones: identifying text cues, drawing a picture, listing the givens, identifying the unknown, and for each one of these, clarifying to herself how and why she chose each word or piece of information. Karen also began to include internal two-way conversation to help walk herself through the process—"OK, self, what do I do next?" As the students grew familiar with this kind of thinking, Karen asked them to do think-alouds themselves, and of course they used the same kinds of inner dialogue. Talking to oneself became a practice that signaled greater sanity, rather than the opposite. Of course, it didn't take long for teachers across the school to adopt the think-aloud strategy, adapting it to their particular subject matter and personal style.

Promote Self-Monitoring

Cris Tovani (2003) found that her high school students wanted her to do their thinking for them. Asserted one student, "I'm sick and tired of you telling the class that it's our job to know when we know and know when we don't know. You're the teacher. Aren't you the one who is supposed to know when we understand something and when we don't?" School too often encourages students to abdicate responsibility and leave all the thinking to their teachers. Students become highly adept at waiting for teachers to simply give them answers instead of taking on challenges themselves.

Downers Grove South teachers support self-monitoring by including "stop and think" guides for a lot of students' reading. They frequently reprint articles, adding boxes along the right margin of the text in which they pose higher-level questions, ask students to explain concepts in the reading, highlight challenging vocabulary, or invite students to indicate their own questions or confusions.

Use Materials Students Can Successfully Read

It's crucial for resistant readers to work with books they can read, rather than simply being defeated again and again by ones they can't. While books beyond their level may just lead average and successful students to have less *interest* in reading, struggling readers are often completely *locked out*. It's very simple: if a student can't read the material, he can't get anything out of it or get any better at comprehending it. Reading researcher Richard Allington (2001, 44–45) summarizes the clear conclusions of one thorough study this way:

> Tasks completed with high rates of success were linked to greater learning and improved student attitudes toward the subject matter being learned, while tasks where students were moderately successful were less consistently related to learning, and hard tasks produced a negative impact on learning. Hard tasks also produced off-task behaviors and negative attitudes.

Downers South teachers approach this in a variety of ways. Many are moving more and more toward nontextbook materials. These are often short articles found on the Web. During Steve's visit to Lisa MacArtney's freshman biology class, the article of the day was on Galapagos turtles and the discovery that one particular species was not extinct as previously thought. Even with shorter, less challenging readings, the teachers often use a strategy or tool to deepen students' thinking. In this case, Lisa—coteaching with Amy Stoops—used a three-column sheet, with the left column containing quotes and vocabulary terms, the middle column asking for connections to what the student already knows, and the right column for generating further questions about each item. Amy modeled the first item herself, had the students help to complete the second item together, and then turned students loose in pairs to complete the rest of the notes.

Biology

Students' success with reading can also include challenging texts, if enough support is provided. The Downers South Social Studies Department is working to help students read college-level articles—but using extensive supports to do so. These include a wide variety of multicolumn notes, often including quotes or statements of larger concepts that students are invited to support or critique, providing evidence for their position.

Social Studies

Build Engagement with the Text

When Jeff Wilhelm (1997) realized how extensively his top readers immersed themselves in the stories they read, he encouraged resistant kids to do the same thing. But they continued to resist, because this simply didn't fit their mental picture of reading. Jeff found two strategies that launched students on the road to engagement by using activity rather than exhortation: drama and drawing. And he introduced these activities not for after-reading enrichment, but for before-reading introduction. Once students experienced some physical, visual, and auditory involvement, they more readily continued it as they moved into their reading.

Social Studies Our visit to Downers Grove South High School happily coincided with a social studies department-wide project in which freshman classes throughout the day participated in a "hunger banquet." This massive role-play focused on world poverty by assigning students randomly to high-, middle-, or low-income categories. Each student received a card assigning a specific identity to him or her. One card, for example, read, "You live in a small village outside Quito, the capital of Ecuador. Your father has a stall selling souvenirs to tourists. When there are lots of travelers, the money is good, but when they stay away, life is difficult." Tables were set with a variety of treats and drinks. The high-income students took whatever they wanted. The low-income kids were severely restricted to a few crackers, and some were permitted no drinks at all. Teachers read excerpts from a speech on poverty by Nelson Mandela, and the classes discussed the issue after the experience.

Student ownership of their inquiry as they read is also a major element of engagement. When Karen Eder starts students on a new unit, she takes them through a "textbook walk," helping them notice headings, illustrations, and other highlights. While many teachers do this, Karen includes a specific next step. It's not quite a KWL, but it does focus on questions. She asks students to each create their own list of questions about the topic, and to keep these in mind as they read. She stresses that it's essential for these to be the students' own questions, not ones supplied by the teacher. She wants students to set their own purposes for reading, and repeatedly reminding them to notice what they are thinking as they read helps them to stay focused. They are often surprised that the text in fact answers many of their questions. And in the process, the students grow much more engaged in the reading. When the questions are provided by the teacher or at the end of a textbook chapter, she finds that the teenagers mindlessly search for answers mechanically, rather than really thinking about what they are reading.

History Taking a different tack, history teacher Brennan Lazzaretto introduced a series of speeches by politicians in the 1930s and in the 2012 presidential campaign by posing a series of possible positions on the government's influence on the economy. For example:

* Too much government money spent on relief programs stops our country's prosperity.
* It is the responsibility of a government to provide for the basic needs of citizens who cannot provide for themselves.

Then as students read the 1930s speeches and viewed videos of the more recent ones, their task was to make notes, with one column for evidence from the speeches supporting a statement, a column for evidence refuting it, and a "so what" column for each side, explaining why the student considered the evidence to support or refute the assertion. Brennan acknowledged that this activity took much longer than a more traditional lesson. But he felt strongly that he was preparing students to become responsible citizens in the community, so the time was well worth it.

Provide Materials in Various Formats

In *There's Room for Me Here* (1998), Kyle Gonzalez, who was a new middle school teacher at the time, describes how taped books can help students become readers. Like most strategies, however, the tapes don't automatically provide a miracle cure without plenty of adjusting by an observant and resourceful teacher. Kyle admits, "Our first day of sustained silent reading [SSR] was an eye-opener: my students were neither sustained nor silent, and they certainly had no intention of reading." She had to gradually discover the type and level of materials her students would listen to. She began a log to keep track of students' reading and tape-listening, to minimize confusion, and to get kids started quickly at the beginning of the period. Brief check-in conferences during reading time helped keep students going. Kyle gradually found solutions to each problem, rather than reprimand and blame kids when things didn't flow smoothly (Allen and Gonzalez, 1998, 62–66).

How Students See It

We met with a group of students in Amy Stoops' Reading Strategies class to learn their perspective on their teachers' many efforts to help them with reading. All of the students agreed that before they'd entered this class, they had little interest in reading, and had no hesitation in admitting that they never read textbook assignments. And now?

> **Sarina:** I have dyslexia, so reading is hard. But knowing all the different strategies has helped me. I especially like text-marking and summarizing.
>
> **Calley:** My dad loves reading and he said it would expand my outlook on life. But when Ms. Stoops said it too, I believed it because it wasn't just a parent saying it.

Miles: This class has helped me develop a habit of reading.

Hal: I asked Ms. Stoops, "What's the point in reading, anyway?" So she sat me down and she printed out an article that told all the different ways that reading could help me. She really took time for me. [Amy explained later that he had been on the verge of dropping out, but was now a very successful student.]

We asked the students how their approach to reading had changed and whether they read on their own, outside of school.

Marisa: I text-mark all the time. It's just a habit with me now. I even mark the romance novels I like to read.

Miles: I'll read biographies of musicians [he plays drums], but not other things.

Marisa: I read romances and mystery novels. I especially like to read about the history of my culture—Mexican American.

Calley: I like reading facts. My brother is a paramedic and I read his medical books.

Steve: So are you thinking about going into the medical field in the future?

Calley: Yes.

Finally, we asked how the work on reading affected their learning in other classes.

Sarina: If you don't understand something, the strategies really help.

Marisa: In discussions, you hear other people's opinions and thoughts. Last period we had a great discussion about Mexican Americans and what's happening with the courses that aren't permitted in Arizona.

Calley: When you express your own opinion, it opens your mind to more thoughts.

Steve: That's so interesting, because many people would think that expressing your own opinion closes you up to other people's ideas.

Calley: Well, you just go into so much more depth than you had ever imagined.

What teacher wouldn't give her eyeteeth to hear a struggling student say that!

THE RAJAH'S WIFE

A BOOKCLUB HIGHLIGHTED TITLE

AMALA JAYARAMAN

AUTHOR OF *TRAVELS THROUGH THE CHAUDHARA*

12

Recommendations from Reading Research

Since the first edition of *Subjects Matter* was published in 2004, there has been a welcome explosion of research on adolescent and content-area literacy. Much, but not all, of this research supports the thrust of the Common Core Standards. In this chapter we will point out some of the key studies and reports that are giving us an ever clearer picture of "what works" in enhancing students' comprehension of the nonfiction text genres that comprise our subject fields.

Among the more influential research summaries:

* *The Handbook of Reading Research*, Volume 4 (Kamil et al., 2010)
* "Adolescent Literacy: A Statement of the International Reading Association" (IRA, 2012)
* "Essential Elements of Fostering and Teaching Reading Comprehension," in *What Research Has to Say About Reading Instruction* (Duke et al., 2011)
* *Improving Adolescent Literacy: Effective Classroom and Intervention Practices* (Kamil et al., 2008)
* "A Synthesis of Reading Interventions and Effects on Reading Comprehension Outcomes for Older Struggling Readers" (Edmonds et al., 2009)

* "Adolescent Literacy, A Policy Research Brief of the National Council of Teachers of English" (NCTE, 2007)
* "Reading Instruction for All Students: A Policy Research Brief of the National Council of Teachers of English" (NCTE, 2012)

These assorted reports share a consensus that the state of adolescent literacy in America needs swift improvement, and offer mostly overlapping sets of research-based recommendations, which we summarize below.

There is also a growing body of research, not just about teen readers in general, but about content-area reading specifically. In a very helpful 2012 research review, Zhihui Fang points out that there are four current approaches to improving students' content-area literacy—cognitive, sociocultural, linguistic, and critical—and that these approaches are backed up by varying degrees of scientific evidence, as measured by the What Works Clearinghouse of the U.S. Department of Education (Kamil et al., 2008).

The **cognitive strategies** approach focuses on explicitly teaching the specific mental "moves" that proficient readers use. This line of work dates from Pearson and Gallagher's groundbreaking 1983 study, "The Instruction of Reading Comprehension," which has since been widely replicated and translated for teachers by authors like Keene and Zimmerman, Harvey and Goudvis, and Tovani, to name a few. The What Works Clearinghouse says that the research supporting strategy instruction is "strong."

The **linguistic** approach focuses students' attention on how pieces of language go together to create meaning on the page. It begins with words, including vocabulary, moves up to instruction about sentence ingredients, and finally to the study of whole-text structures. The research on linguistic approaches is split; according to the Clearinghouse, the explicit teaching of academic vocabulary has "strong" evidence of effectiveness, while working on sentence and text structures (a big emphasis of the Common Core) yields "mixed" evidence.

In the **sociocultural** approach, teachers begin by welcoming and respecting kids' own background knowledge and language. They explicitly teach about different discourse communities, settings, and occasions and try to build bridges from where the kids are toward the use of more privileged and academic language. (This is exactly the approach that teacher Marnie Ware talks about on page 73, where she details how she shows students that embracing technical vocabulary will help them to stop feeling excluded from the academic world.) The Clearinghouse rates the research on sociocultural approaches as "moderate."

In the **critical** approach, teachers "problematize" all texts and authors. Nothing is taken at face value, and there is no deference to textbooks, primary sources, or expert voices. They teach students that all texts are socially constructed, that every word ever published serves someone's interests, and may well work against others'. While this approach is partly about taking a skeptical, critical stance, it's more than that—it's literacy as liberation, and as such it takes some of its main cues from social justice educators like Paulo Freire. Not surprisingly, since proponents of this field rely on qualitative rather than quantitative research designs, the Clearinghouse rates the evidence on this approach to be "weak."

We hope you'll recognize, having read this book, that we draw most heavily on the first approach, the well-documented "cognitive strategies" model, though there are valuable elements of the other three approaches in our repertoire as well.

Drawing upon these sources and many more, we have created the following synthesis of research on "best practice" instruction for adolescent readers across the secondary school curriculum. First, we'll quickly list ten important areas in which research gives us guidance, and then offer some interpretations and further details about each.

Major Conclusions from Recent Reading Research

What Students Read

1.   Students should read a wide range of materials and genres of text in all classes.
2.   Students should read for the same purposes as literate adults, for both information and pleasure. A sense of personal purpose is key to reading success.
3.   Kids need to read a lot; volume, quantity, and practice count.
4.   Students should read plenty of materials written at a comfortable recreational level, and gradually move up toward more challenging text as the necessary supports are in place.
5.   Teenagers need genuine choice of reading materials: much of what they read should be self-selected, based on interest and curiosity.

6. Teachers make their own reading habits and processes visible by regularly reading aloud and by explaining and modeling their thinking about content-area texts.

7. Teachers invite students to routinely talk and write about what they are reading, joining in a community of lively, purposeful discourse.

8. Teachers help their students acquire the repertoire of specific cognitive strategies that proficient readers use to understand general academic nonfiction as well as discipline-specific text.

9. Teachers help students develop the academic vocabulary they need to process increasingly difficult texts, with special attention to those "power" words that reach across disciplines and characterize the language of educated people.

10. Students engage in extended subject-matter inquiries, project- and problem-based learning, and small-group investigations that allow them to explore important disciplinary and multidisciplinary topics in depth, and to share their learning with varied audiences.

Now let's look at these assertions in detail.

What students read

1 **Students should read a wide range of materials and genres of text in all classes.** Teenagers' reading and learning of school subject matter grows when they read the kinds of materials real adult readers do—including a wide range of text, fiction and nonfiction, articles and books, paper and digital, informational and poetic, in a wide range of genres. This broad mixture aids learning in all subjects—from English to math, history to science, art to foreign language (NCTE, 2012; IRA, 2012).

The value of breadth in reading has long been noted in literacy research. Davidson and Koppenhaver's classic 1998 national study showed that successful adolescent reading programs have two distinctive features: giving students access to a wide variety of materials, and spending a high proportion of time on actual reading, as opposed to drills.

The value of breadth was reconfirmed by Strauss (2000), and Biancarosa and Snow (2006) showed that a wide range of reading topics and difficulty levels is an essential ingredient for reading growth. Stephen Krashen (2009) published a compilation of research listing dozens of studies showing positive effects of giving students wide choices and frequent opportunities to read. A recent British study looking at six thousand teenagers revealed that greater amounts of independent reading led to higher scores in math, vocabulary, and spelling (Sullivan and Brown, 2013). For all these reasons, *range in reading* really matters; the Common Core Standards (2010, 10) put it succinctly:

> Through extensive reading of stories, dramas, poems, and myths from diverse cultures and different time periods, students gain literary and cultural knowledge as well as familiarity with various text structures and elements. By reading texts in history/social studies, science, and other disciplines, students build a foundation of knowledge in these fields that will also give them the background to be better readers in all content areas.

As the Core explicitly states, broad reading is not limited to English language arts classes. In many studies, content-area teachers have provided reports of effective use of novels and trade books for teaching subject matter. In one particularly striking study, Leslie Mandell Morrow and her colleagues observed how students learned more science in a program that integrated literature-based study with the science curriculum (Morrow et al., 1997). For several years, the ongoing "Seeds of Science" project by Pearson et al. (2013) has been documenting gains in science knowledge when kids are engaged in reading grade-level trade books.

Wide reading is also necessary for developing vocabulary in various subjects. It is estimated that normally, students learn vocabulary at the rate of three thousand to four thousand words per year, adding up to fifty thousand words or more by the time they finish high school (Anderson and Nagy, 1992; Anglin, 1993). Clearly, no directly taught memorization program alone—ten words a week with a quiz on Friday—can ever achieve this rate of learning. Instead, kids' word knowledge expands as they read widely, acquiring most of their vocabulary through context and repeated exposure (Butler, 2010).

2 **Students should read for the same purposes as literate adults, for both information and pleasure. A sense of personal purpose is key to their reading success.** The purposes in students' heads make all the difference, not only in what they get out of reading in history, math, and science, but in whether they even attempt the work at all. It is well established that motivation, engagement, and relevance are keys to adolescent reading development (Gambrell et al., 2007; Sturtevant, et al. 2006). It's not enough for teachers to pile on reading assignments; kids must experience plenty of self-driven reading for themselves.

John Guthrie and Emily Anderson (1999) identified the larger motivations students may have for reading:

* involvement in the material itself
* curiosity about a particular subject or question
* social interactions with others about their reading
* the challenge of tackling something difficult
* the sense that reading is important
* a sense of efficacy, of confidence about their reading abilities
* recognition for doing well (a more extrinsic motivation)
* competition, proving oneself better than other students (also an extrinsic motive)

Not surprisingly, it is the intrinsic motivations that lead to greater learning in high school subject areas. For example, in one study, students who reported being motivated by a strong interest in physics and believed it was relevant to their everyday and future lives "read more widely, talked to their teachers and parents, and thought deeply about physics applications both in class and out of school" (Hynd, 1999). The role of intrinsic motivation in reading has been borne out in repeated studies (Shunk, 2003; Horner and Shwery, 2002).

Unfortunately, all such motivations for reading decline steadily as students move up the grades (Scholastic, 2013; Clark, 2012; Wigfield and Guthrie, 1997). Repeatedly, researchers find that especially with adolescents, those who avoid reading see it as merely decoding the words, or looking for answers to the questions at the end of the chapter, rather than a personally purposeful exploration (Biancarosa and Snow, 2004; Gambrell and Marinak, 2009).

Interviewing eighth graders, Jeff Wilhelm found that good readers enter deeply into the material they read, visualize what is happening, identify with characters and events, and connect the material with real life. In contrast, those who don't read well experience none of these things, and simply do not recognize that they are possible. Avid student readers are reading not because work is assigned to them, but because their reading matters. As one enthusiastic student said, "I think reading is important because it teaches people to understand life more and understand themselves" (Wilhelm, 1997).

3 **Students need to read a lot; volume, quantity, and practice count.** Like any other skill in life, reading benefits from practice, and quantity counts. A study of over forty-five thousand students who had independently read some three million books showed that volume does indeed matter. Topping, Samuels, and Paul (2007) found that simply reading lots of books was indeed associated with improved reading skill. They also looked at the *quality* of reading—defined not by some rating of the value of the literature, but by how well kids scored on a comprehension test. You might say that quality reading, as defined here, is careful, attentive reading. And the study showed that, especially as kids got older, growth in reading achievement was optimized by kids reading a lot of books with high comprehension—reading plenty of books they could read and understand.

There have been many studies associating high volume of reading with reading achievement as gauged by such customary measures as standardized reading achievement tests. For example, John Guthrie and Anderson (1999) found that higher reading volume related to better reading comprehension in eighth- and tenth-grade students. A meta-analysis by Samuels and Wu (2004) showed that students who have in-school independent reading time do significantly better on measures of reading achievement than classmates who have not had that reading time.

But there has been a controversy about this, which manifested itself during the creation of the National Reading Panel report in 2000. Some researchers pointed out that such data show a *correlation*, and not necessarily a cause-and-effect relationship—in other words, it's possible that some kids read more *because* they're already good at it, and therefore enjoy it, rather than improving because they read. However, studies that look at *assigned* classroom reading time can remove the question of whether the better readers just choose to read more. To address this concern, careful studies also control statistically for past reading achievement, prior knowledge, and motivation (Guthrie and Anderson, 1999). One study on the effect of reading volume randomly assigned students to read for longer or shorter periods for six months. In fact, the poorer readers had stronger gains in comprehension when they read for forty minutes per day compared with similar students who read for only fifteen minutes (Samuels and Wu, 2004).

4 **Students should read plenty of materials written at a comfortable recreational level, and gradually move up toward more challenging text as the necessary supports are in place.** Allowing kids to read plenty of "easy" text in our courses can sound counterintuitive—doesn't it mean dumbing down the curriculum and lowering standards? And what about the Common Core Standards' insistence on "complex" and "grade-level" texts? But research shows that students' reading improves most when no more than 10 percent of material in a text is difficult for them to understand. In other words, kids' learning improves as they have more success with their reading. Actually, it's logical when you think about it: if kids don't understand what they're reading, then how can anything happen in their heads? As researcher Richard Allington (2013) puts it: "You can't learn to read from text you cannot read." When reading is disrupted repeatedly by unknown vocabulary or unclear connections, meaning quickly gets lost (Cunningham and Stanovich, 2001).

Of course, when a student *wants* to try a more challenging book, we don't hold him or her back. And providing plenty of "scaffolding" supports will help students read valuable and engaging but complex material that can be important to their content-area studies (see multiple studies cited in National Council of Teachers of English, 2012). However, the evidence shows that high school students become very frustrated when trying to read textbooks that are difficult to understand, particularly when no supports or reading strategies are provided (Hynd et al., 1997, 1999). It's not for a lack of interest in the subject matter though, because when passages are rewritten to provide clearer explanation and more connections between ideas, the students learn more (Britton et al., 1996; Beck et al., 1991, 1995).

5 **Teenagers need genuine choice of reading materials: much of what they read should be self-selected, based on interest and curiosity.** In high success classrooms, teachers are far more likely to let students choose some of the books they read (Allington, 2001). Content-area teachers who fear that student choice may lead to nothing but trashy novels and fashion magazines can put away their concern. We can understand this by comparing adult Americans' choices to those of teenagers. So what do today's adults choose to read? The top five sellers on Amazon in 2012 were:

1. *Fifty Shades Freed* by E. L. James (the third of the *Shades of Grey* trilogy)
2. *Gone Girl*, a novel by Gillian Flynn
3. The *Fifty Shades Trilogy* by E. L. James
4. *Bared to You—A Crossfire Novel* by Sylvia Day
5. *No Easy Day: The Firsthand Account of the Mission That Killed Osama Bin Laden* by Mark Owen

These selections remind us what grown-up lifelong readers are likely to select. It's important not to romanticize literate adults as people who seek a death match with complex text every time they buy a book. Interestingly, 46.9 percent of Americans reported that they read at least one novel, short story, poetry collection, or play in 2012 (National Endowment for the Arts, 2013). Yet more readers (26 percent) said they enjoyed reading for gaining knowledge or information than for any other purpose (Rainie et al., 2012). Nonfiction rules!

Of course, making a comparison between adult and teen literacy isn't easy. It's difficult to pin down teenagers' reading nowadays because so much of it simply isn't in traditional books (Moyer, 2010). But we know that books like *The Hunger Games* and its sequels are wildly popular. And so is nonfiction. The Goodreads website reports the top three teen nonfiction favorites in 2012 were:

1. *Bomb: The Race to Build—and Steal—the World's Most Dangerous Weapon* by Steve Sheinkin
2. *How They Croaked: The Awful Ends of the Awfully Famous* by Georgia Bragg
3. *Wheels of Change: How Women Rode the Bicycle to Freedom (with a Few Flat Tires Along the Way)* by Sue Macy

This distribution of titles parallels the adult choices above: a mix of serious and lighter fare. Researchers have found that the ability to choose their own reading enhances teens' motivation to read (Krashen, 2009). Frustratingly, though, while choice is a major factor in students' potential engagement, both the classroom opportunities for choice and access to a variety of books are very limited in most schools. (Worth and McCool, 1996; Oldfather and Dahl, 1995). And when book choices *are* available, kids do not have to go it alone. An important role for teachers is helping students to find and engage with appropriate independent materials. Recent studies have shown that kids benefit most when teachers model how to find books and then confer with individuals about their choices (Moss and Young, 2010; Kuhn et al., 2006).

How Students Are Taught to Read

6 **Teachers make their own reading habits and processes visible by regularly reading aloud and by explaining and modeling their thinking about content-area texts.** Whether they are comfortable in the role or not, all teachers are *reading models.* Students benefit when teachers share their reading lives with them, talking about books or articles they are reading, sharing information gained from texts, and modeling a literate, curious adult life (NCTE, 2010). The value of teachers reading aloud fiction and nonfiction texts, even to older students, has long been established by research and by the wisdom of practice (Gambrell et al. 2003, 2007; Guignon, 2010; IRA, 2012). It seems that we are never too old to benefit from being read to. Of course, reading aloud brings the magic of print to life, but it also provides an example of fluent and dramatic reading, which can only result from the reader's deep comprehension of the text.

The reading strategies research described in section eight below (beginning with Pearson and Gallagher, 1983) revealed a gigantic gap in traditional instruction: we had failed to *show* students how proficient readers actually think. In other words, teachers had never regularly and intentionally demonstrated their own thinking as they read. This line of research led to many pedagogical breakthroughs, but arguably the first-among-equals is the *think-aloud*. In this structure, the teacher reads aloud from content-area text, stopping periodically to share her mental processes with students, as we describe on pages 94–97. Think-alouds are part of a broader model of reading instruction called the Gradual Release of Responsibility (Duke, Pearson, Strachan, and Billman, 2011). The first step in a Gradual Release lesson is the teacher demonstrating her own thinking for students; the mantra of this phase is, "I do it, you watch" (Routman, 2003). Next the teacher invites students to try reading with her, then in closely supported groups, and finally on their own—hence the term, gradual release. The What Works Clearinghouse says the evidence supporting explicit reading strategy instruction is "strong," with think-alouds being one of the more prominent modalities (Kamil et al., 2008).

7 **Teachers invite students to routinely talk and write about what they are reading, joining in a community of lively, purposeful discourse.** In the traditional classroom, reading has been a mainly solitary activity, often followed by kids filling in blanks or circling multiple-choice answers at the end of the selection. We now understand that keeping reading silent and private puts a needless lid on kids' comprehension (Horowitz, 2007). Understanding improves when students interact with each other around text (Allington, 2012; Frey, Fisher, Rothenberg, and Heath, 2008). This begins with activities as simple as quick partner "turn and talks" or "think-pair-shares," and works its way up to larger groups discussing longer texts over longer periods of class time, in activities like book clubs, Socratic seminars, or inquiry circles.

Researchers like Nystrand (2006) have shown, however, that for student talk to be effective, it must be focused and well structured by the teacher. Just telling kids to go have a conversation is not effective; they need explicit social skill training before and during such gatherings (Daniels and Steienke, 2011), clear-cut responsibilities, and focused, engaging prompts in order to make the most of peer interaction (Soter et al., 2008).

Unlike peer-to-peer talk, writing in response to reading has not been neglected in American classrooms. But most of it has been restricted to two extremes—either writing short, factual recall answers to comprehension questions, or writing long, polished, high-stakes research papers a few times a year. What's been missing is regular, several-times-a-day writing practice, during which students put the main ideas of the subject matter into their own words, and use these "first draft" texts to interact with classmates. This kind of writing can happen in academic journals or learning logs, on index cards, or in "written conversations" between students (Daniels and Daniels, 2013). Pioneers of such writing-to-learn activities include Fulwiler (2000) and B. K. Britton et al. (1996). More recent studies confirm the value of writing to learn as a tool for enhancing students' comprehension (Bangert-Drowns, Hurley, and Wilkinson, 2004).

8 Teachers help their students acquire the repertoire of specific cognitive strategies that proficient readers use to understand general academic nonfiction as well as discipline-specific text. To many teenage readers, especially those who struggle, the act of reading can be a mystery. They think that reading is a gift—either you've got the mojo or you are "a bad reader." They think that good readers read effortlessly, drawing an arc of perfect comprehension through any text. They have no idea of all the mental work—the recursions and restarts, the grappling, the connecting, the assembly—that goes on in the minds of skilled readers (Burkins and Croft, 2010).

That's why the comprehension strategies research, which began with Pearson and Gallagher's 1983 study, has been so profoundly important. What Pearson and subsequent researchers showed was that effective readers possess a finite repertoire of definable mental operations or "moves" that they use to make meaning of print. But neither teachers nor curriculum developers had been aware of this phenomenon, partly since adult readers use these strategies mostly at the automatic, unconscious level.

While strategy instruction was conceptualized and validated in the late 1980s and 1990s (National Reading Panel, 2000), the work of developing the appropriate teaching structures continues today. Effective and widely adopted approaches have been developed by Harvey and Goudvis (2008), Keene and Zimmerman (2007), Tovani (2003), and others.

Today, teachers implementing "reading strategies instruction" explicitly teach young people the mental operations that proficient readers use—visualizing, connecting with background knowledge, drawing inferences and making predictions, noticing and asking questions, determining importance, synthesizing meaning, and above all, actively monitoring their thinking as they read. We now have abundant evidence that these strategies can be taught to students, and that they result in better comprehension and higher test scores. The What Works Clearinghouse says that comprehension strategy instruction has "strong" research support (Kamil et al., 2008).

You might have heard that some authors of the Common Core English language arts standards were skeptical of the value of strategy instruction, apparently having seen some poor implementations of the approach (Publisher's Guidelines, 2012). It is important to know that this dispute was resolved after an outpouring of objection (and evidence) from the research and teaching community. The final versions of the standards and their accompanying Publisher's Guidelines now fully support the use of proficient reader strategies (National Governors Association, 2012).

9 **Teachers help students develop the academic vocabulary they need to process increasingly difficult texts, with special attention to those "power" words that reach across disciplines and characterize the language of educated people.** There's never been any debate about the importance of vocabulary in the development of strong, effective reading. There have, however, been vigorous controversies about which words to teach, and how to teach them. Since Beck's pioneering work (2002), we have been able to identify the most powerful words for students to learn. As Beck's model explains, most students come to us with an age-appropriate inventory of Tier 1 terms—words that "everyone knows." As they begin studying academic subjects, they will encounter any number of Tier 3 words—technical, discipline-specific terms (*mitochondria, pentameter, phloem*) that are mainly pertinent when studying or working in a specialized field. If we don't continue to actively use these Tier 3 words, they tend to drop out of our vocabularies, with little consequence. But most critical to teach are the all-important Tier 2 words (*matrix, parallel, abstract, erosion, evidence, vector, analysis*). These are terms that are used across many disciplines and that characterize the speech of mature language users.

But how to teach vocabulary best? We know that much vocabulary is acquired "incidentally" through wide reading. But research says that the teaching of some words should be explicit and direct, with teachers identifying key terms in subject-area units or texts, so that readers will have the tools they need to comprehend content-area materials (Butler et al., 2010). Interestingly, there is little research support for traditional list-and-memorize vocabulary work; instead, the most effective approach is to highlight and teach key words in context, while students are actually reading a text. It is very useful for teachers to stop and talk about words along the way (Nash and Snowling, 2006). And this, in turn, can be smoothly delivered via the think-alouds described above, where teachers can stop and demonstrate how they grapple with strange or unfamiliar words. Research also shows that students need multiple exposures to a word for it to enter working vocabulary, but that these repetitions can be provided by pleasant, gamelike activities (Blachowicz and Fisher, 2009; Fisher and Frey, 2008).

10 **Students should engage in extended subject-matter inquiries, project- and problem-based learning, and small-group investigations that allow them to explore important disciplinary and multidisciplinary topics in depth, and to share their learning with varied audiences.** Abundant evidence shows that students are motivated to read when we invite them into important topics, give them reading choices (and responsibilities), and help them to work productively with others in well-structured collaborative groups (Darling-Hammond et al., 2008; Johnson and Johnson, 2009; NCTE, 2008). Students need to become researchers, identifying and pursuing topics worthy of extended study, gathering and winnowing information, creating syntheses and critiques, and presenting their findings in face-to-face, written, and digital formats.

There are many current models of such inquiry learning from which teachers may choose. Project-Based Learning has a strong national organization and substantial research evidence linking the model to enhanced achievement on a variety of the customary measures (Vega, 2012). Harvey and Daniels' "inquiry circles" model (2010) draws upon research in both comprehension and collaboration to structure effective extended small-group research projects, K–12. The Document-Based Question model (DBQ, 2013) from Chicago offers primary source materials that invite students to work like real historians, constructing meaning by examining, sifting, and drawing supportable inferences from complex sets of historical texts. P. David Pearson, who has been so prominent in reading research, is now amid a multiyear study of reading in science, and his work with the Seeds of Science/Roots of Literacy project has shown growth in kids' engagement with and comprehension of interesting science materials (Cervetti, Pearson, Greenleaf, and Moje, 2013).

Conclusion

We think that, taken together, this body of research paints a clear picture of what young readers in content-area classes need—indeed, what they deserve. They should have access to a wide range of interesting reading materials in the field, much of which they choose for themselves with teacher support. They need an abundance of successful reading experiences, plenty of time spent freely reading, in text they *can read and want to read*. They need to savor and play with words, building a wide vocabulary from wide reading.

When students need to move up the ladder of challenge, they need teachers who don't just assign and exhort, but who *show them the way*. These mentors demonstrate their own content-specific reading strategies and explicitly help learners practice and acquire them. These teachers sponsor positive, interactive, and supportive classroom environments where kids regularly talk and write about their reading, and feel safe to take risks, debate, and disagree. These special teachers' signature is *engagement*: they infuse their courses with important, relevant issues and encourage kids to engage with both ideas and the wider community.

Research Works Cited

Allington, Richard. 2008. *What Really Matters in RTI*. New York: Pearson.

_____. 2011. *What Really Matters for Struggling Readers: Designing Research-Based Programs* (3rd ed.). Boston: Allyn and Bacon.

_____. 2013. "What Really Matters When Working with Struggling Readers," *Reading Teacher* 66(7) April.: 520–530

Allington, Richard and Rachael Gabriel. 2012. "Every Child, Every Day." *Educational Leadership* 69(6) March: 10–15.

Anderson, R. C., and W. E. Nagy. 1992. "The Vocabulary Conundrum." *American Educator* 16(4) 14–18, 44–47.

Anglin, J. M. 1993. "Vocabulary Development: A Morphological Analysis." *Monographs of the Society for Research in Child Development* 58.

Bangert-Drowns, Robert, Marlene Hurley, and Barbara Wilkinson. 2004. "The Effects of School-Based Writing-to-Learn Interventions on Academic Achievement: A Meta-Analysis." *Review of Educational Research* 74(1): 29–58.

Beck, I. L., et al. 1991. "Revising Social Studies Text from a Text-Processing Perspective: Evidence of Improved Comprehensibility." *Reading Research Quarterly* 26: 251–276.

_____ et al. 1995. "Giving a Text Voice Can Improve Students' Understanding." *Reading Research Quarterly* 30: 220–239.

Beck, I. L., M. G. McKeown, and L. Kucan. 2002. *Bringing Words to Life*. New York: Guilford Press.

Biancarosa, Gina, and Catherine Snow. 2006. *Reading Next: A Vision for Action and Research in Middle and High School Literacy*. New York: Carnegie Corporation of New York.

Blachowicz, C., and P. Fisher. 2009. *Teaching Vocabulary in All Classrooms* (4th ed.). New York: Pearson.

Bloch, C. and J. Mangiere. 2002. "Recreational Reading Twenty Years Later." *The Reading Teacher* 55(6): 572–80.

Britton, B. K., et al. 1996. *Improving Instructional Text: Tests of Two Revision Methods*. Universities of Georgia and Maryland, National Reading Research Center.

Burkins, J. M., and , M.M. Croft. 2010. *Preventing Misguided Reading: New Strategies for Guided Reading Teachers*. Newark, DE: International Reading Association.

Butler, Shari, Kelsi Urrutia, Anneta Buenger, Nina Gonzalez, Marla Hunt, and Corinne Eisenhart. 2010. *A Review of the Current Research on Vocabulary Instruction*. Reading First. Washington, DC: U.S. Department of Education.

Carnegie Council on Advancing Adolescent Literacy. 2010. *Time to Act: An Agenda for Advancing Adolescent Literacy for College and Career Success*. New York: Carnegie Corporation of New York.

Cervetti, G.N., P. D. Pearson, C. Greenleaf, E. Moje. 2013. "Science! Literacy! Synergy!" In W. Banko, M. L. Grant, M. E. Jabot, A. J. McCormack, and T. O'Brien (eds.). *Science Literacy and Our Nation's Future* (pp. 99–124). Washington, DC: NSTA & STANYS.

Clark, Christina. 2012. *Children's and Young People's Reading Today: Findings from the 2011 National Literacy Trust's Annual Survey*. London: National Literacy Trust.

Cunningham, Anne and Keith Stanovich. 2001. "What Reading Does For the Mind." *Journal of Direct Instruction*. Summer.

Daniels, Harvey, and Elaine Daniels. 2013. *The Best Kept Teaching Secret. How Written Conversations Engage Students, Activate Learning, and Grow Fluent Writers*. Thousand Oaks, CA: Corwin Literacy.

Daniels, Harvey, and Nancy Steineke. 2010. *Texts and Lessons for Content-Area Reading*. Portsmouth, NH: Heinemann.

_____. 2012. *Texts and Lessons for Teaching Literature*. 2013. Portsmouth, NH: Heinemann.

Darling-Hammond, Linda, et al. 2008. *Powerful Learning: What We Know About Teaching for Understanding*. San Francisco, CA: Jossey-Bass.

Davidson, Judith, and David Koppenhaver. 1988. *Adolescent Literacy: What Works and Why*. New York: Garland Publishing.

Designed Instruction. 2013. "Modeling for Learning: Addressing Student Misconceptions." http://www.designedinstruction.com/learningleads/misconceptions.html.

Dillon, D. R., and D. G. O'Brien. 2008. "The Role of Motivation in Engaged Reading of Adolescents." In K. A. Hinchman, and H. K. Sheridan-Thomas (eds.). *Best Practices in Adolescent Literacy Instruction, Solving Problems in the Teaching of Literacy*, 78–96. New York: Guilford Press.

Duke, Nell K., P. David Pearson, Stephanie L. Strachan, and Alison K. Billman. 2011. "Essential Elements of Fostering and Teaching Reading Comprehension." In S. Jay Samuels and Alan E. Farstrup (eds.). *What Research Has to Say About Reading Instruction* (4th ed.). Newark, DE: International Reading Association.

Edmonds et al. 2009. "A Synthesis of Reading Interventions and Effects on Reading Outcomes for Older Struggling Readers." *Review of Education Research*. 79(1).

Fang, Zhihui. 2012. "Approaches to Developing Content Area Literacies: A Synthesis and a Critique." *Journal of Adolescent and Adult Literacy* 56(2): 111–116.

Fisher, Douglas, and Nancy Frey. 2008. *Word Wise and Content Rich. Five Steps to Teaching Academic Vocabulary* (7–12). Portsmouth, NH: Heinemann.

Flynt, E. S., and William Brozo. 2008. "Developing Academic Language: Got Words?" *The Reading Teacher* 61(6): 500–502.

Frey, Nancy, Douglas Fisher, Carol Rothenberg, and Shirley Brice Heath. 2008. *Content-Area Conversations: How to Plan Discussion-Based Lessons for Diverse Language Learners*. Alexandria, VA: Association for Supervision and Curriculum Development.

Fulwiler, Toby. 2000. *The Journal Book*. Portsmouth, NH: Heinemann.

Gambrell, Linda, and Barbara Marinak. 2009. "Reading Motivation: What the Research Says." www.readingrockets.org.

Gambrell, Linda, and V. Ridgeway. 2007. "Assessing Children's Motivation for Reading and Writing." In J. Paratore and R. McCormick (eds.), *Classroom Literacy Assessment: Making Sense of What Students Know and Do* (pp. 50–61). New York: Guilford Press.

Gambrell, L. B., L. M. Morrow, S. B. Neuman, and M. Pressley. 2003. *Best Practices in Literacy Instruction* (2nd ed.). New York: Guilford Press.

Gambrell, L. B., L. M. Morrow, M. Pressley, and J. Guthrie. 2007. *Best Practices in Literacy Instruction* (3rd ed.). New York: Guilford Press.

Guignon, Anne. 2010. Reading Aloud: Are Students *Ever* Too Old? *Education World*. http://www .educationworld.com/a_curr/curr081.shtml.

Gunter, M. A., , T. H. Estes, and J. H. Schwab. 1999. *Instruction: A Models Approach* (3rd ed.). Boston: Allyn & Bacon.

Guthrie, John, and Emily Anderson. 1999. "Engagement in Reading: Processes of Motivated, Strategic, Knowledgeable, Social Readers." in John Guthrie and Donna Alvermann (eds.). *Engaged Reading: Processes, Practices, and Policy Implications*, 17–45. New York: Teachers College Press.

Harvey, Stephanie, and Anne Goudvis. 2007. *Strategies That Work: Teaching Comprehension for Engagement and Understanding*. York, ME: Stenhouse.

Harvey, Stephanie, and Harvey Daniels. 2010. *Comprehension and Collaboration: Inquiry Circles in Action*. Portsmouth, NH: Heinemann.

Hinchman, Kathleen, and David Moore. 2013. "Close Reading: A Cautionary Interpretation." *Journal of Adult and Adolescent Literacy*. March 58(6).

Horner, S. L., and C. S. Shwery. 2002. "Becoming an Engaged, Self-Regulated Reader." *Theory into Practice* 41: 102–109.

Horowitz, R. 2007. *Talking Texts: How Speech and Writing Interact in School Learning*. London: Routledge.

Hynd, et al. 1997. *Texts in Physics Class: The Contribution of Reading to the Learning of Counterintuitive Physics Principles*. Universities of Georgia and Maryland, National Reading Research Center.

Hynd, et al. 1999. "Instructional Considerations for Literacy in Middle and Secondary Schools: Toward an Integrated Model of Instruction." In John Guthrie and Donna Alvermann (eds.). *Engaged Reading: Processes, Practices, and Policy Implications*, 81–104. New York: Teachers College Press.

International Reading Association. 2012. *Adolescent Literacy: A Position Statement of the International Reading Association*. Newark, DE: IRA.

Johnson, David, and Roger Johnson. 2009. "An Educational Psychology Success Story: Social Interdependence Theory and Cooperative Learning." *Educational Researcher* 38(5): 365–379.

Kamil, Michael, et al. 2008. *Improving Adolescent Literacy. Effective Classroom and Intervention Practices*. What Works Clearinghouse.

Kamil, Michael L., P. David Pearson, Elizabeth Birr Moje, and Peter Afflerbach. 2010. *Handbook of Reading Research, Volume IV*. London: Routledge.

Keene, Ellin, and Susan Zimmerman. 2008. *The Mosaic of Thought*. Portsmouth, NH: Heinemann.

Krashen, Steven. 2004. *The Power of Reading: Insights from the Research*. Portsmouth, NH: Heinemann.

Krashen, Steven. 2009. Free Voluntary Reading. *IATEFL Young Learner and Teenage Special Interest Group Publication*. (Spring.)

Kuhn, M., P. J. Schwanenflugel, R. D. Morris, L. M. Morrow, D. G. Woo, E. B. Meisinger, et al. 2006. "Teaching Children to Become Fluent and Automatic Readers." *Journal of Literacy Research* 38(4): 357–388.

Morrow, L., M. Pressley, J. Smith, and M. Smith. 1997. "The Effect of a Literature-Based Program Integrated into Literacy and Science Instruction with Children from Diverse Backgrounds." *Reading Research Quarterly*. 32:54–76.

Morrow, Lesley, Linda B. Gambrell, and Nell K. Duke. 2007. *Best Practices in Literacy Instruction*. New York: Guilford Press.

Moss, B., and T. A. Young. 2010. *Creating Lifelong Readers Through Independent Reading*. Newark, DE: International Reading Association.

Moyer, Jessica. 2010. "'Teens Today Don't Read Books Any More:' A Study of Differences in Interest and Comprehension Based on Reading Modalities." *Journal of Research on Libraries and Young Adults*.

National Council of Teachers of English. 2012. Reading Instruction for All Students: A Policy Research Brief Produced by *The National Council of Teachers of English*. Urbana, IL: NCTE.

National Council of Teachers of English. 2007. *Adolescent Literacy. A Policy Research Brief Produced by The National Council of Teachers of English*. Urbana, IL: NCTE.

National Endowment for the Arts. 2013. *How a Nation Engages with Art: Highlights from the 2012 Survey of Public Participation in the Arts*. NEA Research Report #57. Washington, DC: NEA.

National Governors Association. 2010. *The Common Core Standards for the English Language Arts*.

National Governors Association. 2010. "Note on Range and Content of Student Reading." In *Common Core Anchor Standards for Reading*.

National Governors Association. 2012. *The Common Core Standards for the English Language Arts*. Publisher's Guidelines, Revised May 2012. 392–412.

National Reading Panel. 2000. *Teaching Children to Read*. National Institute for Child Health and Human Development. Washington DC.

Nystrand, Martin. 2006. "Research on the Role of Classroom Discourse as It Affects Reading Comprehension." *Research in the Teaching of English*. 392–412.

O'Brien, David G., and Deborah R. Dillon. 2008. "The Role of Motivation in Engaged Reading of Adolescents." In K. A. Hinchman et al. (eds.). *Best Practices in Adolescent Literacy Instruction* (2nd. ed.). New York: Guilford Press.

Oldfather, P., and K. Dahl. 1995. *Toward a Social Constructivist Reconceptualization of Intrinsic Motivation for Literacy Learning*. Universities of Georgia and Maryland, National Reading Research Center.

Oster, L. 2001. "Using the Think-Aloud for Reading Instruction." *The Reading Teacher* 55: 64–69.

Pearson, P. David, et al. 2013. "Seeds of Science/Roots of Reading." http://www.scienceandliteracy.org/about/howisitbetter.

Pearson, P. David, Elizabeth Hiebert, and Michael Kamil. 2007. "Vocabulary Assessment: What We Know and What We Need to Learn." *Reading Research Quarterly* 42: 282–296.

Pearson, P. David, and Beverly Gallagher. 1983. "The Instruction of Reading Comprehension." *Contemporary Educational Psychology* 8: 317–344.

Rainie, Lee, Kathryn Zickuhr, Kristen Purcell, Mary Madden, and Joanna Brenner. 2012. *The Rise of e-Reading*. Washington, DC: Pew Research Center.

Roden, Phil, and Chip Brady. 2013. Document-Based Questions. www.dbqproject.com.

Routman, Regie, 2003. *Reading Essentials*. Portsmouth, NH: Heinemann.

Samuels, S. Jay, and YiChen Wu. 2004. "How the Amount of Time Spent on Independent Reading Affects Reading Achievement: A Response to the National Reading Panel." Paper presented to IRA 2004 Annual Convention.

Scholastic. 2013. *Kids and Family Reading Report* (4th ed.).

Schunk, D. H. 2003. "Self-Efficacy for Reading and Writing: Influence of Modeling, Goal-Setting, and Self-Evaluation." *Reading & Writing Quarterly* 19: 159–172.

Shanaham, T. 2012. "Disciplinary Literacy is NOT the New Name for Content -Area Reading." http://www.shanahanonliteracy.com/2012/01/disciplinary-literacy-is-not-new-name.html.

Soter, Anna, Ian Wilkinson, P. Murphy, L. Rudge, K. Reninger, and M. Edwards. 2008. "What the Discourse Tells Us: Talk and Indicators of High Level Comprehension." *International Journal of Educational Research* 47(6): 372–391.

Strauss, Susan. 2000. *Literacy Learning in the Middle Grades: An Investigation of Academically Effective Middle Grades Schools.* Talahasse, FL: Florida State University.

Sturtevant, E., F. Boyd, W. G. Brozo, K. Hinchman, D. Alvermann, and D. Moore. 2006. *Principled Practices for Adolescent Literacy: A Framework for Instruction and Policy.* Mahwah, NJ: Erlbaum.

Sullivan, Alice, and Matt Brown. 2013. *Social Inequalities in Cognitive Scores at Age 16: The Role of Reading.* London: London Institute of Education.

Topping, K. J., J. Samuels, and T. Paul. 2007. "Does Practice Make Perfect? Independent Reading Quantity, Quality and Student Achievement." *Learning and Instruction* 17:3 June: 263–264.

Tovani, Cris. 2004. *I Read it, But I Don't Get It.* Portland, ME: Stenhouse.

Vega, Vanessa. 2012. "Project-Based Learning Research Review." http://www.edutopia.org/pbl-research-learning-outcomes.

Wigfield, A., and John Guthrie. 1997. "Relations of Children's Motivation for Reading to the Amount and Breadth of Their Reading." *Journal of Educational Psychology* 89: 420–432.

Wilhelm, Jeffrey. 1997. *You Gotta BE the Book: Teaching Engaged and Reflective Reading with Adolescents.* New York: Teachers College Press.

Worth, J., and L. S. McCool. 1996. "Students Who Say They Hate to Read: The Importance of Opportunity, Choice, and Access." In E. Leu, C. Kinzer, and K. Hinchman (eds.). *Literacies for the 21st Century.* 245–256. National Reading Conference.

General Works Cited

Achieve the Core. 2013. *Student Achievement Partners.* AchievetheCore.org.

Afflerbach, Peter, P. David Pearson, and Scott G. Paris. 2008. "Clarifying Differences Between Reading Skills and Reading Strategies." *Reading Teacher* 61(5): 364–373.

Allen, Janet. 1995. *It's Never Too Late: Leading Adolescents to Lifelong Literacy.* Portsmouth, NH: Heinemann.

———. 1999. *Words, Words, Words: Teaching Vocabulary in Grades 4–12.* York, ME: Stenhouse.

———. 2007. *Inside Words: Tools for Teaching Academic Vocabulary, Grades 4–12.* York, ME: Stenhouse.

Allen, Janet, and Kyle Gonzalez. 1998. *There's Room for Me Here: Literacy Workshop in the Middle School.* York, ME: Stenhouse.

Allington, Richard. 2001. *What Really Matters for Struggling Readers.* New York: Longman.

———. 2008. *What Really Matters in RTI.* New York: Pearson.

———. 2012. *What Really Matters for Struggling Readers: Designing Research-Based Programs* (3rd ed.). Boston: Allyn & Bacon.

———. 2013. "What Really Matters When Working with Struggling Readers." *Reading Teacher* 66(7): 520–530.

Allington, Richard, and Rachael Gabriel. 2012. "Reading: The Core Skill: Every Child, Every Day." *Educational Leadership* 69(6): 10–15.

American Academy of Orthopaedic Surgeons. 2013. "Backpack Safety." http://orthoinfo.aaos.org/topic.cfm?topic=a00043.

Anderson, R. C., and W. E. Nagy. 1992. "The Vocabulary Conundrum." *American Educator* 14–18; 44–47.

Anglin, J. M. 1993. "Vocabulary Development: A Morphological Analysis." *Monographs of the Society for Research in Child Development* 58.

Atwell, Nancie. 1998. *In the Middle: New Understandings About Writing, Reading and Learning* (2nd ed.). Portsmouth, NH: Heinemann.

Bangert-Drowns, Robert, Marlene Hurley, and Barbara Wilkinson. 2004. "The Effects of School-Based Writing-to-Learn Interventions on Academic Achievement: A Meta-Analysis." *Review of Educational Research* 74(1): 29–58.

Barnett, Jennifer. 2013. "7 Ways to Increase Student Ownership." *Education Week – Teacher* http://www.edweek.org/tm/, Jan. 8, 2013.

Beck, Isabel, et al. 1991. "Revising Social Studies Text from a Text-Processing Perspective: Evidence of Improved Comprehensibility." *Reading Research Quarterly* 26: 251–276.

———. 1995. "Giving a Text Voice Can Improve Students' Understanding." *Reading Research Quarterly* 30: 220–239.

Beck, Isabel, Margaret G. McKeown, and Linda Kucan. 2013. *Bringing Words to Life: Robust Vocabulary Instruction* (2nd ed.). New York: Guilford Press.

Beers, Kylene. 2003. *When Kids Can't Read: What Teachers Can Do.* Portsmouth, NH: Heinemann.

Biancarosa, Gina, and Catherine Snow. 2004. *Reading Next: A Vision for Action and Research in Middle and High School Literacy.* New York: Carnegie Corporation 18.

Blachowicz, Camille, and Peter Fisher. 2009. *Teaching Vocabulary in All Classrooms* (4th ed.). New York: Pearson.

Bloch, C., and J. Mangiere. 2002. "Recreational Reading Twenty Years Later." *Reading Teacher* 55(6): 572–580.

Bodanis, David. 2001. *E = mc²: A Biography of the World's Most Famous Equation.* New York: Berkley Publishers.

Brame, Cynthia J. 2013. "Flipping the Classroom." Vanderbilt University Center for Teaching. http://cft.vanderbilt.edu/teaching-guides/teaching-activities/flipping-the-classroom/.

Britton, B. K. et al. 1996. *Improving Instructional Text: Tests of Two Revision Methods.* Universities of Georgia and Maryland, National Reading Research Center.

Brodhagen, Barbara. 2007. "The Situation Made Us Special." In James Beane and Michael Apple, eds. *Democratic Schools* (2nd ed.). Portsmouth, NH: Heinemann.

Budiansky, Stephen. 2001. "The Trouble with Textbooks." *Prism: Journal of the American Society of Engineering Education* February.

Burkins, J. M., and M. M. Croft. 2010. *Preventing Misguided Reading: New Strategies for Guided Reading Teachers.* Newark, DE: International Reading Association.

Butler, Shari, et al. 2010. *A Review of the Current Research on Vocabulary Instruction.* Washington, DC: U.S. Department of Education.

Campbell, T. Colin, and Thomas Campbell. 2006. *The China Study: Startling Implications for Diet, Weight Loss, and Long-Term Health.* Dallas, TX: BenBella Books.

Carnegie Council on Advancing Adolescent Literacy. 2010. *Time to Act: An Agenda for Advancing Adolescent Literacy for College and Career Success.* New York: Carnegie Corporation of New York.

Cervetti, G.N., P. D. Pearson, C. Greenleaf, E. Moje. 2013. "Science! Literacy! Synergy!" In W. Banko, M. L. Grant, M. E. Jabot, A. J. McCormack, and T. O'Brien (eds.). *Science Literacy and Our Nation's Future* (pp. 99–124). Washington, DC: NSTA & STANYS.

Clark, Christina. 2012. *Children's and Young People's Reading Today: Findings from the 2011 National Literacy Trust's Annual Survey.* London: National Literacy Trust.

Clark, Christina, and Kate Rumbold. 2006. "Reading for Pleasure: A Research Overview." London: National Literacy Trust.

Coleman, David, and Susan Pimentel. 2012. "Revised Publishers' Criteria for the Common Core State Standards in English Language Arts and Literacy, Grades 3–12." In *Common Core Standards for the English Language Arts*, 392–412. National Governors Association and the Council of Chief State School Officers. www.corestandards.org/assets/Publishers_Criteria_for_3-12.pdf.

Cunningham, Anne, and Keith Stanovich. 2001. "What Reading Does for the Mind." *Journal of Direct Instruction.* Summer.

Dallas News. 2008. "I Was Told There Would Be No Math." www.dallasnews.com/sharedcontent /dws/news/texassouthwest/stories/111607dntextbooks.268c6c7.html.

Daniels, Harvey. 2002. *Literature Circles: Voice and Choice in Book Clubs and Reading Groups* (2nd ed.). York, ME: Stenhouse.

———. 2011. *Comprehension Going Forward. Where We Are, What's Next*. Portsmouth, NH: Heinemann.

Daniels, Harvey, and Elaine Daniels. 2013. *The Best-Kept Teaching Secret: How Written Conversations Engage Students, Build Knowledge and Grow Fluent Writers*. Thousand Oaks, CA: Corwin.

Daniels, Harvey, Marilyn Bizar, and Steven Zemelman. 2001. *Rethinking High School: Best Practice in Teaching, Learning and Leadership*. Portsmouth, NH: Heinemann.

Daniels, Harvey, and Nancy Steineke. 2004. *Minilessons for Literature Circles*. Portsmouth, NH: Heinemann.

———. 2011. *Texts and Lessons for Content-Area Reading*. Portsmouth, NH: Heinemann.

———. 2013. *Texts and Lessons for Teaching Literature*. Portsmouth, NH: Heinemann.

Darling-Hammond, Linda, et al. 2008. *Powerful Learning: What We Know About Teaching for Understanding*. San Francisco: Jossey-Bass.

Davidson, Judith, and David Koppenhaver. 1988. *Adolescent Literacy: What Works and Why*. New York: Garland Publishing.

Designed Instruction. 2013. "Modeling for Learning: Addressing Student Misconceptions." www. designedinstruction.com/learningleads/misconceptions.html.

Dillon, D. R., and D. G. O'Brien. 2008. "The Role of Motivation in Engaged Reading of Adolescents." In K. A. Hinchman, and H. K. Sheridan-Thomas (eds.). *Best Practices in Adolescent Literacy Instruction, Solving Problems in the Teaching of Literacy* 78–96. New York: Guilford Press.

Duke, Nell K., P. David Pearson, Stephanie L. Strachan, and Alison K. Billman. 2011. "Essential Elements of Fostering and Teaching Reading Comprehension." In S. Jay Samuels and Alan E. Farstrup (eds.). *What Research Has to Say About Reading Instruction* (4th ed.). Newark, DE: International Reading Association.

Durlak, Joseph, et al. 2011. "The Impact of Enhancing Students' Social and Emotional Learning: A Meta-Analysis of School-Based Universal Interventions." *Child Development* 82(1).

Edmonds M.S., S. Vaughn, J. Wexler, C. Reutebuch, A. Cable, K. K. Tackett, and J. W. Schnakenberg. 2009. "A Synthesis of Reading Interventions and Effects on Reading Comprehension Outcomes for Older Struggling Readers." *Review of Education Research* 79 (1): 262–300.

Environmental Protection Agency. 2013. "Light-Duty Automotive Technology, Carbon Dioxide Emissions, and Fuel Economy Trends: 1975 Through 2012." www.epa.gov/cleanenergy.htm .http://www.epa.gov/otaq/fetrends.htm.

Estes, T.H., M. A. Gunter, and S. Mintz. 2010. *Instruction: A Models Approach* (6th ed.). Boston: Pearson.

Facing History and Ourselves. 2013. "Teaching Strategies: Barometer—Taking a Stand on Controversial Issues." www.facinghistory.org/resources/strategies/barometer.

Facing History and Ourselves. 2013. "Teaching Strategies: Four Corners." www.facinghistory.org /resources/strategies/four-corners.

Fang, Zuihui. 2012. "Approaches to Developing Content Area Literacies." *Journal of Adolescent and Adult Literacy* October: 103–108.

Farrington, Camille, et al. 2012. "Teaching Adolescents to Become Learners: The Role of Noncognitive Factors in Shaping School Performance." Chicago: University of Chicago Consortium on Chicago Schools Research.

Feierman, Barry. 2009. "Active Physics by Eisenkraft and Published by Its About Time." Middle School Physical Science Resource Center. http://www.thesciencehouse.org/middleschool /reviews/ActivePhysicsFeierman.html.

Fendel, Dan, and Diane Resek. 2013. *Interactive Mathematics Program: Integrated High School Mathematics.* Mt. Kisco, NY: It's About Time Publishers. http://mathimp.org/general_info /standards.html.

Fitzpatrick, Michael. 2012. "Classroom Lectures Go Digital." *New York Times.* June 24. www.nytimes .com/2012/06/25/us/25iht-educside25.html.

Flynt, E., and W. G. Brozo. 2008. "Developing Academic Language: Got Words?" *Reading Teacher* 61(6): 500–502.

Frey, Nancy, Douglas Fisher, Carol Rothenberg, and Shirley Brice Heath. 2008. *Content-Area Conversations: How to Plan Discussion-Based Lessons for Diverse Language Learners.* Alexandria, VA: Association for Supervision and Curriculum Development.

Fisher, Douglas, and Nancy Frey. 2008. *Word Wise and Content Rich. Five Steps to Teaching Academic Vocabulary, 7–12.* Portsmouth, NH: Heinemann.

Fulwiler, Toby. 2000. *The Journal Book.* Portsmouth, NH: Heinemann.

Gallagher, Kelly. *Readicide: How Schools are Killing Reading and What You Can Do About It.* York, ME: Stenhouse.

Gambrell, Linda, and Barbara Marinak. 2009. "Reading Motivation: What the Research Says." *Reading Rockets Website,* www.readingrockets.org.

Gambrell, L. B., L. M. Morrow, S. B. Neuman, and M. Pressley. 2003. *Best Practices in Literacy Instruction* (2nd ed.). New York: Guilford Press.

Gillen, Chris, and Jasmine Vaughan. 2003. "Reading Primary Literature in Biology." http://biology .kenyon.edu/Bio_InfoLit/index.html.

Glasser, William. *Control Theory in the Classroom.* 1986. New York: Harpercollins.

———. 1998. *Choice Theory in the Classroom.* New York: Harper.

Greenfield, Jeremy. 2013. "Students Still Not Taking to e-Books." *Digital Book World.* (February 7).

Guignon, Anne. 2010. "Reading Aloud: Are Students Ever Too Old?" *Education World.* www. educationworld.com/a_curr/curr081.shtml.

Guthrie, J. T., and N. M. Humenick. 2004. "Motivating Students to Read: Evidence for Classroom Practices That Increase Motivation and Achievement. In P. McCardle, and V. Chhabra (eds.). *The Voice of Evidence in Reading Research.* Baltimore: Paul Brookes.

Guthrie, John. 2008. *Engaging Adolescents in Reading.* Thousand Oaks, CA: Corwin.

Guthrie, John, and Emily Anderson. 1999. "Engagement in Reading: Processes of Motivated, Strategic, Knowledgeable, Social Readers." In John Guthrie and Donna Alvermann (eds.). *Engaged Reading: Processes, Practices, and Policy Implications*, 17–45. New York: Teachers College Press.

Harvey, Stephanie. 1998. *Nonfiction Matters.* York, ME: Stenhouse.

Harvey, Stephanie, and Anne Goudvis. 2005. *The Comprehension Toolkit.* Portsmouth, NH: Heinemann.

———. 2007. *Strategies That Work: Teaching Comprehension for Understanding and Engagement.* York, ME: Stenhouse.

———. 2008. *The Primary Comprehension Toolkit.* Portsmouth, NH: Heinemann.

Harvey, Stephanie, and Harvey Daniels. 2009. *Comprehension and Collaboration: Inquiry Circles in Action.* Portsmouth NH: Heinemann.

———. 2011. *Inquiry Circles in Action in Middle and High School Classrooms* (Video). Portsmouth, NH: Heinemann.

Heller, Rafael, and Cynthia Greenleaf. 2007. *Literacy Instruction in the Content Areas: Getting to the Core of Middle and High School Improvement.* Washington, DC: Alliance for Excellent Education.

Hill, Bonnie Campbell, Cynthia Ruptic, and Lisa Norwick. 1998. *Classroom-Based Assessment.* Boston: Christopher Gordon.

Hinchman, Kathleen, and David Moore. 2013. "Close Reading: A Cautionary Interpretation." *Journal of Adult and Adolescent Literacy* 58(6).

Horner, S. L., and C. S. Shwery. 2002. "Becoming an Engaged, Self-Regulated Reader." *Theory into Practice* 41: 102–109.

Horowitz, R. 2007. *Talking Texts: How Speech and Writing Interact in School Learning.* London: Routledge.

Hubisz, John. 2003. "Middle School Textbooks Don't Make the Grade." *Physics Today* (May).

———. 2012. "What's Wrong with Books?" Middle School Physical Science Resource Center. http://www.thesciencehouse.org/middleschool/essays/books.html.

Hyde, Arthur. 2006. *Comprehending Math: Adapting Reading Strategies to Teach Mathematics K–6.* Portsmouth, NH: Heinemann.

Hynd, Cynthia. 2013. "Reading in Content Areas." http://education.stateuniversity.com/pages/2349/Reading-CONTENT-AREAS.html.

Hynd, Cynthia, et al. 1997. "Texts in Physics Class: The Contribution of Reading to the Learning of Counterintuitive Physics Principles." Universities of Georgia and Maryland, National Reading Research Center.

Hynd, Cynthia, et al. 1999. "Instructional Considerations for Literacy in Middle and Secondary Schools: Toward an Integrated Model of Instruction." In John Guthrie and Donna Alvermann (eds.). *Engaged Reading: Processes, Practices, and Policy Implications*, 81–104. New York: Teachers College Press.

Kirby, Dan, and Carol Kuykendall. 1991. *Mind Matters: Teaching for Thinking.* Portsmouth, NH: Heinemann.

Harmon, Janis M., et al. 2009. "Interactive Word Walls: More Than Just Reading the Writing on the Walls." *Journal of Adolescent and Adult Literacy* 52(5).

International Reading Association. 2012. "Adolescent Literacy: A Position Statement of the International Reading Association." Newark, DE: IRA.

Johnson, David, and Roger Johnson. 2009. "An Educational Psychology Success Story: Social Interdependence Theory and Cooperative Learning." *Educational Researcher* 38(5): 365–379.

Joyce, Bruce and Marsha Weil. 2008. *Models of Teaching* (8th ed.). Boston: Pearson.

Kahn Academy. 2008. "The Mole and Avogadro's Number. At www.wyzant.com/Help/Science /Chemistry/Moles/Kamil, Michael, et al. *Improving Adolescent Literacy: Effective Classroom and Intervention Practices.* Washington DC: Institute of Education Sciences.

Kamil, Michael L., P. David Pearson, Elizabeth Birr Moje and Peter Afflerbach. 2010. *Handbook of Reading Research,* Volume IV. London: Routledge.

Keene, Ellin Oliver, and Susan Zimmerman. 2007. *Mosaic of Thought* (2nd ed.). Portsmouth, NH: Heinemann.

Kornell, N., M. J. Hays, and R. A. Bjork. 2009. "Unsuccessful Retrieval Attempts Enhance Subsequent Learning." *Journal of Experimental Psychology: Learning, Memory, and Cognition* 35: 989–998.

Krashen, Steven. 2004. *The Power of Reading: Insights from the Research.* Portsmouth, NH: Heinemann.

———. 2009. "Free Voluntary Reading." Faversham, U.K.: International Association of Teachers of English as a Foreign Language, Young Learner and Teenage Special Interest Group Publication. Spring.

Kuhn, M., et al. 2006. "Teaching Children to Become Fluent and Automatic Readers." *Journal of Literacy Research* 38(4): 357–388.

Layton, Lyndsey, and Emma Brown. 2012. "SAT Reading Scores Hit a Four-Decade Low." *Washington Post* (September 24).

Lee, Valerie, Julie Smith, Tamara Perry, and Mark Smylie. 1999. *Social Support, Academic Press, and Student Achievement: A View from the Middles Grades in Chicago.* Chicago: University of Chicago Consortium on Chicago School Research.

Martin, Sara, and Fran Needham. 2009. *Sciencesaurus.* New York: Great Source.

McCabe, Cynthia. 2010. "The Economics Behind International Education Rankings." *NEA Today* (December 9).

Met Life Survey of the American Teacher. 2013. https://www.metlife.com/metlife-foundation/about/ survey-american-teacher.html?WT.mc_id=vu1101.

Miller, Donalyn. 2009. *The Book Whisperer.* San Francisco: Jossey Bass.

Moss, B., and T. A. Young. 2010. "Creating Lifelong Readers Through Independent Reading." Newark, DE: International Reading Association.

Moyer, Jessica. 2010. "'Teens Today Don't Read Books Any More': A Study of Differences in Interest and Comprehension Based on Reading Modalities." *Journal of Research on Libraries and Young Adults* 1(1).

Nash, H., and M. Snowling. 2006. "Teaching New Words to Children with Poor Existing Vocabulary Knowledge: A Controlled Evaluation of the Definition and Dontext Methods." *International Journal of Language and Communication Disorders* 41(3): 335–354.

National Assessment of Educational Progress. 2013. "The Nation's Report Card." National Center for Education Statistics. http://nces.ed.gov/nationsreportcard/subject/publications/main2013/pdf/2014451.pdf.

National Assessment of Educational Progress. 2011. "The Nation's Report Card." National Center for Education Statistics. http://nationsreportcard.gov/science_2011/summary.aspx.

National Board for Professional Teaching Standards. 2002. "What Teachers Should Know and Be Able to Do." Arlington, VA: NBPTS.

National Council of Teachers of English. 2007. "Adolescent Literacy. A Policy Research Brief Produced by the National Council of Teachers of English." Urbana, IL: NCTE.

———. 2012. *Reading Instruction for All Students: A Policy Research Brief Produced by the National Council of Teachers of English.* Urbana, IL: NCTE.

National Endowment for the Arts. 2013. *How a Nation Engages with Art: Highlights from the 2012 Survey of Public Participation in the Arts.* Washington, DC: NEA.

National Governors Association and the Council of Chief State School Officers. *Common Core State Standards.* 2010. www.corestandards.org/.

———. 2010. "Note on Range and Content of Student Reading." In *Common Core Anchor Standards for Reading.* National Governors Association and the Council of Chief State School Officers.

National Reading Panel. 2000. *Teaching Children to Read: An Evidence-Based Assessment of the Scientific Research Literature on Reading and Its Implications for Reading Instruction.* Washington, DC: National Institute for Child Health and Human Development.

Next Generation Science Standards: For States, By States. 2012. Washington DC: Achieve, Inc.

Nokes, Jeffery. 2011. "Recognizing and Addressing the Barriers to Adolescents' 'Reading Like Historians.'" *History Teacher* 44(3): 379–404.

Nystrand, Martin. 2006. "Research on the Role of Classroom Discourse as It Affects Reading Comprehension." *Research in the Teaching of English* 392–412.

Oldfather, P., and K. Dahl. 1995. "Toward a Social Constructivist Reconceptualization of Intrinsic Motivation for Literacy Learning." Universities of Georgia and Maryland, National Reading Research Center.

Oster, L. 2001. "Using the Think-Aloud for Reading Instruction." *Reading Teacher* 55: 64–69.

Pearson, David, et al. 2013. "About the Curriculum: How Do We Know It's Better?" *Seeds of Science/Roots of Reading.* www.scienceandliteracy.org/about/howisitbetter.

Pearson, P. David, and Beverly Gallagher. 1983. "The Instruction of Reading Comprehension." *Contemporary Educational Psychology* 8: 317–344.

Pearson, P. David, Elizabeth Hiebert, and Michael Kamil. 2007. "Vocabulary Assessment: What We Know and What We Need to Learn." *Reading Research Quarterly* 42: 282–296.

Pearson, P. David, Jennifer L. Tilson, and Jill Castek. 2011. "The Role of Science Vocabulary in Supporting Students' Academic Language Development" (PowerPoint). International Reading Association Institute 18, May 8. www.scienceandliteracy.org/sites/scienceandliteracy.org/files/biblio/pdpearson/Pearson_Tilson_Castek_IRA_Vocabulary.pdf.

Programme for International Student Assessment of the Organization for Economic Cooperation and Development. "PISA 2009 Key Findings." www.oecd.org/pisa/pisa2009keyfindings.htm.

Rainie, Lee, et al. 2012. *The Rise of e-Reading.* Pew Internet and American Life Project. Washington, DC: Pew Research Center.

Rico, Gabriele. 1983. *Writing the Natural Way.* Los Angeles: Tarcher.

Riddile, Mel. 2010. "PISA: It's Poverty Not Stupid." NASSP Blogs. December 15. http://nasspblogs.org/principaldifference/2010/12/pisa_its_poverty_not_stupid_1.html.

Robinson, Francis Pleasant. 1970. *Effective Study* (4th ed.). New York: Harper & Row.

Roden, Phil, and Chip Brady. 2013. The DBQ Project. www.dbqproject.com.

Roseman, Jo Ellen, Gerald Kulm, and Susan Shuttleworth. 2001. "Putting Textbooks to the Test." American Association for the Advancement of Science. ENC Focus 8(3): 56–59. www.project2061.org/research/articles/enc.htm.

Routman, Regie. *Reading Essentials.* 2003. Portsmouth, NH: Heinemann.

Samuels, S. Jay, and YiChen Wu. 2004. "How the Amount of Time Spent on Independent Reading Affects Reading Achievement: A Response to the National Reading Panel." Paper presented to IRA 2004 Annual Convention.

Samuels, S. Jay and Alan Farstrup. 2011. *What Research Has to Say About Reading Instruction* (4th ed.). Newark, DE: International Reading Association.

Schlosser, Eric. 2002. *Fast Food Nation. The Dark Side of the All-American Meal.* New York: HarperCollins.

Shanahan, Cynthia, et al. 2011. "Analysis of Expert Readers in Three Disciplines: History, Mathematics, and Chemistry." *Journal of Literacy Research.* 43(4): 393–429.

Schlosser, Eric, and Charles Wilson. 2007. *Chew on This: Everything You Don't Want to Know About Fast Food.* New York: Houghton-Mifflin.

Schmuck, Richard, and Patricia Schmuck. 2000. *Group Processes in the Classroom* (8th ed.). Des Moines, IA: Wm. C. Brown.

Scholastic. 2013. *Kids and Family Reading Report* (4th ed.). New York: Scholastic.

Schunk, D. H. 2003. "Self-Efficacy for Reading and Writing: Influence of Modeling, Goal-Setting, and Self-Evaluation." *Reading & Writing Quarterly* 19: 159–172.

Simonson, Shai. 2011. *Rediscovering Mathematics.* Washington, DC: Mathematical Association of America.

Smith, Julia, Valerie Lee, and Fred Newmann. 2001. "Instruction and Achievement in Chicago Elementary Schools." Chicago: University of Chicago Consortium on Chicago School Research.

Smith, Malbert III, Jason Turner, and Steve Lattanzio. 2012. "Public Schools: Glass Half Full or Half Empty?" *Education Week* (February 10): 22–23.

Smith, Michael, and Jeffrey Wilhelm. 2002. *Reading Don't Fix No Chevys: Literacy in the Lives of Young Men*. Portsmouth, NH: Heinemann.

———. 2006. *Going with the Flow: How to Engage Boys (and Girls) in Their Literacy Learning*. Portsmouth, NH: Heinemann.

Soter, Anna, et al. 2008. "What the Discourse Tells Us: Talk and Indicators of High Level Comprehension." *International Journal of Educational Research* 47(6): 372–391.

Steineke, Nancy. 2002. *Reading and Writing Together: Collaborative Literacy in Action*. Portsmouth, NH: Heinemann Educational Books.

———. 2009. *Assessment Live!: 10 Real-Time Ways for Kids to Show What They Know—and Meet the Standards*. Portsmouth, NH: Heinemann.

Strauss, Susan. 2000. "Literacy Learning in the Middle Grades: An Investigation of Academically Effective Middle Grades Schools." Unpub. Dissertation, Florida State University.

Sturtevant, E., Boyd, F. Brozo, W. G. Hinchman, K. Alvermann, and D. Moore. 2006. *Principled Practices for Adolescent Literacy: A Framework for Instruction and Policy*. Mahwah, NJ: Erlbaum.

Sullivan, Alice, and Matt Brown. 2013. *Social Inequalities in Cognitive Scores at Age 16: The Role of Reading*. London: London Institute of Education.

Topping, K.J., J. Samuels, and T. Paul. 2007. "Does Practice Make Perfect? Independent Reading Quantity, Quality, and Student Achievement." *Learning and Instruction* 17(3): 263–264.

Tough, Paul. 2012. *How Children Succeed: Grit, Curiosity, and the Hidden Power of Character*. New York: Houghton Mifflin Harcourt.

Tovani, Cris. 2003. *I Read It But I Don't Get It*. York, ME: Stenhouse.

Trends in International Mathematics and Science Study (TIIMSS). 1999. http://timssandpirls.bc.edu/timss1999.html.

Uhlenbeck, Olke. "Research Interests." Interdepartmental Biological Sciences, Northwestern University. www.biochem.northwestern.edu/ibis/faculty/uhlenbeck.htm.

UNICEF. 2012. Child Info: Monitoring the Situation of Children and Women. www.childinfo.org/labour.html.

Vega, Vanessa. 2012. "Project-Based Learning Research Review." Edutopia. www.edutopia.org/pbl-research-learning-outcomes.

Wigfield, A., and John Guthrie. 1997. "Relations of Children's Motivation for Reading to the Amount and Breadth of Their Reading." *Journal of Educational Psychology* 89: 420–432.

Wiggins, Grant, and Jay McTighe. 2005. *Understanding by Design* (2nd ed.). New York: Prentice-Hall.

Wilhelm, Jeffrey. 2007. *You Gotta BE the Book: Teaching Engaged and Reflective Reading with Adolescents*. New York: Teachers College Press.

Wood, K. 1984. "Probable Passages: A Writing Strategy." *Reading Teacher* 37: 496–499.

Worth, J., and L. S. McCool. 1996. "Students Who Say They Hate to Read: The Importance of Opportunity, Choice, and Access." In E. Leu, C. Kinzer, and K. Hinchman (eds.). *Literacies for the 21st Century* 245–256. Oak Creek, WI: National Reading Conference.

Zemelman, Steven, Harvey Daniels, and Arthur Hyde. 2012. *Best Practice: Bringing Standards to Life in America's Schools* (4th ed.). Portsmouth, NH: Heinemann.

Index

as reference books, 54
role of, 46–49
single sourcing, 56
state opinions on, 48, 58
students and, 57–58
vendors of, 47
Text(s), cross-text integration, 77–78
Texts and Lessons for Content-Area Reading (Daniels and Steineke), 68, 101, 122
"The Truth About *Fast Food Nation*" (PETA), 3
There's Room for Me Here (Gonzalez), 287
Think-aloud strategy, 88, 94–97, 283, 300, 302–303
Thinking strategies
annotating text, 121–123
by coding text, 125–127
of effective readers, 30–32
post-it response notes, 118–120
sketching my way through the text, 131–133
teaching specific, 4
think-aloud, 88, 94–97, 283, 300, 302–303
turn and talk, 134–137
Think-pair-share activity, 134, 300
Tiwari, Guarav, 75
Today's Meet discussion tool, 233
Tough, Paul, 204
Tovani, Cris, 209, 280, 284
"Tracks of a student's thinking" (annotating text), 121
Turn and talk strategy, 96, 134–137, 300

Tweet the text strategy, 138–139
Twitter, 74

U
Uhlenbeck, Olke, 34, 35
Understanding by Design (Wiggins and McTighe), 179
University of California Library, 76–77
U.S. Department of Education, 292

V
Vidal, Gore, 70
Visualizing
clustering and mapping strategy, 155–158
dramatic role play strategy, 110–111
frontloading with images strategy, 100–102
as reading strategy, 30, 88, 89
sketching my way through the text strategy, 131–133
Vocabulary. *See* Academic vocabulary
admit slips strategy, 120, 132, 140–142, 234
predictions strategy, 112–114
preparing list of terms, 113
tree activity, 150–152
word sorts activity, 192–193
word wall strategy, 143–146
Vygotsky, Lev, 92

W
Ware, Marnie, 73, 75, 144, 145, 208

Washington Irving School, 253
Washington Post, 11–12
Westbrook High School (Maine), 224–225
What Works Clearinghouse of the U.S. Department of Education, 292, 300, 302
When Kids Can't Read: What Teachers Can Do (Beers), 283
Where do you stand? strategy, 166–168
White, Jackie, 173
Wiggins, Grant, 179
Wilhelm, Jeff, 110, 205, 285–286, 296–297
Woodbury, Jane, 45
Word meaning graphic organizer, 147–149
Word relationships, 105, 150–154
Word sorts, 192–193
Word wall, 143–146
Writing, summaries, 92
Writing the Natural Way (Rico), 155
Written conversation, 159–162

Y
You Gotta BE the Book (Wilhelm), 205

Z
Zemelman, Steven, vii, 50, 63, 110, 171, 208, 215, 238, 277, 279, 285, 288
Zone of proximal development, 9

About the Authors

Harvey Daniels, also known as Smokey, has been a teacher since 1969. He began his public school career at Chicago's Westinghouse High School, then taught in suburban Lake Forest, and years later in Santa Fe, New Mexico, where he now lives. In between, Smokey received his PhD from Northwestern University, where he later taught linguistics and teacher education classes and coordinated the undergraduate program. Smokey has authored or co-authored 23 books and videos. While he is still well known for his development of literature circles, his more recent work has been in content-area comprehension, inquiry groups, and the explicit teaching of social-academic skills. These days, Smokey is an independent consultant and author, working with kids and teachers across the country. Smokey's wife and sometime co-author Elaine is also a teacher; his son, Nick, is founder of a private pathology company; and his daughter, Marny, is the artist behind Skeletina.com.

Steven Zemelman promotes innovative education in Chicago and across the country. He is founding Director of the Illinois Writing Project and former director of the Center for City Schools, National Louis University. He helped start innovative new schools in Chicago and guided others building teacher leadership and professional community. This led to his Heinemann book *13 Steps to Teacher Empowerment*, coauthored with Harry Ross. Steve's recent efforts focus on bringing teacher voices into the larger public discussion on education through a series of TEDx teacher talks and teachersspeakup.com. He provides talks, workshops, and consulting on these issues, and on literacy instruction, across the country. His wife Susan helps international students learn American culture and teaches literacy for homeless adults. His son Mark is a dancer and artist, and Dan is a jazz pianist.

Smokey and Steve have coauthored many books and videos, filled with practical strategies for making writing, reading, and learning into a richer learning experience for young people.

* *Best Practice: Bringing Standards to Life in America's Classrooms* (1993/1998/2005/2012)
* *Best Practice Video Companion: Watching the Seven Structures That Create Exemplary Classrooms* (2012)
* *Content–Area Writing: Every Teacher's Guide* (2007)
* *Rethinking High School: Best Practice in Teaching, Learning, and Leadership* (2000)
* *Rethinking High School Video: Best Practice in Action* (2000)
* *A Community of Writers: Teaching Writing in the Junior and Senior High School* (1988)
* *A Writing Project: Training Teachers of Composition from Kindergarten to College* (1985)